In Our Opinion

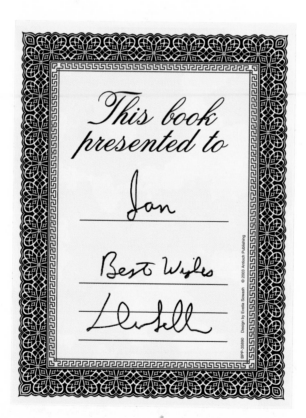

This book presented to

Jan

Best Wishes

In Our Opinion

More than 100 Years of
Canadian Newspaper Editorials

Fitzhenry & Whiteside

Fitzhenry and Whiteside Limited
195 Allstate Parkway,
Markham, Ontario L3R 4T8

In the United States:
311 Washington Street,
Brighton, Massachusetts 02135

www.fitzhenry.ca   godwit@fitzhenry.ca

Fitzhenry & Whiteside acknowledges with thanks the Canada Council for the Arts, and
the Ontario Arts Council for their support of our publishing program. We acknowledge
the financial support of the Government of Canada through the Book Publishing Industry
Development Program (BPIDP) for our publishing activities.

Canada Council   Conseil des Arts
for the Arts   du Canada

Library and Archives Canada Cataloguing in Publication
Sellars, Don
In our opinion : More than 100 years of Canadian newspaper editorials /
[compiled by] Don Sellars.

ISBN 1-55041-987-0

1. Editorials—Canada. I. Title.

PN4903.S44 2006   070.4'42   C2006-902908-3

United States Cataloguing-in-Publication Data
In our opinion : More than 100 years of Canadian newspaper editorials /
[compiled by] Don Sellars.
[256] p. : cm.
ISBN 1-55041-987-0
1. Journalism – Canadian. I. Sellars, Don. II. Title.
071.109 dc22   PN4908.S444 2006

Cover design by David Drummond
Interior design by Fortunato Design Inc.
Printed and bound in Canada

1 3 5 7 9 10 8 6 4 2

For Lynda,

And for Canada's Editorial Writers,

Past and Present

Contents

3 True North

4 Not Our Proudest Moments

8 Slow News Day

9 The Next Generation

Contents

10 War

11 Havoc, Home and Away

12 Workers of the World Unite

13 Balancing the Scales of Justice

14 Sport

15 The Great Outdoors

16 Across This Great Land

20 Getting Close to Home

21 Taking a Stand

22 Inside The Fourth Estate

Tell all the Truth but tell it slant.
— Emily Dickinson

Men get opinions as boys learn to spell.
— Elizabeth Barrett Browning

Writing editorials is like wetting your pants while wearing a blue serge suit. Nobody notices and it leaves you with a warm feeling.
— George Bain

All successful newspapers are ceaselessly querulous and bellicose. They never defend anyone or anything if they can help it; if the job is forced on them, they tackle it by denouncing someone or something else.
— H.L. Mencken

Introduction

Somewhere in a cardboard box in my basement is a yellowed note from the typewriter of Jack Brehl, a splendid writer and reporter at *The Toronto Star*, where I wrote editorials for a living in the 1980s. The pithy memo repeated the classic take on my job by American newspaper columnist Murray Kempton of *Newsday* and the *New York Post*: Kempton called editorial writers "the people who come down from the hills after the battle to shoot the wounded."

Thanks for the reminder, Jack. *Let's lock and reload* I thought, pinning that new note on my office bulletin board.

In eight years of writing thousands of editorials, I used my fair share of ammo. When you're an editorial writer, aiming choice words at a juicy target is like throwing a rock into a pack of dogs. You know when you've hit one. Like the day I nailed a private TV network executive with a short, sharp burst of maybe 250 words on some obscure broadcasting issue now long forgotten.

Next morning, a savage letter to the editor arrived at the paper by fax. Like the best newspaper editorials, the broadcaster made one point exceedingly well: the person responsible for the editorial should be *summarily shot*. This in a country that had abolished flogging *and* capital punishment! The letters editor wanted to cut that juicy bit — it was gratuitous, she said. Let it stay, I begged. She ran the letter uncut, and that was the end of it. I lived to write another day.

Newspaper editorials are sober, passionate, reflective, witty, disturbing, prescient and often as nutty as the people who write them. I think most will agree, after reading even a handful of the entertaining and thought-provoking editorials from Canadian newspapers in this collection which date back to the 1880s.

* * *

You're about to take a guided tour of the passion, anger and occasionally downright (and sometimes deliberately) silly opinions that have filled the editorial pages of Canadian newspapers since the era when the Last Spike completed the transcontinental Canadian Pacific Railway in 1885.

Whether railing against stupidity in government, the high cost of lawyers and the horrors of war, mourning the deaths of Queen Victoria and that old rascal Harold Ballard, pondering the future of lacrosse in 1895, or celebrating home-grown hockey star Brad Richards, "the pride of Murray Harbour," editorials are the personalities of our newspapers, and our communities, from St. John's to Victoria.

But first, a few words of caution are in order. Editorial pages are *not* archives of great Canadian events, this is not a history book, and I am no historian. Editorials are opinions fashioned to stimulate thought or debate on the issues of the day. Frequently incomplete and inaccurate, they speak to overwhelming human emotion in times of crisis or stress and, perhaps as often, to the ebb and flow of community life – especially on those dreaded slow news days when an editorial writer's mind turns simply, to a walk in the woods. The result, then, is not a collection of opinion on landmark events and pivotal figures (although there is a good helping of each here). That is fodder of headline news. Instead, you'll find a mix of opinion reflecting the attitudes, heart and soul of Canadian newspapers – and Canadians – from the last 120 years or so. Represented in this noisy tapestry are bold designs, splashes of local colour, silly patches and a few bad ideas that ended up in the papers for all to see.

* * *

Even in their second début here, many an old edit seems as fresh as ever, sometimes just as controversial. Consider gun control. In 1900, *The Windsor Evening Record* urged a ban on air gun sales to young boys who were using them to "kill birds, smash windows, torment stray dogs, and plug the eyes of the neighbours' cats." In 1912, *The Vancouver Sun* urged authorities to ban concealed handguns and knives. In 1962, *The Toronto Telegram* lamented that we treat guns "like toys."

Other editorials represent a nation's less proud moments, reflecting the bias, ignorance and bigotry of their day. By reprinting them, we remind ourselves of accepted wisdom of days long gone, ideas discredited, discoveries eclipsed. Readers are free to judge for themselves how far we've come as a society.

In 1884, when a smallpox outbreak was traced to a Chinese-owned laundry in Calgary, *The Herald* suggested a boycott of Chinese-owned laundries. In 1912, *The Vancouver Sun* contended that Sikh men make welcome immigrants, but not Sikh women because "we do not want a permanent (Sikh) colony" on the West Coast.

Also resurrected from the millions of newspaper editorials stored on microfilm at The Toronto Star Newspaper Centre in the basement of the Toronto Reference Library are some mighty intriguing, even macabre ideas that once banged around in editors' heads. Are people buried alive? asks one. As government requires us to do more paperwork to collect a pension or qualify for medicare, will we soon be on a treadmill that leads from compulsion to socialism and inevitably to "autocracy and dictatorship"? wonders another. And how about a railway linking Calgary to Paris, with passenger cars loaded for a ferry ride across the Bering Strait and then a train ride across the Russian steppes?

You will also learn what an editorial writer thought about the usefulness of the bayonet in the Boer war ("It is not difficult to carry and it is always loaded."); too many "motors" on Toronto streets in the 1920s; the bizarre use of unwitting Inuit from Quebec as "human flagpoles" in the Arctic; the danger of falling space junk in the '60s; the role of government budget cuts in the Walkerton water disaster of 2000; and the current threat of global warming.

Our oldest specimen is a mid-1800s rant against what's now called the sex trade. With the Canadian Pacific Railway tracks having just reached Calgary, a local editor demanded to know if local police were going to allow a "promising town to become the asylum for the harlots and prostitutes of the east."

One of the most recent edits is a sorrowful *Globe and Mail* tribute to a casualty of the war in Afghanistan: Captain Nichola Goddard, who will forever be remembered as the first Canadian woman combat soldier to be slain in battle.

Through these pages, we capture the sweep and diversity of the country as we skip from city to city, province to province, and coast to coast to coast, through periods of high immigration, women's suffrage, economic prosperity, depression and Canada's slow march toward independence from Britain (and measured distance from the United States).

There are vivid memories of Canadians in the grip of war and trying to prevent it: Vimy Ridge, Dieppe, D-Day and Lester B. (Mike) Pearson's 1957 Nobel Prize for Peace.

We sample the instant reactions of editorial writers to tidings of fire and flood, the Halifax Explosion, the atomic bomb dropped on Hiroshima and the 9/11 terrorist attacks on New York City and Washington, D.C.

We celebrate the accomplishments of Canadian astronaut Dr. Roberta Bondar, our incomparable racehorse Northern Dancer, and the schooner *Bluenose* when she sank to a watery grave in 1946.

We say farewell to a few national figures – the indomitable Pierre Trudeau, Haida sculptor Bill Reid, suffragist Nellie McClung, pianist Glenn Gould, author Margaret Laurence and former Ottawa mayor Charlotte Whitton, among others.

There are milestones to mark: *The Regina Leader*'s stirring farewell to "our old friend" the Nineteenth Century, *The Toronto Globe*'s challenging welcome to the Twentieth, a *Toronto Telegram* centennial ode to Canada's spirit in 1967, the *Ottawa Citizen*'s welcome to the end of capital punishment in Canada, and *The Edmonton Journal*'s pithy prescriptions for the new millennium.

There are fearful editorials about typhoid, smallpox and Toronto's deadly bout with SARS, an early warning about smog, and much confident editorial advice on education, the raising of children, booze, recreational drugs, and gambling.

Particularly fascinating is a group of good-old-days editorials focusing on public health issues, such as *The Vancouver Sun's* 1912 campaign to clean up the city's milk supply, an even earlier one by *The Toronto Globe* to get rid of outdoor privies, and the same editor's prescription for the grip.

Such editorials serve to remind us now how Canadians used to live, what rankled or plagued communities, and what the local editor demanded be done about it. They're slices of cultural history that easily outlast more learned but drier stuff on tariffs and trade, economics, diplomacy and political maneuvers.

There are liberal editorials, conservative ones and a number that defy ideological classification, such as a curmudgeonly critique of the *Mona Lisa* and one editor's lament that readers seemed to know his job better than their own.

Many readers will rightly conclude from the lack of inclusive language in many editorials – "mankind" as opposed to "people" – or from dismissive attitudes toward women, aboriginals and other minorities, that the authors were decidedly white and male. Welcome to Canada's newspaper history. I hope we learned the lesson.

To get into this book, an editorial had to catch an old editor's eye and hold his attention. It had to be fun to read. Passion, conviction, wackiness and sheer crankiness were winning qualities, whereas picky or eye-glazing treatises on time-trapped politics or economics were easily discarded. In addition, I tried to balance political slants and regional viewpoints, and include editorials from small as well as larger papers.

I can't say whether any editorial in this grab-bag collection ever won a Canadian prize for journalism, or was the first to take a particular stand. For that information, please consult the serious historians.

However, a furious (almost incomprehensible) 1937 *Calgary Herald* editorial comparing then-premier William Aberhart to Adolf Hitler, was part of a spirited and ultimately successful campaign by Alberta newspapers to rid the province of Social Credit's odious press control law. On behalf of those papers, *The Edmonton Journal* in 1938 was given a special citation from the U.S. Pulitzer Prize committee, the first such Pulitzer awarded to a non-U.S. publication.

In the latter stages of the book, we plumb some of the deepest purposes and aims of a good editorial page in a free society: to hold powerful institutions and elected leaders accountable, demand open court proceedings, fight obsessive secrecy, and unlock file cabinets and computer data bases in the public interest.

Which brings us to the point of editorials: no matter how authoritative or aggressive its news coverage on the issues of the day, a newspaper without a spirited editorial page fighting for what it believes in might as well dismantle the presses and sell widgets instead.

Canada is a free society. We've made a reputation as a people who prefer to fight with words, not swords. The best editorials are weapons that advance debate, lead a community, illuminate dark corners or inspire lofty thoughts. When prodded by a provocative editorial, readers often respond with a fusillade of letters to the editor raising points, pro and con, that had never occurred to the editorial writer. Society only benefits from the cross-ventilation of ideas. Ironically, it wasn't until the explosion of electronic media that this two-way exchange, a hallmark of newspapers for more than a century, got a new name: interactive journalism.

And what of the future? As papers struggle in a multi-media universe, their circulation figures and advertising linage dipping ominously, the worst thing they could do to themselves would be to gut the editorial page – an asset unique to newspapers, wholly unsuited to TV and radio competitors. As I hope this book demonstrates, editorials are an integral part of our newspaper and cultural heritage. When a newspaper scales them back or shrinks the ranks of editorial writers, it becomes harder for readers to understand the personality of what they are reading, a paper's character and point of view.

Yet, with bean-counters everywhere relentlessly trimming newsroom budgets, laying off staff, closing foreign bureaus or shrinking page sizes to save on newsprint (and make shareholders happier) I fear editorial boards are becoming targets of opportunity.

The newspaper industry already produces free public transit papers that have no editorial page, and thus no point of view. The editorial-free newspaper is a junk-food serving of empty calories hardly likely to win a new generation of engaged readers to the medium of print. If you've never seen an editorial, how can you know what you're missing?

To some in executive suites, editorials are either not worth reading or just a troublesome frill. For one thing, they run on ad-free pages. Also, they annoy advertisers and readers who don't share the paper's institutional opinions and values, or who object to hearing why the newspaper believes so-and-so is best qualified to be mayor.

But that's enough about editorials, their importance, traditions and murky future. It's time the editorial writers themselves be given a turn. Let the chips fall where they may.

Don Sellar
Port Hope, Ontario, 2006

Acknowledgments

The idea for a zany collection of Canadian newspaper editorials popped up years ago in a phone chat with Peter Taylor, an author and long time newspaper and book publishing executive. Peter had called the ombudsman at *The Toronto Star* to bend my ear about something awful he'd read in the paper. An editorial no doubt. A year or so later when I left the *Star*, at last there was time to test the idea. As friend, confidant and handler-in-chief, Peter was indispensable. Always trust someone whose passions include raw oysters.

What made the book feasible was the generous participation of Canadian newspaper publishers, editors and staff members from coast to coast. Most papers willingly gave reprint permissions; all left me free to pick whatever editorials caught my eye.

In particular, thanks to: publisher Bob McKenzie and editor-in-chief Lucinda Chodan, *Victoria Times Colonist*; publisher Dennis Skulsky, *Vancouver Sun*; manager of editorial services Debbie Millward, *Pacific Press*; then-publisher Peter Menzies, and executive editor Ronald Nowell, *Calgary Herald*; president and publisher Linda Hughes, *Edmonton Journal*; president and publisher Greg McLean and editor-in-chief Janice Dockham, *Regina Leader Post*; publisher Andy Ritchie and editor-in-chief Bob Cox, *Winnipeg Free Press*; then-interim publisher Bob Calvert, and editorial page editor John Coleman, *Windsor Star*; publisher and chief executive officer Susan Muszak and librarian Anita McCallum, *London Free Press*; publisher and general manager Jim Ambrose and managing editor Ed Arnold, *Peterborough Examiner*; then-publisher Jagoda Pike and editor-in-chief Dana Robbins, *Hamilton Spectator*; publisher Michael Goldbloom, *Toronto Star*; publisher and chief executive officer

Phillip Crawley and permissions editor Francine Bellefeuille, *Globe and Mail*; publisher Gordon Fisher, *National Post*; licensing rep Leann Swalwell, Canwest Interactive; then-publisher Neil Fowler, *Toronto Sun*; director, electronic information, Julie Kirsh, Sun Media Corporation; publisher Jim Orban and librarian Lois Kirkup, *Ottawa Citizen*; publisher Alan Allnutt and editor-in-chief Andrew Phillips, *Montreal Gazette*; publisher Jamie Irving, *New Brunswick Telegraph Journal*; publisher and chief executive officer Graham Dennis and librarian Louise Higgs, *Halifax Chronicle-Herald*; publisher and general manager Don Brander and managing editor Gary MacDougall, *Charlottetown Guardian*; publisher and general manager Miller H. Ayre and editor Russell Wangersky, *St. John's Telegram*; associate travel editor Susan Pigg, *Toronto Star* (for giving the book its title); librarian Joan Sweeney Marsh, *Toronto Star*; David Michael and many other friendly and accommodating staffers at The Toronto Star Newspaper Centre, Toronto Reference Library; and photographer Cathy Adams, Port Hope.

The professionals at Fitzhenry & Whiteside, especially managing editor Richard Dionne, were a joy to work with. Richard gave the book a shape and flow I didn't know it could have, always gently and patiently pulling an old newspaper hack from the weeds.

Finally, my appreciation to a wonderful family – Lynda, Jamie, Kate and Dan – for unwavering support, aid, and encouragement.

1
An Anniversary Medley

The Nineteenth Century

We now bid goodbye to our old friend, the century in which we were all born, have lived and have had our being. The world has been so often reminded that it has been the most wonderful century that ever was, that we have come to believe it: perhaps because we like to believe it, and perhaps because it is true.

There are, however, doubts on the last point. Great as have been the discoveries and advancement of the nineteenth century when compared with the eighteenth; yet the marvellous intellectual activity and progress that characterized the sixteenth and the seventeenth centuries when compared with the fifteenth equal, if they do not surpass those of the century peculiarly our own.

True it is that we boast of photography, steam and electricity, that have accomplished so much and are on the way of accomplishing so much more; but the sixteenth and seventeenth can appeal to the invention of printing that has achieved as much as any other one thing in the world, as well as to the discovery of the laws of gravitation, the circulation of the blood, and the vast strides made in physical science.

We can boast of Stephenson, of Watt, of Edison, Arkwright and a crowd of inventors to say nothing of Darwin, Tennyson, Goethe, Burns, Adam Smith, Bentham, Hume, Mill, Ricardo and a perfect galaxy of economists and philosophers; but it may be fairly advanced that these are eclipsed by Kepler, Galileo, Copernicus and Volta, by Newton, Bacon, Descartes and Locke, by Shakespeare, Milton, Corneille and Racine, to say nothing of Luther and a host of reformers.

The rivalry as to the excellence of the centuries, we repeat is a question quite open to discussion. One point, however, is quite clear, that it is to the marvellous intellectual activity of the sixteenth and seventeenth centuries that we are indebted for the inventive activity of the nineteenth century. The sixteenth and seventeenth showed the way on which the nineteenth eagerly travelled.

To properly appraise the value of our own times we should remember that the proper study of mankind is – man. With this as a pivotal consideration we find that the progress made has been satisfactory. The Rights of Man is no longer a doctrine: it is a fact, though of only recent recognition.

A giant intellect, such as Gladstone's, in its undeveloped state, believed in slavery as a divine institution, and even the crucial test of the "rights of man," the abolition of slavery, preceded many simpler conclusions from the doctrinal stage. Now, however, the full rights of citizenship to every person morally and physically capable are conceded by all; and this notwithstanding some remnants of old fogeyism discovered in property qualifications in some parts of Canada, and certain privileges of rank and birth that still obtain in the mother country.

They are, however, in the passing-away stage, and do not retard the onward flow of man's assertion of equal rights and opportunities for every citizen. This, then, is the great achievement of the nineteenth century, that individual liberty is triumphant.

Those who have watched the march of events realize the great blessings that have followed a doctrine now so obvious.

But for all that we are still faced with a problem that it would be well the twentieth century should solve. The resources of the world have made nations rich, but still there is the bitter cry of the outcast and the poor. The palatial mansions of the wealthy are side by side with dens where poverty and wretchedness reign supreme, and where the squalor and the misery are so great that the pen and the tongue would alike fail adequately to describe them.

This is at once the mystery and the shame of the nineteenth century; and it is the great question for the coming years to solve. There is a slight consolation in the fact that bad as things are in this respect, they are not so bad as they have been. There is, however, more than consolation in the realization of the truth that so long as there are those who toil not neither do they spin, and who yet consume the labour of those that both toil and spin, just so long will there be the wail of lamentation from those who suffer much and endure long.

It seems monstrous that on a globe so rich in natural resources, there should be people starving in the dens of London, Paris, and New York. It is not that the world is overcrowded – overcrowded, indeed, when the population of the whole world could stand shoulder to shoulder in Assiniboia.

The world is big enough for all and rich enough for all; the problem is to bring the toilers to sow the seed and gather the harvest, and see that those that have sown shall reap and those that have gathered shall garner.

There is always a temptation to endeavour to pry into the future.

We watch the wheels of Nature's
mighty plan,
And judge the future from
the past of man.

And truly the imagination may be excused any flight of imagination, however audacious. Picture the old countries in 1801, with their post chaises, stage coaches, slow, expensive, uncertain postal arrangements, with their narrow and privileged classes, restricted franchises, and indeed divided into but two antagonistic classes – the rich and the poor.

And now regard the scene today with railways and steamboats, telegraphs and telephones, penny postage and equal rights for all. Then look at our prairies, not a hundred years ago but only a quarter of a hundred – the home of the Indian and the buffalo and nothing else; and now see them today, after a few short years, beginning life with the accumulated advantages of civilization ready to hand to start with; and the wildest dreams could not depict a view too extravagant of what may be seen a hundred year hence.

The main point now urged, in keeping with what is written above, is that out here in the west we stand in full citizenship. Not only that, but we start with the knowledge that we are independent as a people, that we toil for ourselves, that what we earn is our own. The idea that a colony is an orange to be sucked by the mother country is an idea of the last century.

It has nothing to do with this century and in nothing more than in features such as this is the progress that has been made during the century so marked, so certain and so satisfactory.

—*The Regina Leader,*
December 27, 1900

3

The New Century and its Problems

Welcome the new century. It dawns upon the world in a wonderful day. The battle for political freedom was the great work of the nineteenth century. The battle for industrial freedom must be the great work of the twentieth. Much has been won from arrogant ecclesiasticism and royal despots. Something is still to be won from great trusts and powerful corporations.

We have gone far in the science of production. We must now advance in the science of distribution. Not every millionaire is an enemy of his kind, nor every demagogue a friend. The best progress will not come through the cursing of capital and the wild projects of levellers, but through the same processes of arbitration and earnest work for reconciliation and a good understanding between capital and labour.

But, first and last, we must work for the freedom of the individual. It will be better if the corporation shall have to depend more upon the state and the individual less upon the corporation.

The citizen who feels that he is free, that he is no man's man, and that while his arms are strong and his head sound, no other human creature can put him upon the street, is better, stronger and saner than his neighbour, who, doing even better, it may be, in this world's work, still feels that a stronger hand has him by the collar, and that he petitions man rather than his Maker for his daily bread.

Yes, we know that revolutionists and Anarchists hold this language. But it will be better not to refuse to listen on that account. Just here is a mighty truth and a mighty danger.

The truth is that the future is menaced by great industrial combinations upon the one hand and great masses of organized workers upon the other.

The danger is that the settlement may come through the ways of revolution rather than through the ways of peace.

Advance and change there must be. The individual must regain at least a measure of his freedom, the trust and the corporation must be content with fair gains and must submit to reasonable public control, and public franchises must be handled for the public benefit.

These are the questions that press upon thinking men and women the world over. They cannot be evaded nor faced back, and it will be well if with the birth of this new century, we dedicate ourselves in the same, earnest, thoughtful considera-tion of these great looming issues, and strive to advance through prudent and well-ordered evolution, to the new conditions that are coming upon mankind.

—The Toronto Globe,
January 1, 1901

Dieppe, August 19

August 19 is the third anniversary of the Dieppe raid – the reconnaissance in force in which the Cameron Highlanders of Winnipeg in company with such units as the South Saskatchewan Regiment, Les Fusiliers Mont Royal, the Essex Scottish and others, figured so gallantly and suffered such grievous losses.

But the heavy sacrifices made on that misty August morning were not made in vain. Dieppe was a stepping stone to victory in that it gained knowledge and information immensely valuable to the success of the amphibious operations in the assault on Europe. As General Crerar said on the eve of D-Day: "The plans, the preparations, the methods and the technique which will be employed are based on the knowledge and experience bought and paid for by the 2nd Canadian Division at Dieppe. The contribution of that hazardous operation cannot be overestimated. It will prove to have been the prelude to our forthcoming and final success."

In these days of final victory our thoughts are with the gallant men who fell at Dieppe and their comrades who laid down their lives in battle before and since that freedom might endure.

—The Winnipeg Tribune,
August 18, 1945

Expo – A Chance to See the Whole World

One hundred years ago, even in the most elaborate dreams of man, no one could have foreseen the technological age of 1967 and the forces for good and evil it has let loose. Even today, because knowledge accumulates more quickly than any man can comprehend, few people can be aware of the major developments in all of the vital areas of human investigation.

Expo 67 provides the opportunity to catch up with the world as it is in 1967 – the world of science and technology, the world of literature and the arts and the challenges of Man and His World.

The challenges today are numerous and varied. The problem of food production and of population control; the causes of war and the weapons of peace; the banishment of individual poverty and control of national wealth.

The list is endless, and Expo in one way or another, touches them all.

A hint of how the themes are dealt with is contained in a special section in today's *Gazette*. There are detailed interpretations of Man and his Health; Man and Life; Man the Explorer; Man and Oceans; Man, His Planet and Space; Man the Producer; and Man the Provider. In addition, of course, 62 separate nations tell the visitor their own stories, which illustrate the diverse ways man approaches life.

The 100-odd pavilions offer a splendid exhibition in themselves, which might be titled Man the Architect and Designer. There are distinctive styles – from the Oriental magnificence of the Thailand Pavilion and the splendour of the mosaic-tiled Iranian national building, both recalling the vision of older civilizations, to the geodesic dome of the United States and the translucent tent of West Germany – inviting imaginative leaps into the future.

The building of the 1,000-acre island complex, where Expo 67 now stands, also is a story in itself. It was a considerable engineering achievement. Only four years ago Expo 67 was a dream on a river bed – a dream which many said was beyond realization.

The Expo visitor will be aware everywhere of the river. It is a commanding reality. The site is crossed with canals and spotted with lakes. Ocean-going ships will cast shadows on one side as they enter Montreal harbour and on the other, begin the long voyage up the St. Lawrence Seaway system.

This is as it should be. The St. Lawrence River has an honoured place in the history of this continent, and especially of Canada. For 400 years and more, it has carried ships from all nations, all kinds of journeys, with all kinds of cargoes. Now it has been harnessed in a new way; conquered but not forgotten; in fact, used to add a dimension to and a picturesque setting for this first international and universal exhibition in North America.

Expo, then, will be an experience in catching up with the world. It does not pass over the problems that advanced technology and scientific achievement have brought, or the problems that still exist.

It puts man's hopes, man's achievements and man's failings on display. It shows the paradoxes and the potential of Man and His World.

Perhaps, too, it may chart a course for the future.

—*The Montreal Gazette,*
April 28, 1967

The Canadian Spirit

What will our beloved nation, young in years – yet we are told, old in temperament – offer to us and to the world in its second century?

Three possibilities predominate in the context of that mixture of the tangible and the intangible we have blended together in our national course. These are a place for ideas, a new environment for man and an early place of opportunity for youth.

There will be – inevitably and one hopes eternally – a love of the land, of the soil, mixed for a time with memories of the various national histories, some of them unhappy ones, which brought most of us here.

For many there will be a recall of what a harsh land it was for the newcomer, but for a few others it will always have been a place flowing with milk and honey. And for all, there is a land where little blood has been spilled in building it, but from which tens of thousands of Canadians willingly went to fight and then lie forever on someone else's battlefield.

All these things we know and they have been explained to us by our poets, our historians and novelists. All these things, race, culture, a military record forced on us by two global conflicts, have both bound us together and separated us. And many more words will be spilled in 1967 in hard-pressed efforts to define once and for all who we are, as the next one hundred years begin.

But surely the Canadian spirit, though born of these important and often conflicting elements, is something else again, a higher dimension of effort and experience which we, by 1967, have captured – hesitatingly, unknowingly perhaps – but have captured nevertheless.

WORLD CITIZENS IN CANADA

George Grant, the otherwise angry and disparaging Canadian intellectual from the Loyalist heritage, once said: "We are the first people to learn how to be citizens in a world ruled by techniques."

If so, this is where we may start in defining the spirit we have generated and with which we will persevere. And as good Canadians, we immediately search for practical applications of what it is we have become and how we will express it.

In an age of suffocating ideologies, charismatic strongmen who bankrupt whole nations, where wars are still fought as "holy," our quiet heritage is a paradise indeed.

But in a "profit and loss" summing up of who we are (the kind of statement which many Canadians still cherish), we have not slept in our paradise. In our society, in spite of its political imperfections, its susceptibility to domination by the larger one to the south, the political dissident, the advanced social planner, the architect motivated by social purpose and not entirely by material gain, a genuine philosophy of international diplomacy have all flourished. Even with the breathtaking technology which permeates it, we have put our vast environment to work for things of the spirit.

A society for ideas.

Where else in a very angry world could a panel of conflicting international experts containing a Cuban-Communist, a U.S. State Department officer and a Catholic intellectual, talk at each other in the embrace of a quiet summer afternoon? Where else than in the atmosphere of the Couchiching Conference?

What other nation with a military record of a nation in two great wars in this century, with a navy once the world's third largest, with a nation industrialized by armed conflict, would consign its men-at-arms to peacekeeping operations?

In the Middle East, for example, where Semitic brothers stalemate their futures through bloody war and non-recognition, our military helped maintain 11 continuous years of border peace.

What other country with our vast territories has experimented so successfully with new techniques to bridge time and space? There are the bush pilots, the company towns, imaginative urban renewal schemes, exciting intellectual palaces in our new universities, combining modern art and utilitarian concepts, where once field and pastures persisted.

PHILOSOPHY A GUIDE

What other country less intent on defining the spirit of man, of control over environment for the benefit of people, has sought inspiration for its great international fair from a philosopher-writer? "To be a man is to feel that by bringing one stone, one contributes to building the world," wrote the late Antoine de Saint-Exupéry, the great but tender Frenchman.

And so Expo 67 became not a *terre des machines*, "machines and their world," but *terre des hommes*, "man and his world."

Inherent in our contribution to ideas and environment is that great blessing of the two old and sophisticated cultures, the French and the English, which have made our history. Hopefully not too late, those living Canadians who still deny a place for each other's race will come to accept the French and English cultures together and the fact we would not have a Canadian spirit without both.

What a Godsend we have been created by men and women who spoke the languages of Shakespeare, Churchill, Molière and Camus. How disastrous it would have been for us in this physically huge nation with all its potential, if the other official language had been, like Afrikaans, a vehicle for the meanest form of racism.

English has largely brought us our technology and our managerial know-how. French has brought us an understanding of diplomacy, some law, a baroque and open nature to our public life. Both our founding languages are assets for the century ahead. Never drawbacks.

YOUTH HAS OPPORTUNITY

And finally, we are a very young nation. Our population is much younger than it was in 1867. More than half of us are under 30. Those of us with personal memories of World War II are being outnumbered very quickly by our own offspring. Those of us with personal memories of World War I are of even earlier vintage, fewer in numbers, in the sere of life.

But our best young people will still be under 50 as our second century approaches its halfway mark.

What will we bequeath them? Will it be that "greater city" the Scriptures promise, but on native soil – where present ideas of politics, religion and conformism will have faded, hopefully merged into new concepts of politics, faith and work, only now on the threshold of acceptance?

Technical and intellectual output we can leave to our young in abundance. How they use it to make the quality of life paramount in Canada's future will be their abiding, lifelong challenge.

—*The Toronto Telegram,*
July 1, 1967

Ready for Viking 1000?

Now that the Cabot 500 celebrations are off and running, and a huge success, it may be time to start planning for a party for the Great Northern Peninsula three years from now. The year 2000 will be the 1,000th anniversary of the Norse settlement at L'Anse aux Meadows, one of the earliest European settlements in the New World. It could be the premier event of the inevitable millennium celebrations.

In addition to their value as a celebration of history, the Cabot 500 celebrations have shown that Newfoundlanders can organize a significant worldwide event that captures the imagination of the world and increases tourism significantly.

Despite part criticism of the concept, the economic and cultural benefits are everything even its most ardent supporters hoped it would be. When you get cover stories in the *Toronto Star*, *Maclean's*, the *Toronto Sun* and coverage on the BBC along with blanket coverage on News-world, all the planning, money and time put into the event have clearly paid off. One has only to compare the festivities at Bonavista and St. John's with the non-event in Cape Breton to see what planning and good execution can do.

While the 1497 voyage of Cabot marked the start of the English empire, the Norse settlement at Vinland was the apex of the Viking empire, a stage in history when fierce Viking warriors explored and settled much of the northern world from Russia to North America. And while their settlement here lasted only a few years, its existence alone was a remarkable achievement.

The flood of tourists that visit L'Anse aux Meadows each year demonstrates the remarkable drawing power of the recreated Viking settlement. That site – combined with the Maritime Archaic Indian, Paleo-Eskimo and Dorset interpretation sites on the Northern Peninsula and Southern Labrador, as well as the Basques whaling site at Red Bay – could form the nucleus of another wonderful year of celebration and commemoration.

It may also be possible to get Leif Ericsson to repeat his famous voyage of settlement. After all, if we can recreate John Cabot, his ship and his crew, and his historic voyage, then recreating a longboat and a bunch of warrior Vikings should be a snap, although sailing from Scandinavia to Cape Bauld may be a bit trickier.

Given the rave reviews the island received from the Newfoundland flotilla, it could also be time for another flotilla of sailboats to visit the island on the south and west coasts of the province. Staging events in order to attract sailors seems to be an idea whose time has come.

And since the tip of the Great Northern Peninsula is one of the most likely sites for the Matthew's landfall (after Bonavista, of course), staging another event to commemorate Viking 1000 might be even-handed justice.

—*The St. John's Evening Telegram, July 5, 1997*

The Millennium Dawns

What resolutions should we write on the big blank sheet that lies before us?

Well, we could round up the obvious suspects: War. Greed. Pollution. Hunger. Separatism. Ten centuries might just be enough to put these scourges behind us.

Trouble is, war and greed aren't really things that can be stopped on Premier Ralph Klein voluntary-compliance model. Everyone needs to be onside, or the prevalence and magnitude of the problem just gets worse.

And hunger? We're at least a century away from figuring out how this might be resolved, and never mind the will to do it. One of the many dilemmas of hunger is how to avoid ruining the economic machinery that has made ending hunger physically possible. The paradox is this: greed and selfishness are both the cause of the problem, and core elements in the only system we know of that generates enough wealth and food to solve it.

And pollution? The truth is, pollution is probably going to solve itself in the next few decades, whatever we might resolve. Necessity will dictate action – and those actions will either work or we'll lose the moderate environment on which civilization's ability to pollute depends.

And separatism? By raising it here, we'd break the only resolution anyone wants on the subject.

So maybe, instead of presuming to tackle these evils directly, we should resolve to do something about their more obvious causes.

• How about deciding "No more rewarding violence" and "No more pretending that we don't reward it." The cold fact is, humanity has repeatedly proved Mother was wrong when she told us, "Violence never solved anything." Experience shows that unless the wielder of violence sets impractical goals or underestimates his opponents, violence actually works like a charm. Where would Israel be today, without the violent determination of its founders and defenders? Would the Palestinians be on the verge of better circumstances without it? Would Ireland exist? Would the IRA, its political supporters and the aspirations of Ulster Catholics matter a fig in Ulster today? Violence put paid to apartheid in South Africa, stopped the genocide in Rwanda, obliterated Hitler and set limits on nutty nationalism in Yugoslavia. True, negotiations, common sense and other trappings of non-violence had their part in some of these developments, but if people had not taken up arms in the first place, few of these issues would ever have reached the point of solution.

• A corollary to the above resolution should, of course, be: "Avoid policies that would push you to the point of violence if you were on the receiving end."

• How about "No more racism"? If we define this charming human habit widely – to include the tendency to lump all varieties of "other" people into groups, and then assign them a lower status and priority than ourselves – we have a core cause of at least half the violent fatalities of the century.

• How about trying to see things through the eyes of others, instead of deeming it proof of the other's inferiority that he does not see things through ours? How about following the golden rule, rather than the pyrite version, which is "Do unto others what seems to be most beneficial to you, and then use the power and/or wealth and/or social influence so obtained to justify your actions and reduce the ability of others to return the favour."

– Or, after our experience through the century with various folk who claimed to know what was best for humanity, we could resolve to ask "what do you mean 'we'?" with a bit more suspicion when people claim to know what the whole community needs.

Except for the advice in *Edmonton Journal* editorials, of course. Happy New Millennium.

—*The Edmonton Journal,*
December 31, 1999

Brave New World of Cyberspace

An Internet search for the classic baseball movie *Field of Dreams* spits out 1.24 billion Web sites in just 0.06 seconds. A search for Shoeless Joe Jackson, the legendary "Black Sox" slugger featured in the film returns 12,900 sites in 0.11 seconds.

As these examples illustrate, the movie's maxim – "Build it and they will come" – seems far more applicable to cyberspace than to any baseball diamond. They built the Web. Everyone showed up.

It's hard to imagine that this door to the new Oz first opened just 10 years ago this past week. It was unlocked not by the titans of capitalism – preoccupied as they were, with standard-technology products – but by Marc Andreessen, a 21-year-old electrical engineering dropout who was earning $6.85 an hour writing boring software code at the University of Illinois.

As Web historian James Wallace tells the story, in 1992 Andreessen, the "big blond kid with the baby face (and lopsided smile) put together a team of like-minded young programmers. For two months, without the knowledge of their bosses, they "worked day and night, living on milk, chocolate-chip cookies, Mountain Dew and Skittles" to produce Mosaic, the first Internet "browser." Better known today as the

Netscape Navigator, Andreessen's browser made it possible to compress space and time to such a degree that a person sitting in front of a computer in Toronto can now follow reaction in Tokyo, London, Melbourne and New Delhi to the SARS outbreak here at home.

Free from the constraints of time and space, teens in Toronto are now able to play computer games in real time against opponents in Auckland, Manchester and Pretoria.

The browser gave the world access to, and an outlet for, vast amounts of information on the World Wide Web, as well as new ways of learning, working, communicating, shopping, banking, stock-trading, travel planning, gambling and advertising – all done with a few clicks of a mouse.

It spawned a host of new industries, and turned countless young computer "geeks" – some with peach fuzz still on their cheeks – into instant millionaires and even billionaires. It has forced us to speak their language – we surf the NET with Yahoo and Google, complain about spam and trojans, and send each other JPEGs, TIFs and GIFs.

The Internet has created new business models, some virtual and some real. It has, for example, led newspapers, including the *Star*, to compete against themselves by offering readers free on-line copies that are updated through the day.

In the realm of virtual business models, however, the rush to media convergence has proved to have few, if any, real benefits in the world of space and time in which shareholders continue to live.

At the core of the new "information age," the Internet is without boundaries, making it an instrument for good, bad and everything in-between.

On one side of the coin, the Internet has, for example, enabled human rights groups to pierce the cloak of secrecy that had long permitted oppressive regimes to abuse their citizens, and by doing so, it has given dissidents in those countries the chance to tell their stories to the outside world. It has given doctors in remote areas the opportunity to review a patient's file with a consulting specialist thousands of kilometres away.

On the other side of the coin, it has become a depository of child pornography, and a powerful instrument of fraud, although it has also given police new tools to combat these crimes.

In the grey zone, it has facilitated the pirating of copyrighted material. Consumers, for example, have access to vast libraries of "free" recorded music, a source of irritation to the recording industry, to say the least.

By making Marshall McLuhan's global village a reality – we are all only a click or two away from each other – the Internet has had an effect on almost every facet of our daily lives.

In just a decade, it as launched us into a brave new e-world, a world of possibilities that we have only just begun to mine.

It's hard to predict where it will take us, because our future destinations can't be found on any map – they exist only in the minds and imaginations of children who have lived their entire lives in the timeless realm of cyberspace.

—The Toronto Star, April 27, 2003

Canada in 2020: A Changed Nation

Gazing into a crystal ball is fraught with peril, especially when done in print. But the occasion of Canada Day 2005 inspires speculation about what this country might look like on this very holiday 15 years from today.

And so, with great trepidation, we dare to dream of Canada in 2020.

From technology to culture, only one thing is certain – that Canada will be a nation dramatically different than we know it today.

On the technological front, based on changes over the past two decades, Canadians will have access to more conveniences and services than they currently enjoy. But life won't necessarily be any easier for most of us.

Fifteen years ago, the Internet existed but was virtually unknown. The hot communication technology of the time was the fax machine astoundingly capable of transmitting a document over a telephone line. Almost nobody had a cellphone. Portable phones that did exist were the size of a cement block and weighed almost as much.

As for having a computer in the home, what possible use could that be?

Technology has marched a long way since then, and it is set to march even faster. Canadians, and the world at large, will likely be plugged in, and electronically connected, in ways hard to imagine today. Futurists paint a scenario where even a mundane object, such as a refrigerator, will routinely send messages over the Internet, presumably important missives such as: "Milk about to expire on shelf 2."

Once-bulky cellphones are evolving into a combined multi-purpose entertainment system and portable office that can be carried in a pocket.

But some of the biggest – and most expensive – leaps into technology are likely in the medical sector, where a revolution is quietly under way to remake humanity. In 15 years, genetic testing will likely be available to parents eager to know not only their unborn child's vulnerability to certain diseases, but also the youngster's intelligence quotient, personality traits and innate talent for certain sports. Genetic engineering may have progressed to the point where some traits could be fine-tuned in the womb. A child born on this day in 2020 could be troublingly perfect, at least if it had the benefit of wealthy parents.

Advances in using stem cells will likely make it possible to grow tissue for a variety of organs; robotic technology will provide artificial limbs of amazing dexterity; leaps in nanotechnology will open the way for microscopic machines to fix the body from within, and the steady pace of drug development will add hundreds, perhaps thousands, of new treatments to the medical profession's chemical armoury.

Canadians rising for the national anthem in 2020 will be a lot older and greyer than today's population, and society will be more in need of medical help than ever. The number of people 90 and over will almost double in two years. And almost one-third of the population will be 60, or older.

Technology will brim with exciting, and costly, new miracles at the same time that Canadian society develops a growing need for those miracles, but limited ability to pay.

Caught in the twin grindstones of those pressures, Canada's publicly funded health-care system might not survive. It simply may

not be able to cover the many possible treatments made available by science and demanded by an aging population. A two-tier private system would comfort mainly the very rich who could afford the best genetic screening, robotics and other treatments for themselves and their children.

On the cultural front, Canadians will likely still enjoy home-grown musical talent, maple syrup, and – for some in Quebec – poutine. But a kaleidoscope of rapidly shifting international offerings will dominate the cultural marketplace. A trendy snack food, shoe style, or telephone ring tone could blossom in Soho, Tokyo or, more likely, somewhere in China, and sweep across the interconnected world in days, or even hours. It would be all the rage until the arrival of the Next Big Thing – likely a day later.

Excitement will be easy to find, but satisfaction will be fleeting.

Citizens celebrating Canada Day in the year 2020 can also expect less real privacy than any previous generation. That's a downside of the online life. Interconnectedness means, quite literally, we are all in this together.

The big change won't be increased government supervision, though. What will grow dramatically is the amount of intimate data on Canadians held in private-sector data banks around the world. It's hard to see how this could be avoided. Even in a new car today, the OnStar system makes it possible for the company providing this service to track a subscriber's whereabouts. If using Highway 407, the toll company running that thoroughfare could also track the same vehicle, via a transponder or cameras.

That's what exists now. In 15 years, the interconnectedness of society, plus advances in computing, might make it possible to follow the activities of almost any Canadian, virtually anywhere.

Then again, maybe not. The only sure way to experience Canada Day 2020 is to be there. Surely Canadians will rise to the future's challenge.

After all, this country endured the Great Depression, and helped win two world wars, to emerge as one of the most tolerant and prosperous places on the planet. That legacy is solid and certain and worth carrying with pride toward whatever lies ahead.

—*The Toronto Star,*
July 1, 2005

2
Farewells

Death of the Queen

"The Queen is dead." Such was the short announcement flashed by the telegraph across the Empire, from Cowes to Regina, at noon on Tuesday last. Simple as are the words, they have given rise to a grief so poignant, a sorrow so profound, that neither written nor spoken language can adequately express their strength or their depth. "Surely nothing dies but something mourns;" but with the death of a Queen so good, after a reign so glorious, it is no hyperbole to say that the Empire is in tears.

The many nations that form the vast British Empire, with their different faiths, of whatever colour, caste or creed they may be, however diverse their customs and their laws, have all ever been one in love for the sovereign that rules over them, and respect for the queenly office she so worthily occupied.

The chief characteristics of Victoria as a Queen were the intense affection she always showed for her people, irrespective of rank or nationality; and the wide

sympathy she had with all that suffered or were oppressed. On two occasions only did Her Majesty exercise the direct prerogative of her position. One was an act of mercy, the other a proof that her ears were not closed to the voice of her humblest subjects. It was this great affection and this wide sympathy that endeared Victoria to her people, as their Queen.

But if our late Sovereign was revered as the chief of the Empire, she was still more enshrined in the hearts of the people for her womanly virtues and lovable qualities. Behind the crown, the sceptre and the mace, there was the woman. Beneath the intertissued robe of gold and pearl there beat a heart full of loving kindness.

It is trite to observe that a monarch's lot is not altogether an enviable lot. "What infinite heart's ease must kings neglects that private men enjoy," and history shows that many sovereigns have been less happy in being feared than the people in fearing.

This must always be the case with a ruler who realises the duties and responsibilities attached to a throne in the way our beloved sovereign recognized them. If she could share in the joys and prosperity of her Empire; she also felt its sorrows and its woes. Queen Victoria did this in a way of which history records no similar example.

The reason of so estimable a quality was undoubtedly her true womanly nature. She showed it at her own fireside, and her warm influence spread from there to every palace, every house, every cot in the Empire. As wife, and as mother, as well as Queen, our gracious sovereign was of the people as well as over them.

It is for such a one the nation mourns. We feel that with a past life so excellent even the darkness of death must have been beautiful to her. While, therefore, grief is profound beyond all expression, the recollection of her virtues, of her love, of her warm and generous heart, should lead those in less exalted positions to imitate her good qualities and copy her kindness and her wisdom.

We mourn her but we love her still; and her life's acts will ever be a guiding star to other sovereigns and a direction to all the peoples of all the nations of the earth.

—*The Regina Leader,*
January 24, 1901

Sir Frederick Banting

Periodically the great medical profession produces a man who is not merely a physician but a discoverer. He is not content to practise his profession in the ordinary way, but through some inner necessity or some vital spark must experiment, engage in research and venture forth towards new goals of achievement.

Such a man was Sir Frederick Banting, whose tragic death in an air accident was reported on Monday. Had Dr. Banting chosen any other profession he would have risen to the top and made history. He was endowed that way. But he chose medicine and it proved to be the ideal field for his peculiar genius, his great energy and persistence, his powers of co-ordination and leadership, his passion and enthusiasm.

And so, less than six years out of medical school (with war service in between) he, with the aid of loyal colleagues, announced a discovery which was hailed by the entire world of therapeutic science as one of the greatest of the century. It brought him fame and once more reflected lustre upon Canada as a leader among nations in the realm of medicine. Among the honours which were subsequently showered on Dr. Banting were the Nobel Prize and a knighthood from his king.

The same devotion to research which led to the discovery of insulin characterized his activities in the intervening years. At the time of his passing he was at work on aviation medicine. The thoroughness and imagination of his earlier experiments marked his most recent endeavours.

As Dean C.J. Mackenzie tells us, he would go up in an airplane to great heights and insist on a dive in order to further his understanding of the problem he was studying – the effect on flying men of the strains which such conditions and manoeuvres produce. The intimation that his researches in this field may rival those which brought him earlier renown is a measure of the magnitude of his loss.

—*The Ottawa Evening Citizen, February 26, 1941*

Nellie McClung

Nellie McClung was a woman who considered no obstacle insurmountable. That was the secret of her success as a teacher, an author, a politician, a reformer and a champion of women's rights. All that she did in her long, varied life was done with a will. Her enthusiasms rode behind a splendid team of her brilliant mind and determined spirit.

Whether teaching in her first school in a little settlement near Manitou or speaking as a delegate to the assembly of the League of Nations, she concentrated on the job at hand.

Nellie McClung was an ardent temperance worker, social reformer and zealot. But her wit and humour saved her from becoming the grim, depressing sort of person some zealots can be. In all the campaigns in which she engaged, she was the smiling, happy champion. As one of her friends put it years ago, "Even the McClung scoldings were good."

But Nellie McClung will be longest remembered here as a writer. Her novels, such as *Sowing Seeds in Danny* and *Second Chance*, are mirrors of the days when settlers were coming to Manitoba. They are filled with the hundred and one interesting things that happened in the daily lives of the homesteaders as they brought homes, churches and schools to the Prairies. They stand as a monument to a great era and a remarkable woman.

—*The Winnipeg Tribune,*
September 4, 1951

Miss Jennie Webster, O.B.E.

"Miss Webster of the General" is dead.

Perhaps younger folk may never have heard of her, as she resigned her post nearly 20 years ago. But to those who served at the Montreal General Hospital between 1900 and 1922, or who were patients there in those years, the very sound of her name is enough to warm the heart.

For 33 years Miss Jennie Webster, O.B.E., was night superintendent of the General. Towards the end of her career, every new patient, or nurse, or doctor used to ask her how she liked being on night duty for so long. She always replied a little brusquely, that she liked it very well indeed.

Perhaps it was because the hospital at night was less cluttered than in the day, and she liked things orderly and well-managed. And perhaps, too, she felt that she was more needed in the dark night hours, which are dismal to many a sick person – hours of pain and waiting.

Her very appearance at the bedside somehow brought a sense of reassurance and command. She made the sick one feel that all was under supervision. Rarely did she visit a patient without seeing at once something that should be done for his greater comfort; and sometimes the nurse who had failed to smooth a pillow, or had left a lamp shining in a patient's eyes, received a sharp word of rebuke.

Yet the nurses thought as much of her as the patients. She was strict but she was fair. And above all she had nursing in her heart as the finest vocation in life. Those who remember her as a probationer recall how she herself was always the first to do the hard jobs – scrubbing floors, or carrying heavy loads up long flights of stairs.

The dark streets about the old Montreal General, often none too well lit, caused her no alarm. She went to and from the hospital unescorted, with the same firm, vigorous step with which she moved about the hospital corridors. If she happened on Cadieux street to encounter noisy and belligerent groups, she never avoided them, but would deliver them a lecture on the wickedness of disturbing the poor sick patients nearby.

"Miss Webster of the General" became a legend and she has left a tradition. Florence Nightingale herself would have found her a nurse after her own heart. She would have done very well indeed in bringing an orderly mercy to the trenches and barrack-hospitals of the Crimea.

—The Montreal Gazette,
October 17, 1952

Farewell, Charlotte

Her legacy is what she was, warts and all – for she wrote it huge across the life of Ottawa in those days when she ruled as mayor.

She refashioned the mayor's office to her unique taste, endowing it with pomp and ceremony, humanity and explosiveness, and – because she was Charlotte Whitton – with guts and brilliance and venom, and warmth.

And somehow, as if to compensate for her diminutive frame, doing it all bigger than life-size. The mayor's office had to be big – had to be made separate and special with cap and gown as well as chain of office – to contain it all.

And why not? For Charlotte Whitton was surrogate for the little man and woman to whom Ottawa properly belonged – using power in their name to run this city as they would have it run. She was there to beat back those with money and influence; to do battle with her fellow politicians, who marched, as she usually believed, to some drum other than her own; and ceaselessly to watch and bully the city staff.

Though sidewalks were left to decay and streetcar rails and potholes lay unmolested through her era, she bulldozed through a heavy load of business. The city adapted itself to growth and works projects went forward, almost always with the Whitton stamp. If backstage manipulation didn't get her what she wanted, a dressing down usually did. Or even a reading from the Municipal Act, though council often suspected that the rulings she produced had been newly minted to suit the occasion.

The contradictions were as brazen as the lady herself. If she exalted the office with pageantry, she didn't shrink from brandishing a fake gun in the council chamber. She could mercilessly carve up a colleague's reputation from the mayor's chair, and then rouse herself in the night to go to a fire, or quietly help out a citizen in need. She could fight the spread of liquor licences in true temperance tradition, but had no qualms about ordering up her own refill of gin when drinks were being passed round.

"She loved her city," her former colleagues will tell you. That love brought her back to the council table as alderman when the mayor's chair had passed to others – smaller now, a little irrelevant, but zealous as ever in her scrutiny of public business.

Beneath it all, though, she was sad, recognizing – more sharply than most of us – that the mayor's office was diminished, and that other governments had pre-empted much of its power. It would take more even than a Charlotte Whitton to bring it all back.

—*The Ottawa Citizen,*
January 27, 1975

Terry Fox

He never thought of himself as a hero, merely as a young man with an errand to run, a message to deliver, a disease to conquer.

The nation caught up with Terrance Stanley Fox rather late on the road between Newfound-land and Thunder Bay, Ontario, but having caught up, it refused to let go.

He was showered with honours and adulation and with 24 times the $1 million he had set out to collect for cancer research with his Marathon of Hope.

He made Canadians proud to share in his dreams of conquest and by his own example of courage, endurance and selfless-ness he uplifted everyone.

On Sept. 3, the day after he was forced to abandon his cross-country odyssey, we observed:

"Once in a while on the face of the earth there appears an excep-tional human being whose words and deeds restore faith in the human race – one who fills us less-er mortals with pride to be a mem-ber of the species, with the inspi-ration to reach greater heights, with a sense of the indomitability of the human spirit."

Terry Fox was such a human being.

He sought nothing for himself, only for those like him, afflicted by cancer.

He brought a new respectability to cancer research, giving fresh life and a new purpose to those engaged in the search for a cure and hope and encouragement to those whose lives continue to depend on it.

He was overwhelmed by honours and tributes from governments and people eager to show their gratitude and affection for what his Marathon of Hope represented and what it accomplished, but never so proud as to accept them for himself.

Terry Fox ran his way into the hearts of millions and the new cancer research facility at the University of British Columbia that bears his name is only one testimony to the success that attended his mission. Surely, there will be many more.

The marathon that this young man started did not end in September. Nor has it ended with his untimely death.

It will never end until a cure has been found for cancer.

How we remember Terry Fox is not so important as that we do remember him – and, just as important, that we do not forget to finish what he started.

—*The Vancouver Sun,*
June 29, 1981

Glenn Gould

In the 50 years of his life, Glenn Gould did little that was bland, much that was brilliant and provocative. His death yesterday – from a severe stroke suffered a week earlier – robs the world of more than a superbly gifted pianist, more than a great interpreter of the music of Bach, more than a perceptive writer and caustic commentator. As both critic and artist, he provided a vital cultural stimulant to the arts simply by being a creatively disturbing influence.

He was called eccentric, and certainly he was unconventional – credited, for example, with leading the way out of dress formality on the concert stage. He cared little for starch in any form. His mannerisms in performance also attracted a good deal of attention –

the facial contortions, the rolling head, the tendency to conduct with any arm that happened to be free, an orchestra that already had a conductor. He had a tendency to sing unsolicited obbligatos to his piano performances.

All of this was, however, part of an artist with impeccable credentials, and was largely accepted as being essential to Mr. Gould's feeling for, and enjoyment of, the music. He himself was, of course, enough of a free spirit not to be at all concerned about what people might think.

The things that did absorb him did so with passionate intensity. Music – "my ecstasy" – was, of course, an easy first. He saw it as an individual experience in which the musician (or listener) stands outside himself and achieves true communion with the music. Sam Carter, co-producer of a new digital recording of the *Goldberg Variations* (an earlier version of which launched Mr. Gould into prominence in 1955) said he was impressed by what he called the "intentionality" of the pianist. "He is striking as a musician because of his absolute knowledge, the way he embodies musical intelligence. There's seldom any question of what Glenn wants and he's able to execute those intentions better than any other performer I know." Mr. Gould's prowling intellect could not be shackled to the keyboard. It burst forth in television documentaries, in radio commentary and in critical writing – some of it for The Globe and Mail. With evident delight, and sparkling wit, he reviewed for us the book about himself written by Geoffrey Payzant, referring to the first chapter as a "quick-and-dirty sketch of Gould's early years – which is, indeed, rather boring, and by no means as brief as it should be."

Mr. Gould's life, alas, was far briefer than it should have been.

—*The Globe and Mail,*
October 5, 1982

Margaret Laurence, Literary Giant

The loss of Margaret Laurence will be felt on many levels. A consummate writer, she was also a friend to other authors, a noted humanitarian and Lakefield's best-known citizen.

Most Canadians knew Margaret Laurence for her books, especially those volumes in which her heroines wrestled with small-town life, surviving to become symbolic of all humanity. In five novels, two story collections, four children's books, essays, criticisms and a book of early memoirs, Margaret Laurence transcended the boundaries of nationality, gender and generations. She left a lasting legacy.

She was also known as a "writer's writer," not just because of her spare and elegant prose but also because she took time to serve with groups promoting the professional interests of writers and because she always had time to encourage and help the neophyte.

Margaret Laurence did not shy from lending her name to causes in which she had an interest and in recent years, was closely identified with the peace movement.

Her list of achievements and honours includes two Governor-General's Awards for her novels, *A Jest of God* in 1966 and *The Diviners* in 1974. She was made a Companion of the Order of Canada in 1971, was writer-in-res-

idence at several universities and served as chancellor of Trent University from 1981 to 1984.

The Stone Angel probably did most to secure Margaret Laurence's place in the hearts of Canadians. The story of Hagar Shipley, the elderly Prairie heroine, is on the reading list of enough English courses to have secured her income in later years. That popularity also gave Margaret Laurence the most painful moments of her public life. She was bewildered by some of her critics, including those who unsuccessfully asked the Peterborough County Board of Education to remove three of her novels from its course list.

If controversy attached itself to some of her books, Margaret Laurence remained a private person. The people of Lakefield – where the author had made her home since 1974 – will recall a homespun woman making her rounds, chatting and visiting just like the neighbour she was. It was this blend of intellect and ordinariness that made her the giant she was.

—*The Peterborough Examiner, January 7, 1987*

Harold Ballard

"There's no such thing as a nice guy," crusty old Harold Ballard was fond of saying. "Mr. Nice Guys are all fakes."

Ballard, who died yesterday at 86, was seldom nice but never a fake. He was one of a kind.

As the majority owner, Ballard turned Maple Leaf Gardens into a gold mine, renting it to everything from church groups to rock groups, circuses to political rallies.

But his beloved Maple Leafs proved after more than two decades of defeat that he was an inept hockey club owner, often trading good players for bad to satisfy his impulsive piques.

He was jailed for theft and fraud in 1972 and raised a stink by saying that he loved the swimming pool, golf course, sirloin steaks, pie and ice cream at Millhaven prison.

He told evangelist Billy Graham that "I'd love to be in your racket" and in a dispute described one of his hockey stars, Darryl Sittler, as "a cancer on the Leafs." On another occasion, he told broadcaster Barbara Frum to shut up and said women were at their most eloquent "on their backs."

That was Ballard. He was a difficult, cantankerous old man, who had a stormy soap opera-like relationship with family, friends, employees and enemies.

His life was a front-page story. About the only thing he kept his mouth shut about was his generosity. He contributed millions to charities and to those down on their luck.

Ballard wasn't all bad. Some will remember him fondly. Others won't. But everyone will remember him as the great grandstander of Maple Leaf Gardens.

—*The Toronto Star, April 12, 1990*

Bill Reid's Vision

It would be difficult to create a more Canadian mix of roots and influences than Bill Reid's.

His mother a Haida, the sea-going people of the North Pacific, his father a Scots-American. Born in Victoria, trained at Ryerson in making jewelry, a CBC broadcaster in his early manhood.

He discovered his Haida roots in his late teens. The great, classic Haida style of art focused the rest of his life. Haida art was also an early influence on another great artist from the Pacific Coast, Emily Carr, and it allowed her to find the vision that would elevate her to the front rank of Canadian artists.

But her purpose was to preserve this art in sketches. She believed it was doomed to be irretrievably lost as the totems rotted in the damp and the carvers fell to disease.

Reid's purpose was not just to preserve Haida art but to restore its vitality. This he did, and more. He gave it a contemporary feel and scale that collectors came to prize, that inspired a new generation of coastal artists and gave them an economic base to replace the one once provided by tribal chieftains and other worthies.

His genius led to commissions to cast the polished black *Spirit of Haida Gwaii* in Canada's embassy in Washington, then the jade-like companion piece in the Vancouver airport terminal.

He called the *Haida Gwaii* his "Ship of Fools" for the unruly cargo of 13 humans and animals squabbling and vying for position in a canoe but "somehow managing to appear to be heading in the same direction" – a better metaphor than he could have known for a Canada of 10 provinces and, soon, three territories. When he died this past weekend, however, Reid's fame extended far beyond his people, his province, his country. His work projected a universal spirit that transcended boundaries and cultures.

His castings, his carvings, his jewelry, to be sure, grace the Royal Ontario Museum, the McMichael Collection, the Museum of Anthropology in Vancouver and the national Museum of Civilization.

But they also can be found in the British Museum in London, in the Musée de l'homme in Paris, in

30

New York, Asia and private collections around the world.

It is not often that people of Reid's universal vision walk the Earth. We are poorer for his death.

We have been immensely enriched by the life he led among us.

—The Toronto Star,
March 18, 1998

Richard's Legacy

As the vehicle that bears the body of the Canadiens' great captain rolls slowly down Ste. Catherine St. toward the state funeral in Old Montreal this morning, the outpouring of public feeling will testify to the extraordinary hero that Maurice Richard was. He was three heroes in one.

The first, of course, was Maurice Richard the sports idol, whose glittering feats grace the record book. The second was the incandescently determined Maurice Richard who foreshadowed and even helped encourage the Quiet Revolution by personifying French Quebec's drive for excellence.

But there's another Maurice Richard. The outpouring of articles and tributes to the man since his death Saturday have spoken little of this aspect of Quebec's hockey hero. He incarnated several athletic ideals that have become rare these days.

The first was team loyalty. Today, as they wander from club to club, most professional athletes' only allegiance is to the highest bidder, and then only briefly. Mr. Richard played for the same team throughout his 18-year career. He also came from the same city where he played, and lived there after his retirement. So when one speaks of Mr. Richard's loyalty to a team, one is really talking about his loyalty to Montreal.

The second ideal was his lifestyle. Mr. Richard didn't know anything about gold chains, substance abuse or girlfriends in every city, and he didn't want to know. He was married to the same woman for 51 years and was a caring father, and the only times he wandered alone out of the hotel during a road trip were to go to Sunday morning mass. He was a straight arrow in an era when that wasn't something that evoked smirks.

Another trait that seems almost bizarre by today's standards was his attitude toward money. Of course, he appreciated it and he certainly deserved to have earned more, but he also knew what greed was and shunned it. In 1972, 12 years after his retirement and at a time when salaries were beginning to take off, the Quebec Nordiques – then of the World Hockey Association – signed him as coach. After two games, realizing that coaching was not for him, he resigned and sent back his paycheque along with an explanation that he did not deserve it.

True, Mr. Richard was no saint. His quick temper did produce occasional on-ice incidents of unsportsmanlike violence. But in his devotion to the team, closeness to the community and his basic honesty, he exemplified the way that many athletes of an earlier era helped elevate pro sports to great heights of public esteem.

Pro sports – not just hockey, but also baseball, football and basketball – are now furiously squandering that legacy. This is not so much the fault of today's athletes, of course, as it is of the commercial interests that have taken over.

Some of his records have been broken, and others probably will be erased. But the aspects of Mr. Richard that will not easily be eclipsed will be his values. For those, he set a standard for which Montrealers will always be grateful.

—*The Montreal Gazette,*
May 31, 2000

Pierre Trudeau, 1919-2000

They are images that feel burned on our consciousness, distilling his very essence: the mask-like face that never aged, the unflinching stare as rioters at Montreal's 1968 St. Jean Baptiste parade threw bottles at him, the giddy pirouette behind Queen Elizabeth's back. Controlled, hidden, his shell as hard as the Canadian Shield, former Prime Minister Pierre Elliott Trudeau was a public figure unlike any other in Canadian history. As Canadians mourn his passing at age 80, those images, so singular, so memorable, are as much his legacy to his country as his political achievements.

Under him, Canada was refashioned for good, and sometimes for bad. It became, like him, a more worldly, more ambitious place. So much of what we are today is his doing: the Constitution, the Charter of Rights and Freedoms, the ideal of bilingualism, the defence of minority populations everywhere across the country, the belief that bravado and brilliance are admirable traits both in people and nations.

Swept to power in 1968 on a wave of Trudeaumania (which looks sillier now, but looked silly then, too), Mr. Trudeau was 49, a millionaire, an intellectual, all qualities which represented a departure from the dull, grey norm that prevailed at the time in Canadian politics. He was prime minister for 15 years and four months, serving the third-longest in this country (after Sir John A. Macdonald and Mackenzie King).

It is impossible to calculate how deeply he affected Canadian life. If he did not succeed in remaking his country into a bilingual, multicultural, efficiently federal state, he pushed it much farther along that road than anyone could have imagined in 1968. The late 1960s might have been known for wild rebellion elsewhere in the Western world, but in Canada our passions were inflamed over having French on boxes of corn flakes.

In the time he was prime minister, Mr. Trudeau presided over:
• The passage into law of the Official Languages Act of 1968, which established French and English as official languages with equal status from coast to coast

• The patriation into law of the Canadian Constitution, culminating in the Constitution Act of 1982, which finally put an end to Canadian legislators having to seek formal leave from Westminster before amending the country's constitution

• The unfinished business of Quebec independence, despite two referendums in which the popular vote went against the province's separatist government. In 1980, Mr. Trudeau was personally credited with spearheading the 60-percent to 40-percent federalist victory.

• Equally, if not as favourably, he was credited with burying the 1990 Meech Lake and 1992 Charlottetown accords that his successors hoped would paper over the divide separating English and French Canada

A man who viscerally disdained nationalism, Mr. Trudeau did not shy from defending Canada's national interests when circumstances called for it. In 1971, when Richard Nixon, the U.S. president, imposed a surcharge on Canadian imports in an effort to correct a U.S. balance of payments crisis, Mr. Trudeau overcame his pride and his dislike of Mr. Nixon and went to beg, successfully, to have the Americans rescind the measure.

Throughout the 1970s, the Trudeau government adopted a number of policies such as the Foreign Investment Review Agency, designed to foster a more economically independent Canada. For the anti-nationalist Mr. Trudeau to promote greater Canadian economic nationalism was an irony lost on no one.

The great political passion of his life remained the status of Quebec, however. While opponents such as the late Quebec premier René Lévesque argued for the collective right of francophone Quebecers, Mr. Trudeau fought for the primacy of individual rights. He believed that the enlightened state would always accord individual rights greater importance than collective or even state rights. This was, of course, the same man who invoked the War Measures Act at the peak of the October Crisis in 1970, sending police into the streets of Montreal in the dead of night to arrest several hundred alleged sympathizers of the FLQ – a move that, while criticized later, was widely supported at the time.

There's no doubt he wanted to solve the riddle of Quebec – his French-speaking compatriots' apparent desire for an independent Quebec within a strong

Canada – in his lifetime. But it was not to be and he, too, remained as much a riddle as his native province: the champion of individual rights who jailed the innocent; the intellectual who disdained Canada's cultural life; a man whose emotional connection to his three sons ran so deep that the death of his son Michel two years ago dealt a crippling physical and emotional blow.

Canada is left a much diminished place by his death. The men and women who have followed him into public life to not seem blessed with the divine fire that glowed within him. Maybe no country can cope for years on end with existential drama and questioning. But we needed him to push us into trying to find out who we are and what we stand for. The fact that we have not yet answered those questions does not reflect badly on him; it is a measure of the challenges inherent in a federation like Canada. Mr. Trudeau had the intelligence and heart to articulate the contradictions at the core of our country and encourage us to have confidence that we can overcome them. For that alone, we should be grateful.

—The Montreal Gazette,
September 29, 2000

Rosemary Brown Made History

As the first black woman to be elected to provincial or federal office in Canada, Rosemary Brown made her name as a pioneer in this country's political history.

But her legacy is as a role model and leader for the community at large.

Brown was a feminist, human rights activist, social worker and educator. Above all, though, she was someone who cared for others and was dedicated to helping the disadvantaged of society.

The former Vancouver politician died Saturday at the age of 72.

Born in Jamaica, Brown came to Canada to study. Her election to the British Columbia legislature in 1972 was an historic moment. In 1975, she gave Ed Broadbent a good run for the leadership of the national New Democratic Party. Broadbent won, but as a black, immigrant woman, Brown knocked down several barriers with her strong showing in the race.

She left politics in 1986 to become a professor of women's studies at Simon Fraser University. In 1993, she was named head of the Ontario Human Rights Commission at a time when it was mired in battles over budgets and office politics.

Brown had no time for such petty squabbles, recalled Rémy Beauregard, who was the agency's executive director during her four-year tenure. "She came in and said the issue is human rights," he said. "It refocused the work of the commission."

One of her chief challenges was stamping out racism, something she had experienced first-hand. And yet she knew there was no "miracle pill" to end it.

What was needed, she said, was a different way of relating to one another. And different ways of teaching our children. "Children are not born with prejudice," she noted.

In 1996, Brown looked back on her busy life. "I've been so lucky. I've had so many wonderful opportunities to do things. They far outdistanced my aspirations."

This community – and Canada as a whole – is a better place for her lifetime of service.

—*The Toronto Star,*
April 29, 2003

3
True North

Canada is All Right

In an article, "The recent progress of Canada," the *New York Sun* still thinks with Prof. Goldwin Smith, or at least as the professor once thought, that the "manifest destiny" of Canada is "political fusion" with the United States. It is safe to say, however, that the *Sun* is mistaken – political fusion as an issue was never "deader" than at present. Canada has amply demonstrated in the past few years that she can live and thrive without her selfish neighbour. The *Sun's* article is worth quoting in part, however. It says:

"The undeniable existence of unexampled prosperity seems likely to prove a decisive factor at the approaching general election in the Dominion of Canada. It is true that Sir Charles Tupper and his fellow Conservatives insist that this prosperity is due to general cases, which have affected the United States as well, and should be in no way credited to the legislative or administrative work performed by the Liberal government. On the other hand, Sir Wilfrid Laurier and his colleagues recall the prediction of disaster made by their opponents during the campaign preceding the last general election, and point out that the preponderance of Liberals at Ottawa has certainly not hindered the attainment of a rate of agricultural, industrial and commercial progress that has no precedent to Canadian history."

After reviewing the statistics of the subject, manufacturing, commercial and agricultural, the *Sun* continues:

"If such things can be done in the green tree, what might not be done in the dry? If in four years the Dominion of Canada can show such evidences of progress, while she is cut off from her natural market in the United States, how tremendous might be her rate of improvement if the tariff wall were levelled through the admission of her provinces into the American union as states? For that market there is no alternative. It is a chimera which Sir Charles Tupper and his friends are chasing, when they demand a preference for Canadian breadstuffs in the markets of the United Kingdom. No such preference will ever be granted, and, when the Canadian agriculturist is once convinced of the futility of all efforts in that direction, he will recognize that his true interests point to political fusion with the great American republic."

Canada has no need or wish to change her political lot. She has much to lose and nothing to gain by fusion, for she is fully as prosperous as her big neighbour. She is supremely happy and content in her isolation from the trust, from the industrial anarchy which periodically shakes the republic to its centre, from the political jobbery and corruption which makes its administration a stench and byword on earth and from all the other gangrenes, social and economic, that threaten the life of the republic.

—*The Windsor Evening Record*, *July 11, 1900*

The Statute of Westminster

The Statute of Westminster which is being passed by the British parliament is the legal embodiment of a principle enunciated by the Imperial Conference of 1926, namely that:

"Great Britain and the dominions are autonomous communities within the British empire, equal in status, in no way subordinate one to another in any aspects of their domestic or external affairs, though united by a common allegiance to the crown, and freely associated as members of the British Community of Nations."

The detailed implications of the declaration of 1926 were dealt with at the Imperial Conferences of 1929 and 1930, and the statute resulting therefrom has been approved by the Canadian parliament and those of the other dominions prior to its adoption by the British Houses.

It sets forth the principle of equal status as outlined above, and proves that, as one result of this, any alteration in the law touching the succession to the throne, or the royal style and titles, shall hereafter require the assent of dominion as well as United Kingdom parliaments.

The dominions must no longer be referred to as "colonies" in imperial statutes. Where the word in future appears it will not apply to them.

The new statute also provides that no future United Kingdom law shall extend to a dominion except by that dominion's request, and a dominion parliament will now have power to repeal any United Kingdom act in so far as it has been the law of that dominion.

Britain's Colonial Laws Validity Act of 1865 is specifically barred from application to any law made henceforth by a dominion.

That is, dominion laws will not be invalid because "repugnant" or contrary to some English statute.

The need for such a provision is illustrated by the fact that a law which had for 40 years been part of the Canadian criminal code,

and which forbade appeals to the Privy Council in criminal cases, was declared *ultra vires* of the Canadian parliament, and therefore void, because it conflicted with a law passed in England in the days of William.

Another provision of the new statute declares the right of a dominion parliament to make laws extending beyond the dominion's territory. Further sections remove handicaps in connection with the merchant shipping act and colonial courts of admiralty act – rules for our admiralty courts will no longer be subject to the appeal of the British cabinet.

There is, in addition, a section especially applicable to Canada since it deals with the British North America Act. It provides that nothing in the new statute shall apply to the repeal, amendment or alteration of this act, or any order, rule, or regulation made thereunder.

This was inserted to ally the fears of those who suggested that provincial rights might be imperilled by the new Westminster enactment.

That enactment may be summarized by saying that it represents an effort to put into legal practice the principle of equality which the dominions and the motherland have alike declared applicable.

It does not give Canada the right to amend her own Constitution, but, apart from that, it confers wide powers and removes many barriers to equality which have hitherto existed.

It is based on the knowledge that (as Mr. Ernest Lapointe recently put it) "the surest method of maintaining an Empire associa-tion is that it should be based on the solid rock of liberty, of autonomy and equality of status. I have no doubt," he said, "that the bonds which unite us, instead of being weakened, are rather strengthened by the new condition, based on the free will of all the citizens of the Empire."

—The Toronto Daily Star, November 30, 1931

The Flag

Patriotism is considered old fashioned in certain pseudo-sophisticated circles today. Such people may scoff at traditional concepts of loyalty to Queen and country; they may take great delight in debunking meaningful institutions. Fortunately, there is little evidence to suggest that the heart of the ordinary citizen is with them.

Patriotism may be old fashioned in the sense that, for many hundreds of years, it has been considered the primary obligation of good citizenship. But it remains a virtue – and a very solid one. It unifies a people.

And, as a focal point of national unity, there is a country's flag. To the cynic, a flag may just be a common, coloured piece of bunting, but tears have been shed for flags and blood has been spilled in their defence.

Canada has had a new flag since February 15. It flies from schools, government buildings and public buildings across the nation. But how meaningful has been its appearance? Was its dedication the event that it should have been? We fear not.

It might have been expected that the unveiling of the new flag on Parliament Hill would be a major Canadian event, shared by communities across the land.

It wasn't, really. There still weren't sufficient new flags to go around, and even a number of those now flying from mastheads seem to vary in their shades of red.

In view of the seemingly interminable period of debate required to get the Maple Leaf flag approved by Parliament, the government could have waited a little longer, giving it time to make the initial flag-raising a truly national event. It seems a date like July 1, Canada's national birthday, would have been an appropriate choice, and would probably have fired the blood of national loyalty more perceptibly than a bleak ceremony on a chilly day in mid-winter.

Certainly, the importance of stressing the flag's significance to our young people had to be delayed unduly. Calgary schools, for example, didn't get around to their flag-raising ceremonies until Friday, three months after the Ottawa ceremony. The whole situation smacks of a lack of co-ordination and planning on the part of the federal government.

Also regrettable is the insistence of certain provinces of maintaining their own provincial flags, thereby driving splinters into national unity.

—*The Calgary Herald,*
May 22, 1965

Feelings of Mixed Peoples

Canada is a country where one should never say that all bets are off, but rather that all bets are hedged. It is a country where we all say, along with Mackenzie King and his kindly spooks, that we'll do it if necessary but not necessarily do it. It is a country of divided loyalties but, in the crunch, surprisingly loyal divisions. It is a country that pulls itself apart in some ways when it pulls itself together in others. Puzzling, exasperating, fascinating, rather endearing really.

There is something very Canadian about the successful strategy of the Party Québécois, a fact reflected in the subtitle Peter Desbarats has given his book on René Lévesque – A *Canadian in Search of a Country*. Some, of course, denounce "étapism," or separation by étapism as underhand, the hiding of the independence candle under a bushel of conventional provincialism. Tricky, true; but it was all done in open convention a couple of years ago, with étapistes and victory going to étapism, as Claude Morin was its prophet.

True to character

The point is not that the Pequistes suckered the electorate with this move, but rather that they epitomized Canadian ambivalence. The Quebec electorate, accustomed like all Canadian electorates to accepting explicitly equivocal positions, found étapism valid and a plurality voted for it. The corollary, explicitly accepted by Mr. Lévesque in return for a chance at power and influence, is that Quebecers may reject the PQ's étapes that would wrest the province out of its Canadianism.

This kind of politics does not make stirring history. Many an essayist has bemoaned the absence of definition, real and symbolic, that might have been given to our country by a little more blood and thunder. Our uprisings have been tawdry, their resolution – as in the execution of the Patriotes, or the hanging of Riel – pitiful. No, if we are to find a mainstream of meaning in the Canadian story it must lie in the Canadian genius for evicting past defeats from the home of new relationships between peoples. Whether we look back to the Battle of the Plains of Abraham, or the loyalist refugee movement after the American revolution, or the suppression of the Indians, or the squeeze put on peoples of many lands who immigrated to Canada as a kind of retreat, we find a thread of reconciliation, of slowly healing wounds and bruises, of gradual assertion of new confidence and aspiration in this land.

Tomorrow is not today

We have a murky politics. But it has saved a lot of lives. It has postponed days of reckoning that, in all humanity, needed to be postponed so that the contending forces could work out some less drastic settlement. As study and pursuit, Canadian politics is a task for the patient and the determined, the supple and the peaceful, the good humoured and the humble. Canada has no ultimate goals. Canada is process and comity, a time and place in successive lives, where it is given to each generation to influence but not determine the fate of the next. No single election, no single referendum for that matter, will settle things once and for all. We are people of mixed feelings in this country. We should know enough about ourselves by now never to anticipate what we expect. Things may turn out a little differently.

—*The Montreal Gazette,*
Nov. 19, 1976

From Sea unto Sea

It was certainly a victory for Canada – a majority of both French- and English-speaking Quebecers rejecting René Lévesque's referendum question. It was certainly a defeat for the Parti Québécois.

The PQ asked the easiest, softest, gentlest question imaginable – do you grant a mandate to negotiate sovereignty-association with assurance that no actual change will occur without another referendum? And they lost.

They lost despite almost four years in power during which they turned every situation to their favour. They lost despite their own victory in the referendum debate in Quebec's National Assembly. They lost despite the rather plodding style of Claude Ryan at the head of the federalist cause.

They lost because Quebecers prefer the security and the liberty of Canada to the uncertainties of a Quebec drawn into itself in a North American sea. They lost because Quebecers have, in fact, found Canada generally responsive to the cultural and economic needs of that province over many generations. They lost because Quebecers recognized the essential dishonesty of the question posed, which actually sought approval for sovereignty itself.

Unfortunately, Mr. Lévesque was less than gracious in defeat. In his first sentence, he spoke of "next time." He referred to the "scandalous, immoral campaign waged by the federalists," he referred to their "calumny." He came close to suggesting the referendum result was less than valid, less than clear. His speech had the underlying effect of perpetuating divisions rather than healing them.

While Pierre Trudeau and all other premiers agree on the urgency of a constitutional conference, we must ask if René Lévesque should attend on behalf of Quebec. His personal convictions and his political career are set against the very purpose of such a conference – a renewal of federalism.

When asked earlier this month what a resounding "No" vote would mean, he replied a return to the "vicious circle" of federalism, the "dead end" of negotiations trying to put "plastic surgery on the face of federalism." Can a man with these convictions and attitudes represent in good faith the interests of Quebecers so clearly expressed yesterday? He faces a profound personal dilemma.

Either Mr. Lévesque must honestly subject his convictions to the democratic will of his electorate and work sincerely for constitutional change within Confederation, or he must step aside. He has no mandate to obstruct, no claim to represent some silent majority of Quebecers allegedly thirsting for independence. Nor can he claim, as he did last night, that the "Yes" vote was but "the last manifestation of the old Quebec," and don the mantle of history-to-come in lieu of the history etched in reality yesterday.

Almost 60 percent of Quebecers refused Mr. Lévesque even a mandate to negotiate sovereignty-association, and it is probably fair to say that another 10 percent voted "Yes" only to strengthen Quebec's hand within Canada. No, Mr. Lévesque must participate in constitutional talks against his personal convictions, or resign. Because he may well win another term as premier, we can only hope his sense of democracy will prevail, that he will not attempt to hold Canada hostage to his personal dreams against the public will.

There is no doubt – as there has not been doubt – that Canadians everywhere are eager to engage Quebec in serious constitutional talks. It was not other provinces, after all, but Quebec that scuttled the Victoria agreement on the Constitution in 1971. And since 1976, under the PQ, Quebec has not been prepared to participate seriously in negotiations. Quebecers do not need to send a message that constitutional change is necessary, they need to send a representative who sincerely seeks change within Confederation.

As Prime Minister Trudeau said last night, we must "take up once again with vision and daring" the renewal of our country.

Our generation now has the privilege to serve as the new fathers and mothers of Confederation, to confirm and re-fashion our community of communities entirely independent of any other power and according to our own lights and consciences.

This is a challenge grand enough for any Canadian in any time, any Quebecer in any time, grand enough, certainly, for René Lévesque. He represents so many deep and positive impulses in his people and in this country. We must pray that he will join everyone seeking a vigorous rebirth of Canada – this precious and blessed homeland.

—*The Edmonton Journal,*
May 21, 1980

Our Arctic

The federal government embarrassed all Canadians and damaged its Arctic sovereignty claims by passively allowing the Polar Sea, a U.S. Coast Guard icebreaker, to venture into the Northwest Passage without permission.

The government apparently has neither the desire to strongly protest the U.S. action nor the will to establish a stronger military and national presence in the waterways off Canada's Arctic islands. This shameful lack of resolve makes Canada's territorial claims in our northern regions a sham.

Unless Canada moves to defend its borders, the U.S. may begin to treat the Northwest Passage as an American lake.

The military implications are troubling. Paul Robinson, the U.S. ambassador to Canada, says his country would become concerned if the Soviets passed through the Arctic waterway.

It's a peculiar argument coming from a country that wants the passage treated as an international strait. The last thing we need is a superpower confrontation in Canadian waters.

The United Nations' International Law of the Sea Treaty recognizes Canada's jurisdiction over its Arctic waters, including anti-pollution measures, and Canadian control over the gateway to the Northwest Passage.

Unfortunately, the U.S. voted against the treaty.

Canada has a legitimate claim to the Arctic waterways. We assumed sovereignty of the Arctic Islands from Britain in 1880. But if Ottawa isn't prepared to beef up our icebreaker fleet, increase surveillance and become the navigational overseer of the passage, then our national boundaries are an illusion; they have no more substance than an Arctic mirage.

If the U.S. insists on mistaking our backyard for its own, then Canada should take this sovereignty issue to the World Court. That action, combined with an increased presence in the Arctic, would show the world we are serious about being masters of our own house.

—*The Edmonton Journal,*
August 3, 1984

The Myth of Canadian Diversity

Canadians cling to three myths about their country.

The first is that it is young. In fact, Canada is well advanced into middle age. At 127, it has existed as a unified state for longer than either Italy (unified in 1870) or Germany (1871). Less than a third of the 18-odd nations now belonging to the United Nations existed in 1945, when Canada was already a mature 78. We were 51 when Iraq and Austria – two countries many think of as old – came into being.

The second myth is that, in everything but geography, Canada is a small country – small in population, small in economic heft. In fact, our population of 27 million is a fair size by international standards, bigger than that of Austria, Hungary, Sweden, Norway, Finland, Romania, Greece, Algeria, Peru and Venezuela, to name only a few. Our economy, by traditional measures, is the seventh-largest in the world.

But the most important myth about Canada – the one that distorts our self-image, warps our politics and may one day tear us apart – is the myth of Canadian diversity. Almost any Canadian will tell you that his Canada is a remarkably varied place. "Canada, with its regional, linguistic and cultural diversity, has never been easy to govern," wrote *The Globe and Mail* when Jean Chrétien became Prime Minister last fall. Provincial politicians routinely parrot this myth to push for greater regional powers; federal politicians repeat it to let people know what a hard job they have.

In fact, Canada is one of the most homogeneous countries in the world. A foreign visitor can travel from Vancouver in the West to Kingston in the centre without finding any significant difference in accent, in dress, in cuisine or even, in a broad sense, in values. A high-school student in Winnipeg talks, looks and acts much like his counterpart in Prince George. Where they do exist, our regional differences are no match for those of most other countries.

Canada may have a few regional accents in its English-speaking parts – the salty dialect of Newfoundland, the rural tones of the Ottawa Valley – but these are nothing compared with the dozens in the United States or Britain. It may have two official languages, but that is unlikely to impress India, which has 14.

To be certain, we have our French-English divide, two "nations" living under one roof. That hardly makes us unique either. Spain has the Catalans and the Basques, Russia has the Tatars, Ukrainians, Belarussians, Chechens, Moldavians, Udmurts, Kazakhs, Avars and Armenians. And, although few would dispute that francophone Quebec is indeed a distinct society, the differences between Quebec and the rest of Canada are diminishing over time. As Lucien Bouchard himself has noted, we share a host of common attitudes – an attachment to the Canadian social system, tolerance of minorities, a respect for government and law.

Even our much-discussed ethnic differences are overstated. Although Canada is an immigrant nation and Canadians spring from a variety of backgrounds, a recent study from the C.D. Howe Institute says that the idea of a "Canadian mosaic" – as distinct from the American "melting pot" – is a fallacy. In *The Illusion of Difference*, University of Toronto sociologists Jeffrey Reitz and Raymond Breton show that immigrants to Canada assimilate as quickly into the mainstream society as immigrants to the United States do. In fact, Canadians are less likely than Americans to favour holding on to cultural differences based on ethnic background. If you don't believe Mr. Reitz and Mr. Breton, visit any big-city high school, where the speech and behaviour of immigrant students just a few years in Canada is indistinguishable from that of any fifth-generation classmate.

This is not to say that Canada is a nation of cookie-cutter people. The differences among our regions, and between our two main language groups, are real. But in recent years we have elevated those differences into a cult. For all our disputes about language and ethnicity and regional rights, our differences shrink beside our similarities, and the things that unite us dwarf those that divide us.

—*The Globe and Mail,*
June 13, 1994

Don't Let It Crumble

"Many students go to college with a bias that Canadian history does not matter," says Professor Robert Ventresca, a historian at King's College, University of Western Ontario. That students should hold little regard for our collective past is not surprising. Six provinces – British Columbia, Alberta, Saskatchewan, New Brunswick, Nova Scotia and Newfoundland – do not require high school students to take even one Canadian history course. The Dominion Institute, a charitable organization concerned about the state of Canada's public memory, wants to change that. So do most Canadians, according to a recent Dominion Institute/IPSOS-REID poll. Eighty-three percent of respondents said high school students should have at least two Canadian history courses under their belts when they graduate.

J.B. Priestly, the famous 20th-century English novelist, wrote in 1957 that "the Canadian is a baffled man." Forty-four years later, Canadians are still baffled by their national identity. Professional historians have not done much to help matters. National history has been out of favour in our universities for a long time. Professor Ventresca knows this all too well. He was recently awarded the prestigious John Bullen Prize for his doctoral thesis, which was judged by the Canadian Historical Association to be the best history dissertation of 2000. But he did not write about Canadian history, which he says is his first love. Instead, Professor Ventresca chose to devote his talents to a study of Italian democracy. The current state of the historical profession in this country made it, he says, "too difficult to write about Canada's national history."

The trend over the last three decades has been a sorry one. Having been encouraged to dwell on personal testimonials that explore experiences based on region, ethnicity, class, family, sex and sexual orientation, historians now think small. On the 100th anniversary of the University of Toronto's Department of History in 1991, one of Canada's eminent historians, Professor Michael Bliss, warned that this particularism was partly responsible for a "withering sense of community" in this country. He reminded his colleagues that "their subject, after all, is Canada." Many did not want to be reminded. His critics implied that he was just another white man saying students needed to study more dead white men – and that nobody wanted that.

But Mr. Bliss is not alone. Seven years later, the distinguished professor emeritus of history at York University, Jack Granatstein, explained in his book, *Who Killed Canadian History?*, that one consequence of recent trends is that "The history taught (in public schools) is that of the grievers among us, the present-day crusaders against public policy or discrimination. The history omitted is that of the Canadian nation and people." On this score, a May 1997, editorial in *Saturday Night* magazine offered pointed criticism of the *Canadian Historical Review*, the principal Canadian history journal: 'Articles in the journal are long and turgid, as limited in scope as they are timid in judgment and questionable in relevance."

The Dominion Institute's poll results show Canadians want to know more about Canada's past. It also reveals that 74 percent of them do not believe Canadian history is boring. Rudyard Griffiths, the executive director of the Dominion Institute, believes poll results show "our Ministries of Education are out of touch with public opinion." We believe they also show that a great many of Canada's professional historians are as well.

It is a disgrace that Canadians should know so little about their country's past. Clearly, high school students should be taught more about the broad sweep of Canadian history. And those students who seek to build on that knowledge in college and graduate school should not be required to write about this or that umbraged group in order to gain academic acceptance. Historical scholarship is one of the pillars of national identity. Governments and universities should not let it crumble.

—*The National Post,*
September 10, 2001

4
Not Our Proudest Moments

The Chinamen

There is nothing in the broad principles of personal liberty, civil rights, or public toleration, nothing in international law or national relations, to prevent a country or a community receiving into its bosom an element which it believes to be hurtful or dangerous to the common good.

If Great Britain does not desire to receive Chinese into her possessions she need not do so, although if she makes treaties admitting Chinese she must respect these treaties while they last. Canada, though a part of the British Empire is in all respects self governing. Australasia stands on the same footing.

While England may admit Chinese into the United Kingdom without restriction, both Canada and Australasia have imposed restrictions which hamper their admission into these countries.

It may be that while a law passed by Canada to absolutely exclude Chinese from our soil might raise a serious question with Great Britain, whose treaties with China are somewhat liberal, there can be no question of Canada's right to so regulate the admission of Chinese into this country as to make it practically prohibitory.

The laws of self preservation are the "higher" law," and all other laws must give way before them. It may be that we cannot say to Chinamen, "You cannot set foot in Calgary," but we can take such measures as will render their stay unprofitable.

The Chinaman who enters our town, if he respects our laws and conducts himself properly, is entitled to the protection of those laws, and must receive it. As a law and order respecting community this is imperative. Mob violence is on every account to be frowned upon, and put down.

We may, if we choose, levy a special tax on Chinese laundries; we may cause them to be inspected, for sanitary reasons, every month or every week; or even without resorting to law at all we may decide among ourselves that these may become nests of disease and we may abstain from sending washing to them.

In this way, by consulting the interests of the public safety, we may render the stay of Chinamen in Calgary useless and, in a short time, without violence, without any interference with personal liberty, we can be rid of what the majority regard as an obnoxious element.

The Chinese, though not here in any great number, are here because they find employment with us. If they did not find this profitable employment here they would seek other fields.

Notwithstanding what has occurred in connection with the introduction and concealment of smallpox by them, they are employed in our hotels, and large quantities of washing are still sent to their laundries by our citizens. It is useless to expect them to leave the town while this is being done.

Moreover, the late exhibition of mob violence will not drive them forth. The Chinese are quick to know that among well disposed citizens the attack on them has only created sympathy for them, and they expect to profit by that sympathy.

If our citizens do not wish their presence here; if they prefer to employ them in preference to the women of their own nationality who would gladly do the work these Chinamen are doing; if they believe the best interests of the community are promoted by their continuous stay amongst us, they will of course continue to supply them with the means of living comfortably here and the Chinese will accordingly stay.

People cannot, of course, shut their eyes to the fact that while there is a strong prejudice against the Chinaman, he seems, to many, to be a necessary evil – to some indeed a necessary good.

He is industrious, apparently never tiring. He is prompt and cheerful in his work and does it well. He obeys instructions quickly. He is civil at all times. In a country where domestic help is scarce, very costly and difficult to manage, it is not strange that many employers rather welcome than resent the advent of the Chinese, through whose labours they get a considerable measure of relief.

Those who object to them point to them as birds of passage, without any stake in the country, having no intention of becoming citizens in the proper meaning of the term.

They hold that they contribute nothing to the expenditure, the progress or the development of the country; that they in no way identify themselves with the country's future; that they live meanly, the bulk of their earnings going to China for investment; that having no married life, no homes and no social stake, they are simply appropriating the labour and moneys which should go to the deserving families who bear the taxes, burdens and anxieties of the country.

Between the arguments based on private interest and those which appeal to the public advantage it ought not to be difficult to decide; and that decision may be freely given without the charge of intolerance or persecution being raised.

Whether the Chinaman goes or stays it will be in accordance with enlightened public opinion. If public opinion wills that he shall stay, he will receive the fullest protection the laws can give him. If public opinion decides that he shall go, the country will not be a loser by his absence.

—*The Calgary Daily Herald, August 5, 1892*

(Editor's Note: In 1892, an alcohol-fuelled mob in Calgary rioted in the town's Chinese district when a smallpox outbreak was linked to a Chinese-run laundry. Although vaccination and quarantine limited the death toll to four, the editorial in The Daily Herald questioned the suitability of Chinese immigrants as Canadians and suggested their businesses be boycotted.)

Keep the Tricolour Off It

Canada's present day racial troubles are due largely to the dual system. A British colony provided for the official use of the French language, and that with other concessions and latitude allowed Quebec has fostered the French-Canadian idea of a new France on the St. Lawrence. No one needs to be told how this system has hampered the growth of the Dominion or retarded the solidification of the provinces into a United Canada.

The Dominion has had too much of the double system, and the French have been catered to and pampered and deferred to more than was wise.

It would therefore be folly to go the length proposed by a Woodstock correspondent, who suggests that the tricolour be incorporated with the British crosses in forming the proposed Canadian flag. Canada is a British colony, and an emblem of France has no place on the flag of a part of the British Empire.

—The Toronto Evening Star, July 3, 1895

Ottawa and the Eskimo Tribes

The decision has been finally made at Ottawa that there will be no interference with "the course of justice" in the case of the two Eskimos who await execution at Herschel Island.

They are to be hanged on the gallows which the judge, the lawyers, clerks, hangman and shall we say the jury, took with them when they went north to try the case this summer.

No doubt the men who are to be hanged killed other men, and, according to the rules, must die.

The rules, however, are of our making. It is a question in the minds of many whether the Dominion of Canada should extend her ready-made white man's law into the sub-arctic and impose it on the Eskimos, a people who are incapable of understanding and availing themselves of the benefits of our laws, but who are to sustain only the penalties.

These laws of ours have been the growth of centuries of human experience in genial climes, where the people have been tillers of the soil, artisans, dwellers in walled cities, accumulators of wealth and comforts. These laws of ours are meant to fit our state of society.

We are a people who read and write, and are supposed to know the laws. We have as judges men who are supposed to be the best in the land, and courts which are supposed to be the dwelling places of justice. Not content with this, we have the jury system, by which a man can claim the right to be judged by his peers. Nor does that complete our safeguards in respect of the law, for we have a free press and a public opinion, both of which can, if they like, exert a corrective influence.

If the white race had been confined to the country of the Eskimos, the white man's law of to-day would never have been heard of. The tribal customs of the native races are the product of their conditions and necessities. The arctic native inherits nothing, bequeaths nothing. His wealth consists of the clothes he wears, the weapons he carries, the food he has skinned and cut up for the coming week. If one man kills a walrus the whole village eats of it, and it is no more his than every other man's.

They have no written laws, for they have no alphabet. They have no jails, for they have no doors but open ones. They have no judges, courts or policemen, and no prisoners. They have no punishment for an offender but death. A man must be a decent and agreeable citizen or he dies. He wants to live, so he behaves. If he doesn't he is regarded as being insane, which he probably is, and a dangerous man, and he is put out of a world in which he does not fit.

It has been resolved at Ottawa, we are told, that white man's law must be respected in the far north. It may be enforced more or less, but one may doubt that it will be respected. We can send up policemen and handcuffs and gallows, with an occasional visit from a judge who brings with him lawyers, constables and all or part of the jury – although why we should keep up the humbug of having a jury when the jurors are not the peers of the person on trial one fails to see.

While we go through these forms, the Eskimos are probably unable to make head or tail of what the white man is trying to do to them. In *The Star Weekly* of Saturday appeared two important special articles about the Eskimos and white man's law. One story is that of Capt. Joseph Bernier's expedition to Baffin Land, carrying a "court" along to try natives for killing a white man. Two white men of the party were drowned en route. The result of the trial was that one native was sentenced to 10 and another to 2 years' imprisonment, but as there are no prisons up that way the men had to be brought thousands of miles back to be put in Stoney Mountain Penitentiary.

One fancies the natives will rather feel that the men taken away have been greatly honoured. With three square meals a day the prisoners, accustomed to gorging at three meals a week, will probably eat themselves to death in short order, or housed for the first time in their lives, develop tuberculosis and be sent home. What the country gets from it is a renewal of the boast that the arm of the law is very long.

It is up to the parliament of Canada to discuss all this and see whether the "foreign" policy of the government in regard to these people is coherent and reasonable, whether there actually is any thought-out policy, or merely a "mandate" to the police to run things the best way they know how.

—*The Toronto Evening Star, November 6, 1923*

Are General Morals Relaxing?

Many people today are deeply concerned over what appears to them to be a dangerously growing deterioration in general morals, not only on the part of the young and the irresponsible, but in the attitude of people who should know better, toward violations of the code and laws of decency. Probably just as many people take the point of view that conditions are no worse now than they ever were, and that the viewers-with-alarm are seeing things through the jaundiced eyes of encroaching age.

For the first group there is confirmation of their fears and for the second a refutation of their theories in a case revealed last Friday at St. Jerome. It developed from one of those week-end parties in the mountains which have become so popular in recent years, and two young men were convicted in criminal court of "sequestration and indecent assault" against a 17-year-old girl.

The girl had been lured to the party in the belief that it was to be made up of boys and girls. When she found herself the only girl there and attempted to leave, she was forced to remain with 13 young men in a St. Sauveur cottage for approximately two days.

"Shameful, inhuman and beastly conduct" was the term applied to the offences by Judge Hermann Barette in lecturing the two accused. But he sentenced them to only three months in jail dating back to the time of their arrest. It does not seem likely that the parents of that girl, or the parents of any girl for that matter, would consider the punishment to fit the crime.

Few are the youngsters who do not clamour at one time or another for permission to participate in the sort of party that girl thought she was going to. Parents are sometimes made to feel inhuman when such permission is withheld. But a little misunderstanding of that sort can hardly be weighed against such an experience as that girl and her parents have gone through. All this may serve as a lesson to other girls and other parents, to make sure of just what sort of a party it is and what sort of supervision it will have.

—*The Montreal Gazette,*
January 24, 1950

Bring Back the Reindeer

The reindeer is returning to Scotland after an absence of 750 years. In the Pacific northwest Laplanders teach Eskimos to herd this animal as a supply of food, clothing and shelter in the barren areas of the north. In Quebec's northern barrens, the caribou, an animal akin to the reindeer, and one which used to exist in huge herds east of Hudson Bay, is becoming extinct.

Eskimos and some northern Indians used to depend almost entirely upon the caribou for their existence. The disappearance of this animal has struck a blow at their economy that the family allowance and the baby bonus by no means repair.

Taking a lesson from the Lapps of Finland and Scandinavia, the Reindeer Council of Britain, in re-introducing the reindeer to the remote northern section of Scotland, foresees the day when Scottish herds may provide Britain with milk, meat, hides and other valuable products.

West of Hudson Bay and on Baffin Island, caribou still exist in great numbers, sufficient to maintain Eskimo bands in a state of adequate nourishment, with attendant supply of hides for clothing, tents and sewing material. East of the Bay, from Fort George right around to the Labrador Coast, where caribou used to roam by the thousands, they are relatively rare. Eskimos and Indians, particularly the Nascopies (a branch of the Montegnais tribe) are suffering from under-nourishment as a result. This makes them more susceptible to epidemic diseases. Not only their economy, but their very lives are in jeopardy.

Even in the barrens where no trees grow there is food for caribou – the same food, moss and lichens, from which the reindeer derive sustenance. Projects for the introduction of reindeer into the Quebec barrens have been discussed from time to time, but never implemented. Quebec's Eskimos definitely are a people worth saving, but the combined efforts of the federal Department of Indian Affairs, of Anglican, Roman Catholic, Moravian and Grenfell missions, and of the Hudson's Bay Company's outposts have thus far been unable to master the difficulties.

So why not reindeer for Ungava, too, with some Lapp instructors for the Eskimos in the art of herding, which is necessary with this semi-domestic animal? And while they are at it, why shouldn't the authorities bring in a few demonstration teams of Finns to show the Eskimos and Indians how to keep clean and healthy in the latitudes in which they live?

—*The Montreal Gazette,*
October 31, 1952

The Lost People

Reporter Charles McGregor's report on the plight of the Indians of northern Manitoba and the instinctive human response to it across the land raise mingled feelings of pride and shame.

The human heart is warm; it is generous. But it can be pitifully forgetful.

It is not enough to airlift food and warm clothing to the Indians of the Thompson-Moak Lake region of Manitoba at Christmastime, when the spirit of giving is at the flood.

The Indians and Métis of the Manitoba northland call themselves the Lost People of Canada. The Lost People – the bitterness in this phrase embodies all the suffering, all the frustration of people who have become misfits in their own land.

The encroachment of the white man's industry, the white man's technology, the white man's civilization, upon the red man's heritage has changed his environment; but it has not changed him.

It is difficult, the white man excuses himself, to adapt the red man to the white man's ways. And here, surely, lies the red man's future.

It is difficult – it is true. But it is not impossible.

The ordinary white person's stereotype of the Indian is the noble red man, stalking the game of the forest, running the rapids of the rivers, fishing the lakes and rivers, nomadic, his spirit unconquered.

But the Indian cannot stalk game in forests denuded for the white man's timber and newsprint, nor catch fish in lakes and streams fished out by the white man's tourist trade or polluted by his mines.

The Indian of Canada's vanishing wilderness can be helped. He can be educated. He can adapt to the white man's society. Indians with the will, the resources – and perhaps a good deal of outside help – have proven this.

But the Indian trapped in privation and squalor need a great deal more help than his white brother has been willing to give.

Every once in a while there is a great outburst of feeling for the plight of the Indian. Then he becomes the beneficiary of the white man's Christmastide generosity, or even a revision in the Indian Act.

And afterward, the Indian is allowed to sink back into his squalor and his privation. And it is not good enough. The Indian of Canada's disappearing wilderness needs a great deal more of the spirit of Christmas the whole year round, every year.

—The Toronto Telegram,
December 18, 1962

Trial Exposes Hate Law

The jury in Jim Keegstra's trial did a difficult job well. It endured three weary months listening to one man's opinions as they emerged in a Red Deer courtroom so mistaken and twisted as to defy belief.

The verdict it delivered yesterday is no surprise to a majority of society outraged that a teacher would wantonly misuse a trust as Keegstra did by using a classroom to promote hatred against Jews.

A fine of $5,000 doesn't seem excessive retribution in the circumstances, although Keegstra appears in the end almost as one of the victims of his own self-righteousness.

But reflection prompts questions about whether society doesn't have adequate means for dealing with such aberrations outside a courtroom.

The trial has demonstrated that the hatred-promotion provision of the Criminal Code of Canada, Section 281.2 (2) is a liability to society.

The best that can be said for it is that, where there is a conviction, it pleases those who see the matter in its narrowest perspective, satisfying them that the particular falsehood at issue has been officially condemned. But that is all; and a heavy price is paid for this small victory.

For one thing, it is transitory. The falsehood has not been exorcised – not even from the mind of the accused who gave it voice. There is not the slightest assurance that it will not soon be repeated.

Meanwhile, the accused has been allowed to spout his twisted notions in a setting that gives them a patina of status, a setting that compels some people to listen and induces many to do so. A prosecution under this bit of legislation is an exercise in social self-flagellation.

A conviction, moreover, brings the power of the state down upon a set of ideas, which is repugnant in itself, even when the ideas are generally perceived as false. And because those ideas are, almost by definition, the product of a warped judgment, a conviction also smacks of persecution of the weak rather than of the wicked.

An acquittal is even more grievous for society. At the very least, it suggests a law so weak that it mocks the notion of law. At worst, an acquittal may give the accused and his notions more credence than they merit and than they could possibly have attained without being brought to trial.

No right-thinking person regards the promotion of hatred as in any way desirable. The point is that society can best preserve its own values by officially tolerating it and can best defeat it by ignoring it. Legislation that seeks to proscribe it is simply a well-intentioned trap.

—*The Calgary Herald,*
July 21, 1985

(Editor's Note: High school teacher Jim Keegstra had been charged with willfully promoting hatred against Jews by a Red Deer, Alberta jury the day before this editorial ran.)

Making Amends

There's no way to sugar-coat the bizarre 1950s experiment in which the Ottawa bureaucracy used 87 unwitting Inuit as human flagpoles in the High Arctic.

Poorly planned and executed, the resettlement project was a denial of basic human rights and a monumental blunder that needlessly put lives at risk.

Inuit were uprooted from Quebec and dumped in the alien Arctic without proper housing or equipment, let alone schools or medical facilities.

For Ottawa, the course has long been clear: reparations must be made to the 17 families sent to the most remote corner of the country, supposedly for their own good.

Yet a recommendation to compensate these internal exiles is curiously absent from Daniel Soberman's report this week on the whole sorry episode.

His 70-page report, issued by the Canadian Human Rights Commission, does a decent job of confirming the injustices done. But in accepting the role of mediator, Soberman pulls too many punches.

The formal apology and moving or travel allowances he recommends are inadequate, considering the mistreatment and deprivation that he ably chronicles.

Indeed, Soberman uncovered damning evidence that local RCMP officers recruiting Inuit settlers in Quebec in 1953 for the experiment were told by then-RCMP inspector H.A. Larsen: "Families will be brought back home at the end of one year if they so desire."

Yet that promise was broken: Soberman says repeated requested by the Inuit to go home to Quebec were routinely ignored – to this country's everlasting shame.

This crucial revelation means the experiment – whether to advance Canadian Arctic sovereignty or, as Ottawa now claims, to better the lives of Quebec Inuit suffering from a game shortage – was founded on a lie.

Indian Affairs Minister Tom Siddon takes surprising comfort from the report. He says it recognizes Ottawa's "primary motivations for the project were humane."

But Soberman says that Ottawa violated its "fiduciary duties" – a position of trust that obliges it to protect natives. For that obvious failure, Siddon is now prepared to apologize, or issue some lesser statement of regret.

Why won't Siddon thank the Inuit for their unheralded contribution to Arctic sovereignty, and compensate them for their mistreatment? It's the right thing to do.

—The Toronto Star,
January 17, 1992

Rob Anders Shamed Himself

If Nelson Mandela doesn't get to be an honorary citizen of Canada, it's doubtful his feelings will be hurt. Mandela, the closest thing our planet has to a secular saint, has already won almost every prize for peace and social justice the world has to offer. The great South African has won the love, the admiration, and the respect of the international community – and justly so.

It is not Mandela who has been damaged by the churlish refusal of Calgary West MP Rob Anders to grant him honorary Canadian citizenship. It is Anders and, by extension, his Canadian Alliance party who look small and vindictive.

He is an embarrassment to Parliament, to the nation and to Alberta. As Conservative Leader Joe Clark has said, he is unworthy of the multicultural city of Calgary that he represents.

Anders' callow incivility does more to embarrass his own party – which supported the government motion – than to reproach the Liberals. Mandela needs no fresh honours. Anders, however, needs some lessons, both in history and manners.

—The Edmonton Journal,
June 9, 2001

5

The Welcome Mat

Valuable Settlers

The level-headed veteran superintendent of Presbyterian missions, who has spent 25 years in travelling all over Manitoba, the Northwest territories and British Columbia establishing churches and helping in mission work, speaking recently of the Doukhobors, who went into the west last year, said:

"They are people of good physique, they are not lazy, they build good houses, and, above all, they are occupying lands that the Canadians left idle for years and years. They don't seek for soft jobs in the cities, where they can wear good clothing and keep their hands clean."

Dr. Robertson said, with emphasis: "There is too much of that among ourselves. The storekeepers speak well of them, and their women have, many of them, married Canadian farmers out there. Why? Because Canadian girls won't go out and become helpmates to the Canadian farmers. And, continued Dr. Robertson, "what better proof of industry could you wish than this? A Galician farmer and his son spaded 24 acres in the absence of the necessary implements, and grew their crops on the land so prepared. These people will make good settlers, their children will make better settlers than they and that is the reason the people of the east should look after them."

Dr. Robertson's opinion in this matter is worth the opinion of a thousand politicians who are more intent upon making political capital than desirous of settling up our immense extent of country.
—*The Windsor Evening Record, May 15, 1900*

The East India Question

That the people of Eastern and Western Canada are at irreconcilable odds on the question of Hindu immigration to this country is made apparent on every occasion that the matter comes up for discussion in the older provinces.

The public on the Coast are undoubtedly opposed to the settlement in this province of East Indians. Our clergy in British Columbia, or at least many of them, have expressed themselves as in agreement with the general view taken by the people here, and, according to a despatch from London (Ont.), containing a report of the session of the National Council of Women, now being held in that city, the same opinion is shared by the representatives to that gathering, from this province.

The members of the council who reside in Eastern Canada, however, are favourable to Hindu immigration, and at yesterday's session of the council they introduced a resolution, which was heatedly discussed, asking the government to "allow Sikh women to enter Canada or to send back the Sikh men."

Undoubtedly, the discrimination in the rules of the immigration department against East Indian women strikes one at first view as being unfair, and if the members of the women's council who reside in the east limited their efforts in the matter of this immigration to seeking to have the sexes placed on an equal footing their position would at least be a logical one.

The trouble is, that behind their demand for the equality of the sexes, exists a strong sympathy in favour of permitting the free entry of all East Indians. The attitude of the people on the Coast, undoubtedly, is that we do not want East Indians at all, but if we are to have them, or at least some of them, it shall be the men only, because we do not want a permanent colony of them, and one which would increase as a natural result of families being located here.

British Columbia's reply to the demand of the Women's Council, that either Sikh women be allowed to enter Canada or that the Sikh men already here be sent back, will probably be that if the Sikh men wish to live with their wives they are welcome to go back to India.

The opinion held by the members of the council from British Columbia was shown by the resolution proposed by Mrs. Whyte, that the government should be asked to "order no relaxation of the existing regulations regarding the admission of Hindu women."

Mrs. Whyte , too, was undoubtedly right in her assertion that the situation is not understood by the women of the east. That she subsequently withdrew her statement does not make it any the less true.

A question such as this must, to be understood, be studied at close range, and it is at close range that it has been studied by the people here. Their conclusions, therefore, are much more worthy of respect than those of people who live three thousand miles away and who never see a Hindu unless it be one travelling through the country.

But we have the conditions created in certain parts of South Africa by a large East Indian immigration to that country to teach us what might result here if free entry were allowed to these people. However, there seems reasonable assurance that matters will continue as at present in regard to the entry of these people, except, of course, in instances in which Hon. Robert Rogers, on the advice of Mr. H.H. Stevens, M.P., exercises "acts of grace."

—*The Vancouver Sun,*
May 30, 1912

The Plight of Japanese-Canadians

The Co-operative Committee on Japanese-Canadians, composed of representatives of the national Y.M. and Y.W.C.A., churches, social agencies, trade unions and student organizations, this week appealed to the Prime Minister to prevent in Canada what is said to be a Nazi-like action against a minority group.

The committee claimed evidence that Canadian citizens of Japanese ancestry were coerced by government agents to renounce their citizenship and sign to go to Japan under the so-called "voluntary repatriation plan." The agents are claimed to be R.C.M.P. officers who requested from Japanese-Canadians in relocation centres their "voluntary applications to go to Japan after the war or sooner, where this can be arranged." The "repatriation offer" was made, it is claimed, in a threatening manner and it is said that a large number have been thus intimidated to sign up for what may for many turn out to be deportation to a country they have never known, and whose social and militaristic system they dislike.

It is hoped the prime minister will institute an inquiry into this alleged practice, for it is entirely contrary to the policy he announced a year ago with respect to the Japanese in Canada. He stated in parliament:

"We must not permit in Canada the hateful doctrine of racialism which is the basis of the Nazi system everywhere. Our aim is to resolve a difficult problem in a manner which will protect the people of British Columbia and the interest of the country as a whole, and, at the same time preserve, in whatever we do, the principles of fairness and justice.

"What is clearly needed is the establishment of a quasi-judicial commission to examine the background, loyalties and attitudes of all persons of Japanese race in Canada to ascertain those who are not fit persons to be allowed to remain here. To some extent, of course, the task has been carried out through the examination and internment of suspicious or dangerous persons. It cannot be assumed that all those who have been interned are disloyal. The government's intentions would be to have disloyal persons deported to Japan as soon as that is physically possible. There may also be some persons who will voluntarily indicate a desire to proceed to Japan.

"Those persons who wish to remain here should be allowed to do so. However, they should not be allowed once more to concentrate in British Columbia. There is little doubt that, with co-operation on the part of the provinces, it can be made possible to settle the Japanese more or less evenly throughout Canada. It is the fact of concentration that has given rise to this (the Japanese) problem."

Unfortunately, the government did not appoint the commission. Instead, someone is said to have instituted action that is said to be contrary to that proposed by Mr. King. The suggestion is that an attempt has been made to solve the problem by removing the Japanese from Canada by a trick called "voluntary repatriation."

But "repatriation" is a wrong term in the case of 70 percent of the Japanese in Canada. The Dominion census of June, 1941, showed that of approximately 24,000 Japanese in Canada, close to 15,000 were born here and over 3,000 are naturalized. The Dominion labour department reported that the Canadian-born Japanese, especially those brought up in the cities and larger towns, for the most part learned only enough Japanese to converse with their parents, and that only 12.5 percent (of the older people) do not speak English."

Is there danger of disloyalty from the Japanese in Canada? Concerning this, the Prime Minister stated in Parliament in August, 1944:

"It is a fact that no person of the Japanese race born in Canada has been charged with any act of sabotage or disloyalty during the years of war. Surely, it is not to be expected that the government will do other than deal justly with those who are guilty of no crime, or even of any ill intention. For the government to do otherwise would be an acceptance of the standards of our enemies and the negation of the purposes for which we are fighting."

If any have been coerced into signing an application to return to Japan, they should be released from such pledges. Some who signed are said to have been 16-year-old children.

—*The Toronto Daily Star, August 7, 1945*

Unrestricted Movement for All

The general aim of the government's proposed immigration legislation is to place an annual ceiling on the number of landed immigrants without discrimination against any national, racial or ethnic group. Consultation with the provinces will help achieve the bill's aim of limiting immigration to the country's absorptive capacity.

Since there are about 800,000 applications for landed immigrant status on file, some objective criteria must be applied to ensure steady population growth. Aiming at a population of about 30 million by the turn of the century, Immigration Minister Bud Cullen has set an average goal of 140,000 landed immigrants a year, slightly less than the current level but close to the minimum net figure of 100,000 suggested by a parliamentary committee. Certain anomalies in the law, like the ban on "morons," have been eliminated, the UN definition of refugees will be incorporated in the new act, and deportees will be allowed to re-apply after one year.

The bill discriminates between immigrants and citizens, however, in its provision to encourage new Canadians to settle in small towns. Additional points would be awarded to an applicant who agrees to live and work in outlying areas and stay for at least six months. His landed immigrant papers would be granted on arrival at destination and they might be cancelled if he were to leave before the mandatory six months were over.

An automatic distinction is thus created between the immigrant and citizen whose unrestricted mobility is a cherished right. This clause was no doubt introduced to answer complaints from some quarters who feel threatened by black, brown and yellow skinned men and women concentrating in large cities.

After a year of public hearings, the parliamentary committee rejected the notion that immigration contributes to unemployment, scarcity of housing and urban congestion in metropolitan centres. "Even without immigration," said its report, "the largest cities in Canada would face the problems endemic to urban growth. Immigrants represent only one tributary of the great river of Canadians who have gone to settle in cities, in ever increasing numbers in the course of a century."

Efforts to encourage settlement in small towns should be directed toward all Canadians, whatever their status. The manpower department has a mobility program under way to encourage and assist people to move in labour-short areas. These can be applied to landed immigrants without the additional restrictions on their movement proposed in the new act.

—*The Montreal Gazette,*
November 26, 1976

Don't Nix Nannies

Amid all the flagrant disasters plaguing the Canadian immigration system, the nanny program has been the most consistent crowd pleaser – a singular success. There is, therefore, a perverse predictability in the federal government's decision to turn it back into a failure.

Under the program now under review, nannies who work in Canada for two years, and who meet fairly stringent requirements to upgrade their education and prove their self-sufficiency, are rewarded with status as landed immigrants. The program was established in 1981 with two goals. First, it was an avenue by which Third World women might better their lot. Second, it provided a guarantee that nannies who came to Canada with temporary worker status were not exploited by unscrupulous employers forever threatening to send the nanny home.

Both nannies and employers who have taken part in this scheme say those goals have been met admirably and Canada has benefited from new and eager immigrants who are introduced and acclimatized to Canadian culture at no expense to the government.

Now, because of an obscure court case, the government has become paranoid about a nanny loophole and killed the program. That's a mistake. If there's a loophole, Parliament should act quickly to close it, but not at the expense of legitimate immigrants and the Canadians who benefit from their labours.

—*The Vancouver Sun,*
December 21, 1991

We Can't Let our Population Stagnate

P.E.I.'s stagnant population numbers threaten everything from health transfers to economic growth, so it's a fair question to ask: what is being done to get those numbers up?

More to the point, Islanders should be wondering why we do such a poor job of attracting immigrants to our province and keeping them.

This week Islanders learned that there are 135,294 people living in the province, an increase of 0.5 percent since 1996. By comparison Canada's population grew by four percent and Alberta's population grew by 10.3 percent.

Our negligible growth rate suggests P.E.I. is stagnating, something intolerable in a province obsessed with economic diversification and desperate for year-round jobs.

Our failure to keep pace could end up costing P.E.I. when Ottawa calculates transfer payments and could leave us politically marginalized as Parliament expands to reflect population growth in other areas.

Premier Pat Binns seems to recognize the importance of adding to the population. He has set himself a target of one percent annual population growth.

The best source for that growth isn't P.E.I. obstetrical units; the best sources are the Charlottetown Airport and the Confederation Bridge. In other words, newcomers.

Immigrants add vitality to an area by adding new residents who are largely young, highly motivated and eager to carve out places for themselves. They add not just human potential but also the financial capital of their life savings to an area's economy.

But they are staying away from P.E.I. in droves. The Island gets just .07 percent of immigrants to Canada. Even of the refugees that are initially settled on P.E.I., three-quarters end up relocating to one of Canada's major cities.

It's time for the province to start taking action to attract more newcomers to the province and to do a better job of retaining them. Part of that will be uncovering and eliminating the barriers that the Island and Islanders throw up in the way of new settlers.

Improving our appeal to immigrants will require a concerted effort and an unblinking examination of what is best and worst in our province.

Immigrants offer a lot of what Prince Edward Island needs. The Island should take a close look at what it offers immigrants.

—*The Charlottetown Guardian, March 16, 2002*

6
Opening Our Eyes –Slowly

The Mormons

A good deal of needless and more or less offensive criticism both of the Executive Committee and the Mormon church has followed the incorporation of the "Alberta Stake of Zion" by the North West Legislative Assembly during its last session. On the principle that "public men are public property" the Executive cannot of course object to being criticized, but that criticism should at least be fair and based on fact.

Our Mormon fellow citizens, who have immigrated to Canada, are entitled to exactly the same rights as any other settlers in this free country as long as they confirm to the law of the land. The principal objection to the Bill of Incorporation, from within as well as outside the assembly was directed not so much against the powers sought to be conferred by the bill, as against the Mormon church generally.

It has been suggested in more than one quarter that the Assembly in passing the bill recognized the Mormon religion. This statement is absolutely without any foundation in fact, but even supposing that it were literally true, what then? In Canadian law all forms of religion which are not inconsistent with law are equal. Belief in the Mormon religion involves no legal disability, and nobody who is familiar with the history of the Dominion for the past few years will suggest that the late Sir John Thompson, who certainly could not be accused of indifference to

73

law or morals would have been instrumental in allowing these people to settle in Southern Alberta, had he not been satisfied that his doing so was proper and in the best interests of the country.

That the Mormons are good settlers there can be no doubt. They are sober, industrious people, who mind their own business and find plenty to do. Their settlements at Cardston and Mountain View are among the most prosperous and progressive in the Territories. Their social life as far as can be ascertained is entirely in accordance with the law of Canada.

The objection to the Mormons is based for the most part – if not altogether – on the fact that the members of that church practiced polygamy in the State of Utah. If they do not practise polygamy in Canada, the only objection against them falls to the ground. If they do practise polygamy in Canada, they are guilty of a violation of a law of the land and are amenable to that law in the same way that many other too-much married people who were not Mormons have been made amenable. But so long as the Mormons conduct themselves as law-abiding citizens, they are entitled to all the privileges enjoyed by other law-abiding citizens. The outcry raised against them without proof betrays a lack of that spirit of British fair play of which we are so proud and which we are so fond of talking about.

—*The Calgary Daily Herald, January 19, 1898*

Northern Example

In the air tragedy that brought death to Will Rogers and Wiley Post, Eskimos of the Alaska barrens played a part that deserves honourable mention. The scant details of the disaster, as they have come by radio from Point Barrow, are evidence that courage, presence of mind and compassion are among the human qualities that modern progress has not improved upon. The Eskimo who saw the crash and ran to Point Barrow, 15 miles in three hours, to bring help to the wrecked aeroplane, and his fellows who, before help came, had contrived to free the body of Will Rogers from the wreckage, were worthy actors in as strange and moving a drama of contrast as the records of progress can show.

Time, for the Eskimo, has jumped the slow centuries of unfolding invention. Progress has come on him by air without so much as a wheel to roll before it. Wagons and motor cars alike were things he never saw before the aeroplane descended upon him. Innocent of its beginnings in telegraph and telephone he must learn to accept radio as an accomplished miracle. Progress builds its great flying boats, invents its wireless and, telescoping time and space, brings its daring apostles crashing from the skies to die among the wastes that through the centuries have defied progress. Whereupon primitive man, the native of the wastes, does quickly, bravely and compassionately all that can be done in the tragic circumstances.

If as is said, the finest of civilized man's impulses is to give help where help is needed, undaunted by difficulties or the terrors of the unknown, the Point Barrow Eskimos have passed the civilization test with honours.

The only question is whether civilization in general can come up to the Eskimo standard. Late news from Africa makes it appear doubtful.

—The Toronto Globe,
August 19, 1935

Pardon, M'sieur

For quite a long time English-speaking Canadians – who are a pretty docile lot – have accepted the seemingly capricious seating arrangements on Trans Canada Airlines planes in a moderately tolerant way.

They may have been tempted to curse in a rather quiet and unobtrusive way, the clerks who sold them tickets for space that could not be supplied at take-off time. But they haven't learned to do it in a voice loud enough to disturb the other people squirming in the air terminal while waiting for their flights.

What the airline people call, in their sophisticated vocabulary, the "oversell" is a generally accepted necessity of modern airline operation and a nasty nuisance. The "oversell" by airlines is the practice of selling more seats on a plane than the plane can accommodate on the assumption that quite a few prospective passengers will chicken out before take-off time. If the airlines hadn't found by experience that this is a sensible procedure, they obviously wouldn't be doing it. They would be scheduling more planes instead and selling all the seating space they could because, after all, the airlines are in business and the more the merrier.

Unfortunately, however Monsieur and Madame Lucien Saulnier reserved first-class space on a TCA flight the other day and were told when boarding the flight that all first-class space was occupied and that they could have economy-flight space instead.

M. Saulnier, who is chairman of the Montreal City Executive, felt badly about the incident and interpreted it as a slap in the face for all his fellow French-Canadians. Segregation, in fact.

It is highly unlikely that there was any such motive in the minds of the TCA personnel who manage the ticket sales. Their motives and reasoning may at times be difficult for the lay traveller to fathom, but even the most frustrated of these hesitates to attribute their decisions to racial, linguistic or national bias.

There must be a great deal of sympathy with M. Saulnier. The sympathy will come from the large number of people of every colour, creed and nationality who have been entangled at one time or another in the airline "oversell" situation.

"Pardon, m'sieur," we say sincerely.

But please, M. Saulnier, do not think that this is a manifestation of anti-French Canadian sentiment. There does not appear to be any such sentiment these days. On the contrary, in Ontario there are many voices eloquently raised from day to day pleading for a greater understanding and appreciation of the rich vein of French-Canadian culture that is a treasure in our land.

English-speaking children now are not told to stand up and cheer over the victory of General Wolfe on the Plains of Abraham. They are encouraged to study the French language so that they may participate more usefully in the affairs of the nation in which a French-speaking element is such a very valuable part.

—*The Toronto Telegram,*
December 3, 1962

Racism: It's Time it was Confronted

The evidence is sadly overwhelming: the disgraceful discrimination against visible minorities marches on.

True, steps have been taken in school programs, employment equity initiatives, inquiries, reports and tribunals to gradually overcome what most of us realize has been an ongoing scourge. Regrettably, these steps have only made discrimination against minorities arguably less overt today than it was a decade ago.

As *Star* reporters Royson James and Leslie Papp wrote in a series of articles that ends today: "We concluded discrimination isn't something you find, but something that finds you."

Much of it involves ignorant and often racist clichés that whites apply to minorities. For example, a nationwide survey that involved police officers found these attitudes:
• More than one in five officers agreed "some breeds of people are naturally better than others"
• Some 73 percent of officers agreed immigrants often bring discrimination on themselves
• More than 56 percent said laws guaranteeing equal job opportunities for minorities already go too far

These attitudes are not exclusive to police officers, but are shared by Canadians in many walks of life.

The failure of some minorities, particularly immigrants, that most often starts in school usually carried right through to the job market.

Despite some effort, these groups are not well represented in positions of responsibility in the public service or the private sector, including the media. And since they don't see themselves reflected in these fields, they are less likely to try them out. A vicious circle ensues.

A number of explanations can be advanced. But the root cause is a pervasive racism that starts with the colour of skin. It is an obscenity.

In patchwork ways, especially in neighbourhoods, for example, that have become black ghettos, the schools are trying to educate black children with black as well as white teachers. It's working, but in limited ways.

The schools, however, are a good place to start. It will need sensitive teachers and a bureaucracy that is committed to success for minority students.

It follows that the public service and private sector will have to seek minority employees rather than wait for them to knock on doors.

There is much to be done.

How much longer can people be judged on the colour of their skin, rather than their character?
—*The Toronto Star,*
January 17, 1989

Colour-Blind Justice

Justice should not only be blind – meaning impartial – but colour-blind. Prime Minister Brian Mulroney got that right in appointing Julius Isaac as chief justice of the Federal Court of Canada.

Judge Isaac has had a solid career. He's a graduate of the University of Toronto, practised law in Saskatchewan and Ontario, spent 18 years in the federal justice department, and in 1989 was appointed to the Supreme Court of Ontario.

He's also black. Skin colour should neither be a qualification nor a detriment. Mr. Mulroney's appointment, which he took a long time making, acknowledges that. No one can say that the Grenada-born Judge Isaac is a token of anything. He was chosen on what Mr. Mulroney clearly believes are his merits.

The black community predictably is delighted: no black has ever been appointed to such a high place in the Canadian judiciary. Judge Isaac himself, wisely we think, restricted himself to saying that he was "very pleased." His accomplishments said the rest.
—*The Vancouver Sun,*
December 27, 1991

Remember What You Fought For

It is more than a little sad to see this issue in the news again, only days before the celebrations set to mark the 50th anniversary of D-Day. We are speaking, of course, of the decision by a majority of the delegates to the Royal Canadian Legion's national convention to reject a resolution that would have allowed Sikhs, Jews and members of other faiths to wear religious headgear in the public areas of Legion halls.

All sorts of excuses have been rolled out in defence of this decision. None of them stand up to scrutiny. Some say Tuesday's vote – with about 1,960 of more than 2,500 delegates siding against the motion – was at root a conflict over regional autonomy, a struggle for power between Dominion Command and the local branches. To some extent, it seems to have been.

But while it's fine for Legion branches to ask for autonomy from the national headquarters, why would anyone demand the right to capriciously exclude other Canadians, some of them fellow veterans?

Admissions policies will now be left up to the individual branches. According to Ken Allaire of the Newton, B.C. branch, which started this whole furor by excluding five turban-wearing Sikhs on Remembrance Day, 1993, this means that "if the Sikhs choose to open a branch of the Legion, they're totally welcome to open a branch."

The implication is that this is what they'll have to do if they want to get inside a Legion hall in some parts of the country. Yarmulke-wearing Jewish veterans will presumably have to open their own separate branch as well. How can one applaud such an outcome? Can men who fought together for the cause of freedom in time of war not sup together in time of peace?

There are those who say the rule against wearing headgear within Legion halls exists as a sign of respect for fallen comrades, and must be enforced without exception. But surely in this case the spirit of the law supersedes its letter.

It should be obvious to anyone that a Sikh veteran such as Pritam Jauhal, a retired Lieutenant-Colonel in the Indian Army who was excluded from the Newton hall last Remembrance Day, meant no disrespect when he wore his turban that day, as he does every other day.

Many Legion branches understand this: the Moose Jaw, Sask., branch agreed last December to allow headgear to be worn for religious reasons. Explained local president Keith Acott, "That doesn't mean the guy wearing the ball cap will get in." Perhaps the rule that hats must be doffed in a Legion hall can remain – with the understanding that the Sikh turban, a religious symbol that Orthodox male believers wear at all times, is not a hat.

The day after Mr. Jauhal and four other Sikh veterans were excluded from the Newton hall, Dominion Command issued an apology, condemning the actions of the local Legion officials, and saying that while branches determine their own dress rules, those rules are normally applied with "common sense."

Dominion Command, whose chairman resigned last Tuesday after his motion to admit people wearing religious headgear was defeated, said last Remembrance Day that "it is hoped that Canadians will not assume that the extremely poor judgment and bad manners of a very few Legion members is representative of all Legionnaires."

It is doubtless true that these actions are not representative of Canada's veterans – and it is time the majority stood up and said so.

—*The Globe and Mail*,
June 2, 1994

Same-Sex, Same Old Story

Ontario's same-sex benefits bill was defeated in a free vote yesterday, even after the NDP government watered it down by removing a provision that would have given gay and lesbian couples the right to adopt children. The government saw the provision as too contentious for the province's legislators and sacrificed it in a vain attempt to salvage at least those parts of the bill that would have extended employee benefits to same-sex couples. The battle over same-sex benefits will be fought another day. In the interim it is worth considering whether future legislation should include measures providing for homo-sexual adoption.

Polls this week showed that although a small majority of Ontarians supported extending employee benefits to same-sex spouses, many balked at the idea of permitting gays and lesbians to adopt children. But it seems likely that if Ontarians had a better understanding of the real issues behind the call for adoption rights for homosexual couples, at least some of the opposition to the idea would vanish.

The majority of people looking for the right to adopt as same-sex couples are lesbian women living in a long-term conjugal relation-ship in which one of the partners has a child. (Some gay men live in similar relationships, but it is much less common.) The adop-tion would be a means of formaliz-ing a parental relationship that already exists – that is, the non-biological parent is sharing in the upbringing of her spouse's child and the couple want that relation-ship recognized by law.

It is not merely on a point of principle that people want that recognition. Without legal ac-knowledgment of the relation-ship between the child and her mother's partner, the non-biolog-ical parent might not be able to sign the child out of school to go to the dentist, authorize a field trip or consent to medical treatment. And if the biological parent were to die, her partner would have no right to raise "their" child.

Even if the biological parent names her partner as her child's guardian, there is no guarantee that the guardianship would stand. Guardianship is no more than a statement of intent by the deceased parent for her child's future. It is easily challenged in the courts by relatives who might want to argue that it would be in the best interests of the child to reassign custody.

The matter of adoption rights for gay and lesbian couples can also be seen as one of the rights of the child. Without a legal tie between a non-biological parent and the child that he or she has helped to raise, the child has no legal right to financial support from her parent's partner if the spousal relationship breaks down.

It is also possible – depending on the conditions of individual employee-benefits plans – that extending benefits but not spousal rights to same-sex couples could leave the children of same-sex couples without the same access to extended health care that the children of heterosexual couples enjoy. Some plans might cover a same-sex spouse but refuse benefits to what is technically an unrelated child.

There is also considerable inconsistency in a law that allows single homosexuals to adopt children but will not permit a stable and loving homosexual couple to do so.

The current law governing the adoption of children in Ontario – the Child and Family Services Act – takes as its basic test of any decision on a child's welfare the question of what is "in the best interest of the child." Surely it is not unreasonable to assume that very often the best interest of a child is in creating a legal framework for the family in which he or she has been raised.

—*The Globe and Mail,*
June 10, 1994

Canada's Top Ranking Conceals Hardship

For the sixth straight year, the United Nations has ranked Canada first among 174 nations in terms of human development – a concept that measures not only a country's wealth, but how that wealth is used. We can take pride in a U.N. assessment that says, "Canada has been very successful in translating income into the well-being of its people." Just how successful can be seen in the comparison of our income and our quality of life: although we only rank 13th in terms of per capita GDP, we surpass every wealthier country in the broader measure of the quality of life.

However, just as no single word could ever describe all the facets of a painting, no one statistic can capture all the dimensions of a country's quality of life. For that reason, the U.N. augments its Human Development Index with other indices to provide more breadth, depth and perspective to the picture it paints of life around the world.

For example, according to its Gender-related Development Index, the U.N. ranks Canada No. 1 in ensuring that women get access to education and health care. We drop to fourth spot, however, in creating economic and political opportunities for them. The Scandinavian countries all have a higher proportion of women in their legislatures, in scientific and technical professions and in high-paying jobs than Canada.

But where we really lag as a country is in our efforts to combat poverty. Of the 17 high-income countries ranked by the U.N., Canada comes in ninth, trailing Sweden, the Netherlands, Germany, Norway, Italy, Finland, France and Japan.

Compared with most European countries, Canada – like the bottom-ranked U.S. – leaves it very much up to the market to determine how our national income is shared.

And with globalization, the U.N. says, the dominance of markets has produced "a grotesque and dangerous polarization between both people and nations." On one side are the winners, reaping the rewards of free trade and free enterprise; on the other side are the losers, coping with the effects. The U.N. believes globalization – "the growing interdependence of the world's people through shrinking space, shrinking time and disappearing borders" – can create greater opportunities for people everywhere. However, too many people are denied those opportunities because uncontrolled markets shut them out.

The growing gap between rich and poor in Canada is a sign that we are letting that happen in our own country. The per capita income of the richest 20 percent of the population ($42,110) is seven times that of the poorest 20 percent ($5,971).

But embracing globalization doesn't have to mean that we must accept an inequitable sharing of the benefits that it can bring.

The stark contrast in income distribution between Sweden, with its relatively low poverty rate, and the U.S., with the highest, demonstrates that we do have a choice in how we divide up what we have achieved.

Most Canadians will not be surprised that the U.N. thinks their country is the best place in the world to live. But the U.N.'s rosy statistics aren't likely to provide much comfort for those without a job, a home, or a decent income.

Only by bringing them into the mainstream will we truly become the best country in the world. And that should be our No. 1 goal.

—*The Toronto Star,*
July 13, 1999

Let the People Go

Chief Leo Friday of the Kashechewan First Nation, on Ontario's James Bay coast, received test results on the reserve's drinking water on Friday, Oct. 14 and issued the usual notice to the residents to boil the water. He also declared a state of emergency because many of the 1,600 residents were sick with dysentery or with skin infections from the contaminated water.

The reserve's water system, designed for 800 people, had often malfunctioned since it was installed five years earlier, leading to frequent boil-water notices. But the disease outbreaks sparked more concern. Over the next couple of weeks, the Ontario government evacuated residents to Sault Ste. Marie, Ottawa, Sudbury and Cochrane for treatment of their ailments. Ontario Premier Dalton McGuinty publicly urged the federal government to take an interest in the case. The Defence Department soon turned up with its DART emergency water treatment equipment. Prime Minister Paul Martin and Indian Affairs Minister Andy Scott promised to build new houses for Kashechewan at a rate of 50 a year and to repair the water system and all the other malfunctioning water systems of First Nation communities.

Neither government, however, came up with means of making Kashechewan a good place to live.

The community's economic base consists of the cash and services that arrive from Ottawa. People stay there because it is the only home they have known and because they would lose their band-supplied houses and welfare payments if they moved away. As a result, the population has grown rapidly and overwhelmed the water system.

When more houses are supplied and the waterworks expanded, the population will again increase. But there will still be nothing to do in Kashechewan, no means of earning a livelihood, no education or recreation beyond what the band supplies.

Kashechewan therefore raises the vast problem of Canada's Indian reserves — the wretched conditions in which many of Canada's 270,000 Indian reserve residents live and the dim prospects they face. Grand Chief Phil Fontaine and the Assembly of First Nations advise the government to improve reserves by spending the necessary funds to build the houses and other facilities the residents need. The government has agreed to do that for Kashechewan.

Apart from Indian reserves, Canadians have for years been moving away from the smallest and most remote communities and gathering in the largest and best-equipped cities to seek better jobs, better schools, better entertainment, better lives than small, remote communities can provide.

People of the First Nations know the limitations of reserve life: 60 percent of them already live outside reserves. Despite the exodus from reserves, however, many reserves show rapidly growing population while other cities and towns in the boreal forest, the tundra and the grasslands have been shrinking.

The city nearest to Kashechewan is Timmins, whose population dropped by eight percent to 43,686 in 2001 from 47,499 in 1996. Kashechewan's population was not counted in 2001, but it was 1,004 in 1996 and it is currently said in news reports to be 1,600 or perhaps 1,900.

Timmins has a Shania Twain centre, two golf courses and all the other amenities you would expect in a small Ontario city, yet its population is shrinking. Kashechewan's fondest hope recently was to scrape up enough government grants to buy a pool table so that the young people would have something to do other than drink and inhale solvents. The houses are wretched and the water makes you sick. It is a hell-hole and yet the population is growing.

The difference is that Kashechewan is an Indian reserve and Timmins is not. People who leave Timmins can sell their house, take their skills and their wealth with them and make a new life somewhere else. People who leave Kashechewan have nothing to sell because Canadian law forbids private ownership of reserve property. They have few skills because there are no jobs in Kashechewan, no means of learning a skill and no reason to make the effort. People in Timmins are free and mobile while people in Kashechewan are in effect prisoners of the Indian reserve system into which they were born.

More spending by Prime Minister Paul Martin to upgrade the Kashechewan waterworks and replace the houses will not make the people there more free, more mobile or better able to enjoy the abundance of choice and opportunity that is available to people in

Timmins and in the rest of non-reserve Canada.

The immediate solution for Kashechewan must include safe drinking water and good houses. But a proper solution must include hope, mobility and freedom, including the freedom to move anywhere in Canada without losing the rights of the aboriginal people who gave up their land so that Canada might be settled and developed.

The government should let Kashechewan people and other reserve residents take the cash value of their housing benefits, their welfare payments and the rest with them when they leave the reserve. As long as they are required to give up their rights and their income when they leave, then of course they will stay and Canada will never be able to afford them a decent, Canadian life. Mr. Martin should unlock those fetters, though chiefs and councils tell him not to, and let the people go.

—*The Winnipeg Free Press, November 6, 2005*

7
On the Subject of Women

Women Enfranchised

The women of Manitoba are now on an equality, so far as provincial matters go, with their sisters in Australia, New Zealand, Norway, Finland, Sweden, Denmark, Iceland, and a large section of the United States. In England, Ireland, Scotland and Wales women vote in all elections except for members of Parliament.

Henry George put the whole matter in a nutshell many years ago: "The natural right of a woman to vote is just as clear as that of a man, and rests on the same ground. Since she is called on to obey the laws, she ought to have a voice in making them.

John Stuart Mill said that "to have a voice in choosing those by whom one is governed is a means of self-protection due to every one."

Sir Robert Stout, for a long time premier of New Zealand – a very shrewd Scotsman, by the way – said the effect of woman suffrage in his country was beneficial. It interested women in questions of State.

In woman suffrage countries, none of the predicted evils from franchise extension have arrived. Much positive good has resulted.

The deed is done in Manitoba. A long-sustained and just agitation has borne fruit. From Knox Church pulpit, nearly 25 years ago, Hon. Joseph Martin, then a member of the Manitoba

Legislature, publicly declared his strong belief that women should be enfranchised.

One of the women leaders, after the passage of the Bill yesterday, declared that franchise extension would be far from a panacea for all our ills. Thousands of women, granted a most sacred privilege, are just as ignorant, and, worse still, just as heathen in their politics, because of their partisanship, as thousands of men. The campaign of education on the exercise of the franchise must now begin.

—*The Winnipeg Evening Tribune, January 28, 1916*

(Editor's Note: Women in Canada did not gain the right to vote in federal elections until 1918. Denied the franchise at this time, however, were Inuit and Status Native women, and women from several Asian groups.)

The "Persons" Case

The decision of the Privy Council must not be misunderstood. It has not been decided that women must be appointed to the Senate of Canada, but only that they are not precluded by our federal constitution from being so appointed.

—*The Toronto Evening Star, October. 22, 1929*

(Editor's Note: In 1928, the Supreme Court of Canada ruled that women were not "persons" eligible for Senate seats. When the British Privy Council overturned the ruling the next year, The Toronto Evening Star applauded, with one hand, in a 40-word editorial "note.")

Varied Roles

There's a story out of England that Anthony Eden, usually self-possessed in the House, can be disconcerted more by the brilliant and persistent Ellen Wilkinson, a trades union official and one of the members from Manchester, than by anyone else, particularly at question time.

When conversation turned recently to the upsetting influence of Helen of Troy, the foreign secretary is said to have remarked, humourously but ruefully, "We all have our Ellen," which in a country where so many h's are dropped is a bright enough rejoinder. There are some eight women members in the British House of Commons, including Viscountess Astor and the Duchess of Atholl. There is no woman in the present British ministry, although Margaret Bondfield had a cabinet post in the Labour government. There are no women cabinet ministers at Ottawa or in the provinces. Mary Ellen Smith, who died in 1933, was in a B.C. government. Agnes Maphail and Martha Munger Black are the only women in the Canadian House of Commons. There are no women in the Ontario legislature and Mrs. Plumptre is the only representative of her sex now in the Toronto city council.

In the United States, Madame Perkins is the first woman to hold a cabinet position, secretary of labour. Mrs. Carraway, the only woman in the Senate, has become the senior member from Arkansas owing to the death of her colleague, Senator Robinson.

Women are making more advance, in public status, in the Turkey of Mustapha Kemal and in republican nationalist China than anywhere else.

On the whole, the way of active feminism in public affairs has receded, and women are taking up again, unconsciously or deliberately, their traditional role of exercising influence in their own homes and among their own friends rather than in the din of public life.

They have behind them now, however, the prestige of the franchise in a way they never had before and, whether publicly or privately, their power is being constantly exercised for worthy causes.

—*The Toronto Daily Star, July 19, 1937*

Employed and Married

Miss Frances Perkins, United States Secretary of Labour, thinks it is "quite all right for married women to remain in business." Miss Perkins has had unrivalled opportunities of forming an expert opinion on this vexed question, but there are plenty of other experienced men and women who find it impossible to agree with her. Company officials, employment service agents, welfare workers and others have expressed themselves in the most decided terms on the complications arising in industry and in the homes through the employment of married women who are under no economic necessity to work for wages.

It all depends upon the particular circumstances. Each individual case must be judged on its own merits; to make a sweeping pronouncement, one way or the other, is not only unfair, but foolish.

Correspondents of the *Spectator* have, as a rule, shown a sympathetic, judicious spirit in discussing the pros and cons of the problem. Young women, naturally enough, are incensed at their inability to secure work because, as they sometimes find, desirable positions in offices and factories have been given to married women who have no real need to augment the family income.

In instances where a husband already has steady employment, the charge of selfishness may not be unjustified. But where the man's employment is precarious and where ill health or other mis-

fortune has overtaken him, the action of the wife who assumes the responsibilities of the household and so maintains the family's independence is surely deserving of nothing but praise. This is generally admitted by the single women workers themselves. It is the double pay envelope that causes the discontent and criticism.

It is interesting in this connection to note the views of Miss Mary McMahon, of Toronto, described as "director of a large staff of women," who holds that there are too many men in Canada whose earnings are inadequate for the support of their families to challenge the right of the wife to "earn a salary to keep her family comfortable." But, she continues, the majority of married business women admit that "if they could start all over again they would remain out of business after marriage and establish a permanent home."

It is to be hoped that this reflection, given as a result of practical, personal experience, will be duly weighed by those to whom it applies.

—*The Hamilton Spectator,*
November 10, 1938

"How I am Stuck on it All"

The Royal Canadian Mounted Police is a man's force and the *Royal Canadian Mounted Police Quarterly* is a man's magazine. But in the current issue of the magazine is an article by a woman.

She is Mrs. Verda Betts. Her husband is a member of the R.C.M.P. Last year she went north with her husband and their family into the Yukon. It is only a very brief article but it is remarkable for the way it pictures how good life can be in the "new North."

The quarters for families of members of the Force are well built houses, with electricity. Pleasant furnishings are provided. The children can go to good schools, built and maintained by the Department of Resources and Development.

Perhaps to some housewives who live in more settled parts of Canada homemaking in the Yukon may seem uninviting. But Mrs. Betts loves it. The children are thrilled by the outdoor life and the sight of many animals – foxes,

wolves, buffalo and caribou. They are gaining first-hand knowledge of the vast country and have followed the courses of great rivers from the air while travelling in comfortable Police aircraft.

As far as dress is concerned, Mrs. Betts has discovered that this is one of the few parts of Canada where you can dress warmly and still be in style. And the feminine winter wardrobe can be augmented with colourful native handicraft, which may even be cherished as souvenirs in later years.

Nor is life as rushed with useless activities as it is in cities. There is time to develop one's interests and hobbies. And as Mrs. Betts says: "Home life takes on the atmosphere of peace and contentment which mean so much in the world today."

It is part of the fascination of Canada that there are so many homes scattered under so many different skies, from prairies to sea shore, and from great cities to the far north. And Mrs. Betts reminds Canadians elsewhere that life is still very good in Canada, even in the northland that many might think of as forbidding.

But she believes that only those Canadians who have lived in northern Canada can come to understand what Robert Service meant when he wrote:

"The freshness, the freedom, the farness,
O God! How I am stuck on it all."

—The Montreal Gazette,
October 3, 1952

A Public Act of Violence

The Ontario government's $5.4 million program to crack down on wife-beaters is just one step down the long road to breaking the cycle of violence faced by hundreds of innocent women and children. By more effectively prosecuting wife-beaters and increasing family counselling and improving shelters for battered women, Queen's Park will start chipping away at one of our least recognized social problems.

Many still consider wife-beating *a family matter* best dealt with in the privacy of the home. Wrong. It is, in the words of Attorney-General Ian Scott, "a public act of violence." It's estimated as many as 4 in ever 10 women are battered by their mates.

That brutality has enormous social costs. It rips families apart, condemns many women and children to a life of virtual slavery, condemns many women and children to a life of virtual slavery, teaches children that violence is acceptable and puts those who try to intervene at enormous personal risk.

Yet, it's the victims who continue to be victimized: women and children must hide in hostels while the bullies are released from police custody within hours of being charged and are often free to return home. Those convicted often get a mere slap on the wrist – most are fined and put on probation. Few go to jail or are ordered to get counselling.

While battered families can often get help, there are still few counselling programs for wife-beaters – about three in all of Metro Toronto. Queen's Park plans to spend $1 million on new programs, but they are primarily aimed at entire families rather than the men who most need help. The government's initiatives, while admirable, are not comprehensive enough.

Scott's pledge to "make the legal process more responsive" to family violence is welcome – but it must be followed through, as strongly as government measures against drunk driving. And so must earlier commitments from the province to increase the amount of affordable housing.

Meanwhile, women are being turned away from Ontario's 80 shelters. While the government's long-term solutions are being put into place, where will they stay?

—*The Toronto Star,*
September 18, 1986

Equal Exposure

In our breast-obsessed era, a topless woman is destined to turn the heads of pedestrians – some of whom, duly scandalized, may dutifully turn her in.

But by baring her breasts, Guelph philosophy student Gwen Jacob has exposed the contradictions of a society that sells sex and markets nudity by night, but can't countenance it in the full light of day.

Police arrested Jacob for flaunting her body and flouting the law in downtown Guelph. Yet when two men strolled by similarly undressed, they went unmolested.

Now, Jacob stands charged with the Criminal Code offence of public indecency. Naturally, her defence strips the law to its essentials: men and women are equal under the Canadian Charter of Rights and Freedoms.

In court, Jacob said a man asked her to "turn around" so he could check whether her breasts were "better than my wife's." But his wife, Diane Pettifer, found the display disgusting – and contacted police.

Pettifer testified that the errant breasts dangerously distracted passing drivers. And the crown submitted expert evidence that the breast is an erotic sex organ.

But what about other potential road hazards such as deep cleavages, bare knees, exposed navels and painted toenails? And what about nursing mothers recklessly breastfeeding their newborns in public places? Or topless male bodybuilders flexing their biceps?

The court ruling is due next month. But now is the time to end the absurd double standard on bare chests: women work legally topless inside carwashes, taverns, and movie studios, yet they can't walk to work in their uniforms.

Women elsewhere face dress codes compelling them to cover their faces, hair, arms and legs. Yet Canadians think it absurd to force veils on women, just as some Europeans refuse to cover their breasts on the beach.

Why then can Canadian men publicly bare their chests while women are dragged into court? Surely, the solution is to treat men and women equally under the law.

And if Canadians think it tasteless to go bare-chested on tennis courts or in the courtroom, fair enough – ban it for both sexes.

—*The Toronto Star,*
November 25, 1991

(Editor's Note: In 1992, an Ontario court judge convicted Gwen Jacob of indecent exposure and fined her $75. On Dec. 10, 1996, the Ontario Court of Appeal overturned the ruling and the City of Toronto then passed a bylaw allowing women to go topless at municipal pools, beaches and buildings.)

A Twinkle in the Sky

At night, long ago, the child would try to escape the Earth in her dreams. Her bed became her spaceship. In her imagination, she could do anything.

She would pretend to be an asteroid in space, or a galactic adventurer collecting the red sands of Mars with Commander Tom. Alone in the darkness, staring at the distant stars beyond her window, she was free of all the limitations of life in a middle-sized Canadian town. She could be anybody, and so she became Flash Gordon "roaring across the planet Mongo." A child full of dreams and possibilities.

She grew older. Her parents, both teachers, encouraged her to go exploring beyond the frontiers of conventional girlhood. She loved sports and thought she might like to be a phys-ed teacher. She turned to science after an exciting school research project on the life cycle of tent caterpillars in which several squirming generations bred in the kitchen refrigerator. She was the curious kid on the block, and fortunately, nobody in authority tried to harness her spirit. Perhaps they knew it was impossible.

She became a doctor, then a university professor in neurology.

She wrote articles for research publications, gave lectures, earned a PhD, five honorary doctorates and many commendations for her science. For fun, she learned to fly a plane, ride in hot air balloons, enjoy canoeing, cross-country skiing, fishing, cycling, target shooting, squash and French lessons. In her words, she became "an organized cyclone," a whirlwind of ideas and interests, and most important of all, a happy person.

Inside the woman, however, was a small girl who still yearned for the freedom of space beyond Earth.

Roberta Bondar is in free flight on the *Discovery* today, happily working on her 42 experiments, living and breathing her childhood fantasy. Canadians are fiercely proud of her achievement, as they were in 1984 when her only Canadian predecessor, Marc Garneau, flew into space. Knowing how long, and how hard, Bondar prepared for the flight, we are almost out there with her.

"I shall become part of the twinkle in the night sky."

Tonight, we hope, thousands of Canadian children will lie in their spaceship beds and ponder the impossible, beautiful things that can happen in the course of an ordinary life. Up above the world so high, like a diamond in the sky, Roberta Bondar is sending them a message that matters. Dream.

—*The Edmonton Journal,*
January 23, 1992

A Judicious Appointment

Madam Justice Beverley McLachlin is the first woman to hold the powerful position of chief justice of the Supreme Court. That is progress. Even better, though, is that there is no suggestion that the arbitrary qualification of sex had any bearing on the decision.

A small-town Albertan whose early judicial career was forged in B.C., Justice McLachlin has earned her reputation as an uncompromising individual whose loyalty is to the law, not social or political doctrine. We wish her well.

—*The Vancouver Sun,*
November 5, 1999

8

Slow News Day

The Nuisance of Tips

From time immemorial one of the unpleasantnesses in British hotels has been the tipping system, and in the past few years the same pernicious system has so invaded our own land that the civility of waters must now be purchased. Eternally they have their hands behind them.

This is unfair, even dishonest. When a guest registers at a hotel the landlord really enters into an agreement that at a certain rate he will provide meals, beds and attendance; but when the guest takes his seat in the dining room he often finds that he fares badly until he lines the waiter's hand.

Of the best hotels this is especially true, and the proprietor who first takes a stand against it will have the approval of the travelling public.

The servants in hotels, just the same as the servants of any other institution, should be paid a salary that would place them above the station of beggars; and if the pres-

ent hotel rates are too low to permit of this the rates should be raised so that guests can know really what they are expected to pay.

Nor are hotels alone in this respect. The same system has invaded the barber shop, the restaurant and the railways; so much so in railways that commercial travellers are allowed in their expenses a certain amount for tips to baggage men.

The thing should be stopped. Employees should be paid reasonable wages and subject to instant dismissal for accepting money on the outside.

—*The Toronto Evening Star, August 10, 1895*

Cattle and Customs

The Toronto Globe says that an international question of considerable importance has arisen in the North-West Territories. It appears that large numbers of American cattle cross the line, gorge themselves with the succulent grasses of Canada, and return to Montana with the plunder. The cattle first break the laws of the United States by carrying grass across the border in a partially manufactured state, contrary to the provisions of the Dingley Act. They refuse to furnish invoices, pay duty, or otherwise comply with the customs regulations of the two countries. They resemble "the beast who takes his licence in the fields of time, unfettered by the sense of crime, to whom a conscience never wakes."

The Mounted Police of Canada are working in harmony with the riders employed by the ranchmen of Montana, making common cause against the lawless beasts, but it is said to be impossible to prevent cattle straying over an imaginary line. A report presented to the western stock-growers points out that while better feed and water may tend to draw the Montana cattle to our ranges, storms from the north in winter have a similar tendency to drive our cattle into Montana. "A certain reciprocity in such matters suggests itself as being the wisest course under the circumstances."

We foresee a lengthy controversy over this matter, continues the *Globe*. The advocates of reciprocity will be denounced as disloyal. Canadian cattle, it will be said, will come back from Montana full of American ideas and grass, while our good Canadian grass will help to build up the cattle of a foreign land. The construction of a wire fence three or four hundred miles long will be proposed as a means of keeping the cattle in the land of their allegiance, and also of encouraging the iron industry. The cattle of the west seem to have no more respect for boundary lines than the capitalists of the money centres.

—*The Regina Leader,*
May 23, 1901

How to Address Royalty

One of the "side shows" if we may be pardoned so irreverent an expression, incident to the royal visit to Canada, is the little discussion that has arisen on the proper mode of addressing a royal duke. According to the instructions issued from head quarters down east, the proper form and style is, first the superscription of rank and titles, and then "May it please your royal highness," and that mode has been adopted in almost all the addresses presented to the Duke of Cornwall since he landed in the Dominion.

The most authoritative works on etiquette, however, declare that after the superscription of rank and titles, should come simply the word "Sir," and that is the form set forth in Mr. John A. Cooper's excellent work just issued entitled "The New Century Perfect Speaker." One may naturally ask, therefore, Which is correct?

The answer is simple. Both forms are equally correct, but they mean very different things. The first form is merely an admission of superiority of rank, whereas the second is a declaration of respect.

"Your majesty," "your royal highness," "your grace," and similar modes of expression are a polite recognition of the rank of the person addressed; but they are nothing beyond that. They imply no sentiment whatever.

They are purely conventional and simply satisfy the rules of courtesy.

With "sire" or "sir," however, the case is quite different. The word "sire," as everybody knows, means "father;" and when the King is addressed as "sire" it is an indication that he is regarded as "the father of his people." There can be no higher title than this. It is not conventional, not a mere recognition of rank. It carries with it the incidents of fatherhood and sonship.

Love, care and protection on the part of the sire; affection, obedience and reverence on the part of the subject. In addressing the sovereign, therefore, the phrase "your majesty" denotes courtesy; the phrase "sire" denotes loyalty.

—*The Regina Leader,*
September 26, 1901

The Age of Cake and Cackle

Have Nova Scotians ceased to read? This is a question which we should put to ourselves; and insist upon a thoughtful answer. Of course, most of us read the newspapers that is to say the headlines, the "jokes" and the "local columns." We all read the "best sellers," and in consequence pride ourselves on being quite literary. Beyond that, what?

If there are those who do read in the old-fashioned way, they are duly ashamed; and carefully conceal the fact. One might frequent almost any society in Halifax indefinitely and scarcely ever hear a real book mentioned. Jazz has superseded poetry. Bridge has given thought its quietus. Not that jazz and bridge may not be serviceable in their way, and more or less timely; but surely the flounces are not more important than the garments of life.

Men have been living and thinking and recording their thoughts for thousands of years. They of old thought at least as wisely and clearly as the best of us today. Would it not be worth while to revert to their wisdom sometimes and to talk it over with one another? Might it not do us good to read, to think and to speak in terms of other than the blatant present?

We have it on high authority that "reading maketh a full man; conference, a ready man." Where there is neither reading nor conference the inference would seem to be that emptiness and dullness are to be expected.

In the days of not so long ago there was not only sound reading but systematic arrangements for "Conference." There were literary societies for the winter evenings, debating clubs and mechanics institutes.

What has become of them? Are we so wise, so "advanced," that we no longer have need of mental improvement? Is there nothing higher or better in life than eating, playing and chattering? Is no social movement longer possible, otherwise than by means of "grub" and garrulity? Can Christianity itself only be promoted by cake and cackle?

—*The Halifax Herald,*
March 24, 1920

He Ran with the Ball

The hundredth anniversary of rugby football was celebrated the other day at the famous Warwickshire school which gave the game its name. There is a table at the school which

Commemorates the exploit
of
WILLIAM WEBB ELLIS,

Who, with a fine disregard to the rules of football as played in his time, first took the ball in his hands and ran with it, thus originating the distinctive feature of the Rugby game.

A.D. 1823

In other games than football – in the games of industry and business as in the games of science and literature – epochal changes have been achieved by men who have refused to let the past govern the future. The fact that certain things have been done certain ways has meant nothing to these innovators. They have gone ahead and changed them – "with a fine disregard to the rules of football." They have taken the ball in their hands and run with it, to the astonishment and indignation of people who were shortly afterwards to imitate them.

But for one man who makes a change and succeeds, many attempt to make a change and fail. That is because their changes are for the worse, or unnecessary, or, in some cases, attempted before the world is ready for them.

There are writers who throw aside all the established forms of verse and literature, and who think that their product must necessarily be better because it is different. There are artists who discard all the principles of perspective and colour-harmony and wonder that their daubs are not appreciated.

It may be that some who desire to alter things which are already right attempt the change because they are themselves too lazy or too incapable to do these things in the established way. The men and women who achieve wise changes and who inaugurate great reforms are undoubtedly the men and women who make the world go round.

It does not follow that every change is good. Not every football player can be a William Webb Ellis with success.

—*The Toronto Evening Star, November 19, 1923*

Mystery Upon Mystery

Life is chiefly a matter of electricity, according to Dr. George W. Crile of Cleveland, who has been delving into the matter for many years.

Reading a paper before the American Philosophical Society at Philadelphia, Dr. Crile declared that man seems to be fundamentally a sort of glorified storage battery. As long as the battery remains charged, the machinery can function, and the individual can carry on his daily work, whether the job be writing poetry or playing professional baseball. When the battery runs down, however, the daily work has to be given up; the man dies.

Apparently the old expression, "the vital spark," is a good one. If our clever scientists are going to keep on demonstrating that we are kin to the crackling of an electrical generator, rather than to the stars and the wind, as we used to think, we would do well to keep that expression in regular use.

Dr. Crile's researches are extremely interesting, and there is no doubt that they add immensely to the store of human knowledge. Yet it would be a mistake to suppose that they really clear up the fundamental mystery. Life may be a matter of electricity, as Dr. Crile suggests; but what scientist will arise now to tell us what electricity is? We have only exchanged one mystery for another.

During the last century, mankind has found out a great deal about itself and about the world it inhabits. It has dispelled the old fables by which primitive men sought to interpret the puzzles of existence, and has substituted for them a series of far less interesting formulas and equations. But it is really no nearer the root of the matter than it was before.

The ancient Aztecs believed that the creator of the world made a set of clay figures, blew life into them with his nostrils, and sent them forth to inhabit the world – which, by the way, he had trampled into shape with his feet. The modern scientist believes that man is a very complicated sort of storage battery, moving about on a speck of cosmic dust as long as his charge of electricity lasts. Both conceptions are interesting. Neither clears up the ancient mystery.

We tear down the old curtains of ignorance only to find an endless vista of new ones. And if this leaves room for doubt and disquiet, it also leaves room for faith and boundless hope. The technicians may have reduced you to an electrical equation, but what of that? You are still unexplainable.

—*The Victoria Daily Times, May 4, 1929*

Silk Hats, etc.

What punishment, if any, do a silk hat and claw-hammer coat deserve in these days of tension? What seems clear is that section of the jobless population doesn't take to them, unless possibly to remove them or destroy them.

We read that unemployed paraders in London the other night looked menacingly upon a flock of silk-hatted, claw-hammered folk trooping out of one of the theatres. They looked so menacingly, in fact, that this section of the theatre-going population beckoned the police, asking protection.

We're not sure that the jobless wanted to batter up those men wearing those particular hats and coats. It is not established that they had anything against them personally. Like a few theologians, however, they appeared to accept the situation symbolically. To those jobless men those "plug" hats and split-tail vestments probably were a symbol of at least "three squares" a day, a sizeable wad of bills in your jeans and a bit of leisure thrown in without need for worry about financing it. There may even have been a full-fledged "parasite" or two in the entourage. The whole situation was tantamount to a red flag being waved in the face of a bull.

However, maybe we shouldn't be too hard on the silk-hatted folk. Maybe some of those London hats have been doing duty at least since the depression came upon us three years ago. Perhaps, in other words, they are being worn out of enforced frugality. As a matter of fact, maybe some of them aren't wholly paid for. They may be more of those shrunken assets we hear about.

This is so much punishment in itself, and perhaps a bit more lies in the actual wearing of these head pieces. Outside of one "Al" Plunket, we have yet to view a single human soul who looked really comfortable in a silk hat.

So those London unemployed might well eave those theatre crowds to stew in their own juice. Theirs, on more than one point, may be an agony no less poignant than their own.

We once asked a Canadian why he wore a silk hat to a theatre in London. He said that it was easier to get a taxi-man when wearing a high hat. The taxi fellows apparently felt that a man with a silk hat ought to be good for a better tip – perhaps a sixpence instead of a threepence.

—*The Regina Leader,*
November 3, 1932

Leave the Rooster Alone

The danger that besets many worthy campaigns is that they may be carried too far. Take this matter of night noises, gradually becoming worse – rumbling street cars, screeching brakes, auto-horn honking, motorcycle cut-outs, iron-shod horses hauling iron-tired delivery wagons along streets that should be silent. Something should – in fact must – be done about these if city folk are to get any sleep at all during these hot nights.

All well and good; but here enters the danger of excess of zeal. There are extremists who would stop the rooster's greeting to the dawn; his intimation to the sun that it is time to begin its climbing of the orient sky. Do objectors to chanticleer's early activity not know that it has a place in the scheme of nature?

Since the dawn of time this bird's first order of the day has been to notify mankind that it is time to get up. What cares he if times have changed, and if sleepy-headed man never sees a sunrise – except on the way home from his foolish occupations? Nature intended man to sleep at night, but he will not; and chanticleer knows the world isn't any the better for that.

Let the campaign against man-made noises go on vigorously. There are plenty of these to occupy the time of the most zealous workers for a quieter night in the city; but don't interfere with the exultant notes of a wide-awake rooster. He is merely discharging the duty nature allotted to him.

Of course, it is unlikely that the time ever will return when humanity will have slept its fill by sunrise. That would be too sane a procedure for the silly world of today. If city and suburban folk, especially, retired at a reasonable hour, they would not wax wroth when the neighbour's rooster "proclaims the dawn." Instead, they would leap blithely from bed, singing:

Hark, hark! I hear
The strain of strutting chanti-
cleer
Cry cock-a-diddle-dow.
—*The Toronto Globe,*
July 30, 1935

Jeeves, Will You Please Carry On

The servant problem, in North America, is not new. It has existed since pioneer days, when the vast opportunities of the new land made a fetish of "equality." There grew up the opinion that it was degrading to attend to the personal wants of others, even in public service jobs such as barbering or waiting on table.

The result has been that these necessary – and often comparatively lucrative – positions have almost always been filled by Europeans or Asiatics. Only in the taxi-driver (who feels he is "his own boss" anyway) has North America produced a public servant who exists in any numbers.

In bad times, of course, certain sections of the North American community have been forced, unwillingly, to accept "menial" jobs. But they have seldom had the training to do the job well and almost never have they had the enthusiasm to learn how. When times are good, these native sources of service labour dry up. When times are as good as they are now, North America must look very largely to foreign countries for her servants, public or private.

These traditional sources are proving a disappointment. Though the positions are no longer "menial," though pay and privileges and working conditions have improved enormously, other jobs seem too attractive for the New Canadian or New American to resist. Perhaps, too, the newcomer, in adapting himself to his new community, finds his old pride in a job well done overcome by the American prej-udice against the "flunkey."

More than this, these overseas sources are themselves drying up. The traditional English butler, so beloved by novelist and playwright, may soon be a thing of the past. For there are fewer and fewer English homes which can afford to have butlers – or even to train them for export.

The result, of course, will be a greater expansion of a trend already well-established. North America will produce more and more machines to do more and more "menial" chores. But no one has invented, as yet, a machine which will dust the house, or polish the floors, or make dinner, or do the shopping all by itself.

Until that day, Jeeves, will you please carry on.

—*The Montreal Gazette,
October 15, 1952*

A Sneer for Mona

A tourist from this side of the Atlantic once stood before Leonardo da Vinci's *Mona Lisa* and found that the portrait did not move him. He said to the guide: "I don't see why everybody gets so excited about this picture."

"Sir," replied the guide, "the portrait is not on trial. You are on trial."

Custom dictates that one should show a proper amount of awe over the news that da Vinci's masterpiece is being transported from Paris to the National Gallery in Washington under heavy security. The word is that it has been insured for $100 million during its sojourn in America.

After all, it's not just a picture. For four and a half centuries critics have showered it with rhapsodic praise. The fact that it comes from the hand of a multi-faceted genius should be enough to make lesser men fearful of casting aspersions on it.

Yet, like the child who questioned the emperor's new clothes, we can't see it for beans.

Call us clots, dolts, oafs, peasants, Philistines. What's all the fuss about?

Granted that La Gioconda's hands have telling touch of character and that the chiaroscuro is something for professional artists to become lyrical about. But save us from that inscrutable expression of the cheeks and lips, that smile which is really no smile! Or is it a sneer?

The rankest amateur becomes no authority when he discusses this feature. The comments are so commonplace that they pall.

Give us rather Raphael's portrait of *Maddalena Doni* or Carot's *Dame a la Perle*. At least here we don't get pedantic lectures about outer expression reflecting inner life.

If this is heresy, you buffs who fancy yourselves experts, make the most of it.

—*The Toronto Telegram,*
December 15, 1962

Ingathering Time

After the first few light frosts have laid tentative, testing hands on the fields and gardens, there comes the time of ingathering. It is a generic term of Biblical association, and it refers to the harvest season when a husbandman reaps the result of his work. As a man sows in this world, so also shall he reap; and the injunction covers both the tangible and intangible rewards of living.

It is good to work in the garden on a sun-drenched, tenth month day when the blue jays are bugling above the sugar lot and the chickadees are chanting in the old Russet tree at the end of the yard.

It isn't necessarily glamorous work to fork out the carrots and beets; pulling the turnips and cabbages can become a bit monotonous. But there is a deep satisfaction in growing one's own food and storing it against the time of cold and snow.

Sometimes in a mild October a man can get an extra cutting of sweet, frost-limp rowan, and the tangy, nostril-tingling fragrance of new mown hay fills the air. It is good to harvest the Greenings and Northern Spies, Blue Pearmains and Kings from the old orchard on the hillside.

A man takes satisfaction in looking at the vegetables and fruits in the earth-floored house cellar. The bins of Green Mountains, the boxes of fruit, the shelves of fruits and vegetables, the jars of jams and jellies paint a picture in the soft glow of the lantern.

Ingathering is a special time of year. As the colours flame on the hills and then the bonfires of autumn burn out, as bare trees make etchings on the ridges and goldenrod becomes grey ghosts along the roadsides, the countryman works along at his harvesting and gets ready for the winter.

—*The Saint John Telegraph Journal, October 19, 1981*

9
The Next Generation

Air Guns

"Mr. H.H. Penny's boy was struck by a bullet from an air gun. These air guns are in the hands of every boy and are becoming dangerous. Dealers should be stopped selling them." The above is the tenor of a very brief item handed in to this paper. About this time every year the small boy in the Canadian hamlet, town or city develops a fondness for the air gun or the catapult.

It's an objectionable phase of the spring fever. The birds are arriving and the small boys' sporting blood – inherited from his forefathers, who would sooner shoot than eat, and often had to shoot, before they could get anything to eat – stirs within him, and he begs, borrows, buys or steals an air gun or a catapult.

He would prefer a Maxim or a Howitzer, for the more deadly the weapon the better he likes it, but they're too expensive and cannot be readily carried in the hip pocket.

Having got his weapon he proceeds to kill birds, smash windows, torment stray dogs, and plug the eyes of the neighbours' cats. He shoots at everything living or dead, and develops considerable skill as a marksman at other people's expense.

The small boy with an air gun or catapult is a dangerous nuisance, and should be suppressed.
—*The Windsor Evening Record, April 6, 1900*

A Public Bathing Place

The season is upon us when the youthful, as well as the more mature minds, naturally turn to the pleasure of a plunge in the clear, health-giving water that passes our doors. The same lack of proper facilities where this health-giving luxury can be enjoyed without offending decency still.

We hope that there will be no fining of boys as long as this condition exists. To do so would be to discourage cleanliness, which good authority says is next to godliness. The indifference or stinginess or something that makes our rulers neglect such a necessity as a place where people can take a plunge into the river should not be encouraged. Let the boys and men use the means nature supplies if no other is provided. If regard for health will not move our authorities let the people be shamed into providing a place where bathing can be enjoyed. Our river front is now nearly all taken up by railways and the lives of a number of our children have already been sacrificed in their desire to reach the river for a swim.

The absence of such a necessary convenience as a public bathing place is a crying shame and a reproach to the city.

—*The Windsor Evening Record, May 15, 1900*

Happiness and Success

Ask any father what his chief ambitions are, and he will inevitably close his list by remarking, "and, of course, I want to make sure that my kids have a happy childhood."

This is the most natural emotion imaginable. A child, because of its dependence and helplessness, can be lonelier and unhappier than most people dream. Every parent wants to make the period of childhood as joyous and carefree as possible.

But a disturbing thought is raised by a recent interview in

which Joseph Hergesheimer, one of the most gifted novelists in the United States, suggested that a happy childhood may not lead to a successful manhood. Remarking that he himself had taken to literature because he had been unhappy and discontented, Mr. Hergesheimer said:

"Nobody amounts to anything if they have had a happy childhood and youth. Happy people are so adjusted to life, they just live. We have to seek something to convince ourselves that we amount to something. We have to surmount obstacles – otherwise we do not believe in ourselves."

Mr. Hergesheimer has put his finger on one of the oldest conflicts in the world – the conflict between man's desire to find happiness and his desire to amount to something. The two do not often go together. Accomplishment ordinarily springs from discontent, whether we like to admit as much or not. It is not without significance that most of our great leaders in politics, industry and commerce began life as poor boys. There are many great men who would not have reached their high positions if sharp, bitter circumstances had not compelled them to go without playtime, as boys, and dig in to amount to something.

To be sure, there are exceptions from the rule – but they are not very common. For the old proverb, after all, is right: genius is 1 percent inspiration and 99 percent perspiration. And the man who is willing to work his head off to get what he wants is usually the man who was compelled to do that from his early youth.

Unfortunately for our dreams of universal happiness, it is discontent that makes the world move forward. This has been true since the cave man, miserable and hungry because he was too slow-footed to catch game, invented a bow and arrow so that he could kill it from a distance; and it always will be true, down to the day when we shall have wiped out poverty, ended disease and learned how to travel to Mars.

Most of us, of course, will continue to try to give children happiness and let them take their chances on accomplishment. But while we are doing it, we might as well admit that some poor youngsters from an orphan asylum may outdistance them in the race for success.

—*The Victoria Daily Times, May 3, 1929*

111

The Magnetic Quintuplets

All the efforts of patriotic organizations to promote Canada's tourist trade must face a new challenge, issued unofficially by the quintuplets. This summer the North country is swarming with auto travellers whose main purpose is to see the famous Callender babies. During the winter and spring, as Dr. Dafoe puts it, persons wanting information about the quintuplets wrote to him; now they are arriving in person. So the worthy doctor must decide whether answering letters or groups of interrogators is the easier job.

All roads in the North country now lead to Callender. Auto markers from nearly every State over the border may be seen on cars rolling to and from the little Northern village. Daily the attraction increases. Well on in their second year, the Dionne babies are putting on a better show. They kick up their heels, clap their tiny hands and gurgle all kinds of greetings.

Soon visitors may see five little noses flattened against the window panes, and each baby face an animated interrogation mark. What are all these people doing around here? Did they never before see quintuplets? That is exactly the point: they never did.

And there will be finger-marks, too, on the window panes. If science has found a way to keep 10 handfuls of fingers clean – then, indeed, science has made progress.

So, in view of all this, the tourist business about Callender is establishing new records. And next summer it will be still better. Then the quintuplets will be playing about the front steps of whatever home they occupy; and they will be talking a strange jargon of French and English – the youngest bilinguists.

And the beauty of it is that this special tourist trade hasn't cost the country much. The quintuplets have done their own advertising, in their own way. They arrived; they lived; and there they are, the finest drawing card in the North country. Everyone is eager to see a new baby; but to see five new baby sisters is an event in the life of even the most blasé tourist from a land that has many attractions but no quintuplets.

—*The Toronto Globe,*
July 30, 1935

Unfair to Themselves

Do young people sufficiently appreciate the benefits they receive from free education? In the first place, do they realize that though, for them, such education is free, some people have to pay for it?

Parents and citizens in general, in their school taxes, make possible this provision of elementary and higher education for every child in the state. The cost is heavy, but taxpayers cheerfully bear it, in the knowledge that nothing is of more importance to a country than that its young citizens should be well-informed, intelligent and alert, capable of holding their own in the competition of life, within their native land and outside of it. But the financial strain is great, and there is even a suggestion that the school-leaving age be reduced in this province so that those boys and girls who are not profiting from the instruction should be permitted to work and earn and so relieve school expenses. This solution, however, would create new problems.

If students only realized what they are losing when they refuse to take their school days seriously, they would quickly change their attitude. There are some who honestly try to do well but who, in spite of their best efforts, never get very far. They are not to blame. But there are plenty of others who do not even try.

They are wasting their time and public money, and perhaps, if they persist in the obstinacy and are content to be mere "seat-warmers" instead of scholars, the suggestion that they should be asked to take their departure is not such a bad one, after all. They are putting a serious handicap on themselves, but it is no one's fault but their own. If they prefer to remain ignorant and idle and undeveloped, they cannot expect to reap the reward of industry and discipline.

It is estimated that only about 27 percent of those who enter high schools complete the prescribed five-year course, and only 7 percent of the total number of high school entrants proceed to a university. Many, of course, go to technical and commercial schools, to follow their natural bent, and they are right in so doing.

In fact, the government of this province is encouraging scholars to pursue the particular course of training for which they are best adapted. It is the indifferent – those who fail to benefit as they should from any kind of instruction, whether given in collegiates, technical institutes or commercial schools – who are the real problem.

It is not that they are lacking in ability, but that they are blind to their own interests; and it is becoming increasingly apparent that they cannot be permitted to stand indefinitely in their own light in this way, an impediment to themselves and others. Let them take heed and mend their ways while there is time.

—*The Hamilton Spectator, November 5, 1938*

Young Canadians and the U.S.?

What do young Canadians in high school think about the United States? The question is both interesting and important. For these are the Canadians who are about to enter adult life and to play their part in determining the attitude of Canada towards her nearest and biggest neighbour.

A scientific effort to find the answer was undertaken by Dr. J.E.M. Young, Professor of Education in Brandon College, Brandon, Manitoba. The results of his survey are given in the September issue of *Canadian Education*, the official publication of the Canadian Education Association.

Dr. Young's survey is limited to English-speaking Canadian high school seniors, but he has gathered evidence from all 10 provinces of Canada. He found that there is no pronounced "forness" or "againstness" in the attitude of the students towards Americans. The prevailing attitude is one of neutrality.

There were slight variations in the degree of favourableness. Newfoundland and New Brunswick are the most favourable. British Columbia and Ontario the least so. English-speaking Quebec is just about the middle.

One striking feature of the

survey is the fact that the teachers and the schools had comparatively slight influence in forming the students' attitudes. By far the biggest influences were printed material and contacts with American visitors and tourists. Radio programs and the movies came next. School influences were almost at the bottom of the list.

It may be said that the absence of any positive school influence proves that the schools themselves have been neutral in the matter. But perhaps it proves that the schools have been ineffective. Dr. Young raises the very pertinent question whether the teaching of tolerance, mutual understanding and goodwill is not part of the school's job. Perhaps, he suggests, it ought to be part of the curriculum in teacher-training institutions.

In any case, the survey shows that young Canadians are coming to the question of Canadian-American relations with an open mind. Whatever attitudes they will form, will be formed as adults. If young Canadians are not being educated for goodwill, at least they will face the issue without prejudice. And that much, at least, is satisfactory.

—*The Montreal Gazette,*
October 8, 1952

There Should be More Halloweens

Despite the introduction of comic books, radio and television into their lives, children will celebrate Halloween, this Friday night, in traditional fashion. If the weather permits, Montreal streets will be patrolled by hordes of pint-sized ghosts and witches and cowboys and Indians. Girls will be dressed in Brother's clothes, with fierce burnt-cork mustachios and good measure. And young boys will clump along in Mother's shoes, occasionally tripping over a drooping edge of the voluminous house dresses they borrow for the evening.

The distinctly Montreal touch will be provided by the cuffs and collars of heavy sweaters which will peek out of the most fancy costumes. The last day of October in Montreal is no time for deciding to "be" a hula dancer or a South African tribesman. Dressing up as an Eskimo is much more sensible.

Why does the attraction of Halloween remain so much the same, decade after decade, when so many other factors in children's lives are changing? The idea of "dressing up," or play-acting, is always dear to children, of course. But there is more to it than that.

On Halloween, children make their own fun. Most of them "design" – or scrounge – their own costumes. It's participation game. In an age and a part of the world where so much entertainment, for both children and adults, is mechanical or spectator, such opportunities are becoming increasingly rare.

So many apartment-bred children have no opportunity to learn how to play. Without a room of their own, confined to a small corner of the adults' quarters, they never know the fun of turning a whole room into a country store or a pirate ship – or the control cabin of a space rocket. They grow more and more dependent on radio and television and comic books, which do their imagining for them and thereby rob them of one of the most treasured experiences of life.

No wonder they become nervous and irritable and "difficult."

Perhaps there should be more Halloweens in the year.

—The Montreal Gazette,
October 28, 1952

Don't be an "Academic Dumpling"

Dr. Claude Bissell, president of the University of Toronto, in his first convocation address to the students warned them against the fallacy of finding success and happiness in becoming the "well-rounded man and woman," a sort of academic "dumpling." The undergraduate, he said, ought to bring to the university intellectual passion and the ambition to translate this passion into knowledge and accomplishment. "After you graduate there will be time enough to adjust to your environment... And to secure that happy state of well-roundedness and togetherness favoured by self-styled specialists in social engineering."

The president of Varsity hoped undergraduates would not spend their energy trying to meet the specifications of the academic organization man. They ought not to be afraid of being thought lopsided or angular; they should emphasize intensity and concentration. They must retain their belief in the freedom of the human spirit and respect for the individual – and be themselves individuals.

The university graduate reflects the community in which he lives. Its pattern becomes his pattern. Where you find undergraduates passive and tractable you will find the community itself stagnant. Dr. Bissell said that in general the men and women who have given leadership after graduation have not been campus politicians, "all-round students," but men and women with the intellectual passion.

This is not the whole story however; many a "campus politician" and a "joiner" have done remarkably well and given leadership after entering the competitive world of business and politics. With them, as with the scholar, success depends upon hard work and passionate dedication to the service of ambition. The Achilles' heel of our higher education is that so much emphasis is placed on salary-earning capacity and relatively little on the sciences, medicine, and the teaching profession. The Russians reward scientists and teachers with three things: prestige, larger salaries and more personal freedom. Similar rewards with us fall to the lot of the leaders in business and trade.

As long as the undergraduate feels that he places himself in an invidious position by giving himself to teaching and the sciences, we shall possess fewer top quality men in these professions, and one day may pay for it by falling behind in the race for knowledge and power.

—*The London Free Press, September 27, 1958*

Barring the Beatles

In the bizarre world of the teenager, international incidents are not created by revolts in the Dominican Republic or Communist subversion in Vietnam.

To the adolescent brigade, such problems are trivial compared to such earth-shattering revelations as the fact that the Beatles soon may be barred from entering the United States.

In the teenager's world, international incidents are not created by power-hungry totalitarian and military dictators, but by the squares who comprise the British Musicians Union and the American Federation of Musicians.

In the never-never existence which many teenagers pursue before they are forced to assume responsible adulthood, the diplomatic problems which grey the temples of their parents must play second guitar to the question of whether the scrapping of the treaty between the two unions, governing exchange of popular music entertainers, will staunch the trans-Atlantic flow of teenage "culture."

If the men in the U.S. state department and the Pentagon aren't sleeping nights these days because of Vietnam and the Dominican Republic, they might find some consolation in the fact that their offspring are also tossing and turning in their beds in fretful fear that the world is coming to an end because they may be denied the presence of a quartet of mop-headed, yowling Liverpudlians.

—*The Calgary Herald,*
May 28, 1965

Teach, Don't Preach

Edmonton public schools must be used to teach the curriculum, not to preach the gospel.

Some students in Grades 1 and 5 have found their way into fisticuffs after returning Bibles distributed in school. One hopes these were isolated outbursts of intolerance and that most chil-

118

dren have learned religious tolerance at their parents' knee. Yet that tolerance should not be tested by religious propagation in public schools.

It has been proposed that parents be advised of such activities and allowed to withdraw their children from attending them. That would not suffice. Children should be left in class (where the law requires them to be), and all religious propagation should be withdrawn – whether by the Gideon Society or by the followers of Buddha, Mohammed, Krishna or Sun Myung Moon.

Teaching religion – not preaching it – is another issue. Teachers may well instruct their students about the religions of the world in an historical or philosophical context, to expand awareness and to stimulate critical and creative thought. But not to promote religious faith.

Our schools already are strained by their efforts to achieve intellectual objectives and to impart practical skills. They have no time for religious propaganda. Nor should they confuse the student as to the place of the public school – it is a place to exercise and expand one's intellect – not one's faith.

Our society still respects the right to religious propagation – on the street corner, at your doorstep, over the air waves and inside places of worship. Our public schools, however, exist for another purpose – education. This must not be compromised.

—*The Edmonton Journal,*
May 31, 1980

Dealing with Young Offenders

Justice Minister Allan Rock is going to be belted from the right for failing to be "tough" enough on crime, but Ottawa's plan to revamp the Young Offenders Act, which governs the treatment of 12-to-17-year-old criminals, follows a moderate, sensible course.

Mr. Rock has offered a triad of amendments: tougher penalties, more information about offenders being shared between police and community officials and, most promising, a proposal to promote the use of so-called alternative measures.

Although some critics have been calling for violent youths, even very young lawbreakers, to be treated as adults, the government's reforms tread delicately, and rightly so. The current maximum sentence for those tried in youth court is five years. Mr. Rock would increase that to 10 for first-degree and 7 for second-degree murder. Teen-aged murderers sent to adult court already face life in prison, and Ottawa would slightly lengthen the time they would have to wait before becoming eligible for parole. Youths are rarely transferred to adult court now, but under the government's proposals, 16- and 17-year-olds charged with serious violent crimes would be sent to the adult system as a matter of course, unless a judge felt that their best hope of rehabilitation lay in youth court. This proposal may not change much – which may be the best outcome – since judges retain a great deal of discretion in deciding where youths will be tried, and where they will serve their sentences. Dramatically increasing the rate of incarceration is no quick-fix solution, and Ottawa appears to appreciate that.

As an example of this, Mr. Rock's proposals try to encourage the use of punishments other than custody – such as victim restitu-tion or community service – when dealing with non-violent youth criminals. This is promising talk. Yes, people should pay for their crimes – but we as a society should have enough rational self-interest to aim to make the method by which they atone for their misdeeds one that discourages them from re-offending. Too often, prison does not accomplish this. The threat of prison may be something of a deterrent – although criminologists have long argued over how much of a deterrent it is – but the experience of prison all too often only broadens and deepens the pathologies that led to the commission of a crime in the first place. It is not for nothing that prisons are often seen as training schools for criminals. How different are youth holding facilities?

All this talk about alternative measures may, unfortunately, be nothing more than talk. Ottawa has ponied up no new money, and besides, much of the administration of justice is left in the hands of the provinces. Some provinces already have programs for alternative measures, but they are not used nearly enough. As an illustration of this, Statistics Canada reported this year that 35 percent of sentenced adult offenders were admitted to prison solely for failing to pay a fine. The same shortcomings are to be found in the youth correctional system. According to the government, an alarmingly high one-third of all young offenders are sentenced to custody. Worse still, half of those sentenced to custody have committed non-violent property offences. Isn't there a better way for them to unlearn criminal behaviour and repay their debt to society – perhaps even repay the person whose property they damaged – than putting them behind bars?

—*The Globe and Mail,*
June 3, 1994

Searching for Education

University students are supposed to be poor – it's part of their lifestyle.

So when the Council of the Students Union at Memorial University puts out an appeal for contributions to its food bank, people might be excused for not responding.

But they would be wrong.

New statistics released by Statistics Canada indicate that more young people between the ages of 16 and 24 are living at poverty levels than any other age group. And since the bulk of most students are that age, it follows that many students are also living from hand to mouth. A well-stocked food bank on campus would be a great help.

The new study by Statistics Canada examined the experiences of 35,000 individuals during a three-year period to see how people got into and then out of poverty. This study is now giving us new insight into the financial circumstances of all Canadians.

Between 1994 and 1995, 11 percent of young people between the ages of 16 and 25 were living below the low income cut-off (a measurement of when people are living in distressed circumstances, which is sometimes referred to as the poverty line). More important, the study also showed that another eight percent of this age group who had been doing OK in 1993 fell below the low income cut-off line in 1994. Only five percent were able to rise above this line in 1994.

The result was more young

adults were living at low income levels than any other age group in society.

Fortunately, young people who have it rough when in school, usually climb out of poverty when they enter the workforce. They manage to climb out of near poverty faster than any other age group in society. In contrast, children living below the low income cut-off line have had a tendency to stay there for longer periods of time.

Nevertheless, the study does indicate that most young people do have to make significant sacrifices if they want to live better in the future, and a great part of that sacrifice is to live in relative poverty for a few years.

A food bank that helps students and their families survive for a few years is a good idea. This is especially true since existing food banks are already swamped with requests for food aid (though, unfortunately, not with food donations at this time of the year).

Sacrificing for your education is one thing, but going hungry because of it is an entirely different matter.

—*The St. John's Evening Telegram, July 16, 1997*

Good Behaviour in the Stands

The Sherwood-Parkdale Rural Minor Hockey Association has made a good decision in requiring parents to take a good behaviour pledge in signing up their kids for play in the 2002-2003 season. The move acknowledges the fact that the association is experiencing difficulty with confrontational parents and it delivers the message that it won't be tolerated.

Starting this fall, parents registering their kids will have to sign a pledge – the wording of which is still being drafted – promising not to harass anyone at the rink. The decision came after a recent meeting of volunteer coaches who have been expressing a growing concern about dealing with aggressive behaviour. In bringing in the requirement to sign a good behaviour pledge, association president Mike Deighan said the group risked losing volunteer coaches en mass if the concerns were not addressed.

The matter is a subject of debate not only here but throughout North America. Thomas Junta, the Massachusetts father of a young hockey player, was convicted of beating a coach to death at a hockey practice. He became a household name during his trial recently precisely because of the disturbing nature of the case.

It's fair to say that it was a wake-up call to all minor hockey fans and their organizations, all of which have their share of minor, or even major, confrontations from time to time. What that extreme case illustrated was the need for all parties to regain their perspective on what kids hockey is all about.

Remember when minor hockey groups flogged the slogan "Don't send your kids to the rink, take them"? The clear message was that it wasn't necessarily the game that was important for the kids, but the total experience, namely that of having fun, experiencing camaraderie with your team-mates, whether it be through winning or losing, and learning sportsmanship.

Having mom and dad in the stands was seen as reinforcing the child's self-esteem. No one said it better than hockey great Wayne Gretzky following Canada's recent Olympic gold medal win in men's hockey: there's nothing more satisfying than looking up into the stands and seeing your dad, he reflected during an interview.

No one person is to blame for the increasing violence in hockey – on or off the ice. But each person involved in the game – players, coaches, parents – can do his or her part to minimize the problem. The Sherwood-Parkdale Rural Minor Hockey Association should be congratulated for bringing in a parents' good-behaviour pledge to remind us all of this.

—*The Charlottetown Guardian, March 5, 2002*

123

10
War

The Bayonet

The information that the Boer government has ordered bayonets for its army does not prevent the Ottawa Journal again advancing the now old and somewhat discredited theory that modern rifles and ammunition have rendered the bayonet useless. The Journal says:

"When one stops to think that the modern soldier of any army carries a magazine rifle with from 5 to 10 cartridges in the magazine, the futility of the bayonet needs little arguing. Supposing that 10 British soldiers with fixed bayonets get within 50 yards of a single Boer armed with a Mauser, and had to charge at him over even but that brief space of ground, the Boer could bring down the whole 10 before they could reach him. The Mauser rifle carries 10 cartridges in its magazine, and the man with the weapon has but to pump the bullets out almost as fast as he can consecutively press the trigger."

The theory looks all right. Indeed in some recent wars bayonets have been little used. Even so long ago as the American Civil War, but little work was done with the bayonet. And in Cuba there was none at all. But the British soldier has found the bayonet to be useful in every war. But for the bayonet the little British square at Abu Klea would have been crushed by the overwhelming weight of the enemy.

The bayonet was exceedingly useful at Tel El Kebir, and at Omdurman it was not entirely useless. In the Boer war the British bayonet has been very useful, not only for the actual work it did, but for the moral effect it produced upon the enemy. And but for the bayonet Ladysmith would undoubtedly have fallen prey to the great bodies of Boers who attempted to rush the place.

We don't think the British war department will throw away the bayonet for some time yet. It is not difficult to carry and it is always loaded.

—*The Hamilton Spectator, February 8, 1900*

Canada and Conscription

A few days ago, Dr. W.A. Riddell stated at Geneva that Canadians, in the main, were opposed to the idea of conscription. Public opinion in this country will be generally behind Dr. Riddell in this contention, with the qualification that in times of national emergency, when our country is threatened in such a way as to need all available manpower, conscription might become necessary.

In the late war there was a very sharp divergence of opinion on the question of conscription. Hundreds – one might almost say thousands of gallant Canadians of both races did their duty in the firing line, but remained honest opponents of conscription. Thousands of others unable to go to the trenches opposed the plan in the Dominion, and yet their loyalty to the allied cause was never questioned. Altogether it is most doubtful if in any other war of the world's history such a measure could have been adopted in this country. That it was a vital necessity for ultimate victory, however, was the opinion of the majority.

Coercion in any shape or form is anathema to the average Canadian. Moreover, another strong characteristic of our people is their independence. Intensely loyal to the British connection, they are at the same time acutely sensitive to any suggestion of interference or patronage from any other part of the Empire. There is not a doubt that if the Old Country were again threatened by a great European combination, Canadians in large numbers would go to her aid, but they would go entirely on their own initiative.

If the League of Nations can make some real headway in limiting the principle of conscription, both in peace and war, they will be going a long way towards their ultimate objective of international disarmament.

—*The Victoria Daily Times, May 6, 1929*

A Chance for Hitler?

There are signs that Adolf Hitler, the National Socialist, or Fascist, leader in Germany, will be given a chance at the Chancellorship of the republic. In the new crisis brought about by the forcing out of the von Papen government, Hitler has been renewing his plea of last August that he be entrusted with the reins of administration, this by virtue of his heading the strongest party in the state.

But he has been approaching President von Hindenburg more humbly on the subject than he did before, this probably by reason of the sharp falling-off in electoral support he experienced in the latest elections for the Reichstag.

Hitler's first representations to the President were in the nature of a demand; this time they have been in the nature of a request. And, surveying the whole situation, von Hindenburg has entrusted Hitler with the task of forming a Cabinet if he finds out, after consultation with other part leaders, that he can carry on reasonably harmoniously in the Reichstag.

So the possibility is that before the present week is out, Germany will have a Fascist regime as Italy has, though not with the same virtually unchallenged sway, for, for instance, where Communism is relatively weak in Italy, it has become a highly formidable factor in Germany, and no doubt it would seek to give a Fascist government trouble. Whether or not a Fascist government is to come into being will depend, of course, upon the reaction of other party leaders to the idea of Hitler as

Chancellor. Will he be able to get assurance of their co-operation?

Hitler emphasizes two virtues, as he sees them, about a Fascist regime. He virtually undertakes to put the "Reds" in their place by telling von Hindenburg that the Fascists are "Germany's last bulwark against Communism," and he says that he would consider it his cardinal task, as Chancellor, "to get the jobless off the streets and into productive work."

A government headed by Hitler might make for stability in Germany and it could hardly be regarded as a negation of democracy, as has been charged against the Mussolini regime in Italy, inasmuch as it has been pretty well rooted in popular support, so much so, as has been indicated, as to represent the strongest party in the state.

And if it were able to carry out its pledge to put the jobless to work, it might take care of a lot of Communist agitation and disturbance by that very course. A lot of red might be taken out of thousands upon thousands of "Reds" by providing them with steady work.

The present week may see still further history written in Germany. The situation is packed with interest.

—*The Regina Leader,*
November 25, 1932

War in Art

To obtain an art record of Canada's part in the present war, as recommended in the annual report of the National Gallery, would not cost the taxpayers much money. In the last war Canada acquired a collection of paintings, forming "the most important art record of that conflict in existence," at a relatively low cost. It is proposed that steps be taken now to acquire a similar record of this conflict.

When people think of paintings by eminent artists, they think of fancy prices. But under the plan suggested by the National Gallery the cost would be small if the same proceeding as in 1914-1918 were followed. Under the guidance of Lord Beaverbrook, Canada enlisted the services of some of the most famous British and Canadian artists of the day. Had they been paid market prices for their work, the War Memorials pictures would indeed have cost a fortune.

But what Canada did was to make the artists honorary Captains, pay them accordingly and acquire their work. In those days the artists were only too eager to do their bit on such terms. In these days there are artists in Canada and Britain just as eager to serve under like conditions. Such famous men as Augustus John, Sir William Orpen, D.Y. Cameron, Paul Nash, A.J. Munnings, Edgar Bundy, Wyndham Lewis and C.R.W. Nevinson were enlisted in the last war and produced a priceless collection at army pay rates.

Canada led the way in this enterprise and was followed by Britain and later the United States.

There would be no need to engage quite so many artists this time (especially since one of the between-wars problems has been the housing of the War Memorials paintings), but that at least half a dozen recognized artists should be put to work at once in Canada and in Britain is obvious. The acquisition of a record of this war in paint could be regarded as a national obligation to Canadian posterity. It would permanently depict a decisive period in the course of Canadian nationhood.

—*The Ottawa Evening Citizen, February 24, 1941*

Crusade Berlin

Vancouver was just making ready for bed Monday night when D-Day, June 6, dawned over the English Channel. The invasion was on. The Second Front had arrived. General Eisenhower issued his official announcement.

Later in the day, Mr. Churchill stood in his place in the Commons, declared everything was proceeding "according to plan – and what a plan!" he added. The greatest plan, the most carefully thought-out plan of all military

assaults in the world's history.

From the French Coast, which for weary years has been altogether in German hands, General Sir Bernard Montgomery was also heard from. What he said was cheery and reassuring.

Thus we have arrived at the climax of the war. Thus we learned that the Canadians are in the van of attack. Our own men who have been ceaselessly preparing during the impatient years of hard going for the great test that will settle the trend of civilization. Here is Andy McNaughton's dagger pointed at the heart of Berlin come true, just as he had painted the picture of the coming battle. Eleven thousand planes, 4,000 ships moving across in the night to land on the beaches at daybreak – the beginning of a new day for the oppressed peoples of Europe.

Scores of thousands of sorties had already softened up that invasion coast during the last months and weeks. Now new thousands of winged invaders accompanied the ships and the infantry to fend off the Germans, to help with the landings which by noon had become pretty well established. Paratroopers descended from skies, skilled men these and very brave, dropping suddenly on a soil they had never seen, knowing nothing except from hearsay of the conditions they would find when they landed. Or how quickly they would meet death.

But all fired by the joy and assurance of coming victory. Reinforced by the knowledge that every possible contingency had been foreseen by their leaders, every possible interference provided against – and in these circumstances each man willing and eager to take his chance with the luck that should be his in the crusade that Eisenhower foretold. "You are about to embark on a great crusade," was the word that the Allied commander had spread around at ports and beaches and even to the men already aboard the ships. And he continued: "The eyes of the world are upon you and the hopes and the prayers of all liberty-loving peoples go with you. We will accept nothing less than full victory."

The last words are spoken. It is finally up to the foot soldier. The air umbrellas and the tanks and the rocket guns and all the other inventions of expert warmakers were there to help, but in the last analysis the enemies of Germany depended on a man with his rifle who would leap ashore and scramble up a bank. Many a bank and beach was to be bathed in his blood before the day was out. But then a good percentage of him and his fellows would get through and as they surmounted the breastworks overlooking the Channel they would be able to see ahead the road and the route to Berlin. Some who scrambled ashore this morning will live to go right down that terrible road, making it a road of glory and achievement in the cause of right and decency in the world.

It was the Germans who "broke" the news of the invasion. It was on our radios last night at 10 o'clock Vancouver time. A mere rumour at first. Then the news commentators, shy of another Joan Ellis "incredible error," warned the public not to believe anything until it was confirmed from Allied sources. Hours later, it was confirmed. It was confirmed with embellishments which left no doubt that the assault which is to dwarf all others in history was actually on. One of the early bulletins related to the landings of parachute troops on Jersey and Guernsey, where it is safe to say they would get an enthusiastic welcome.

It is evening now in Britain and in those war-strewn shreds of German-occupied France which have been dearly won today into Allied hands. The sun is going down on the first day of what must be final victory for our arms. The initial stage

of the invasion has been accomplished. After all, the Allies have had a good deal of practice at this job.

They swooped down on Sicily, they conquered at Salerno, they stuck it out at the Anzio Beachhead. Now they have established themselves in a position incomparably more difficult. But they are close to home and to reinforcements. There will be a constant stream of new men with rifles and more tanks and guns and more of everything required that can be brought in within an hour or two. They will be backed up as no other expedition has ever been backed up before. They will get supreme protection from the air. Anyway, they will stick. Nobody will turn back now.

The Germans have freely admitted the ability of the Allies to make a landing. But they boast the Allies cannot hold it when the period of counterattack in force comes two or three weeks from now. That will be the great testing time.

Before the week is out Germany expects to be attacked from four directions at once. On the East, Russia has three divisions for every two that the Germans can possibly muster. From Italy the air war will be intensified. In Corsica, another army has been waiting probably to attack in the South of France. New landings from Britain may be attempted in Holland. From many quarters the enemy will be pounded. He cannot be over-strong everywhere. The weak spots will be ferreted out.

But our eyes and hopes must be fixed on that period of greatest danger towards the end of June when the character of the battle will have been tried out and the Germans, with methodical thoroughness, will mass their formations for the supreme counter-attack.

They were not able to drive the Anzio Beachhead people into the sea and this time they will again fail. No matter what their weight of weapons or the enemy's ferocity, the Allies will not give up what they are winning this week. Supposing all other factors break evenly, British and U.S. and Canadian superiority in airpower will turn the scales.

With good luck the crusade for Berlin may be settled and the war within sight of ending in 60 to 90 days. At the worst, it may take us all summer to establish ourselves completely in France, with the march to Berlin put off until next spring. So we look ahead hopefully and wish our fighting men God Speed.

—*The Vancouver Sun,*
June 6, 1944

Victories of Peace

Award of the Nobel Peace Prize to Lester Bowles Pearson of Canada comes as high recognition to one of this country's outstanding citizens and leaders. It is proof positive of the tremendous esteem in which Mr. Pearson is held in the top councils of world affairs. It reflects lustre and prestige upon Canada.

The Nobel award is accompanied by no citation of a recipient's achievements. In the case of Lester Pearson, the world needs no reminder that he is an international citizen of first rank who has devoted outstanding talent and vast capacity to the cause of peace in several crises in which the scales teetered between peace and war. He was president of the United Nations General Assembly in 1952, when the Assembly's major achievement was to work out the Korean armistice. He fathered the idea of the United Nations Emergency Force, which brought peace efforts into focus last year in the Suez crisis.

Mr. Pearson's service to Canada gives substance to the concept that this country has a role to play in world affairs as a linchpin of peace and brotherhood. He is one of the most attractive figures to emerge in our public life, and he has earned an immense popularity.

Some of the great prizes of Canadian life have been his, while his career is still in full course. He was one of the dedicated band of young men who built Canada's foreign service. He rose to the post of permanent head of that service before stepping into parliamentary life and eight brilliant years as the finest foreign minister Canada had yet produced.

His secret of success, known to his associates and sensed by Canadians of all walks of life, has been a tenacious capacity for the arduous, elusive, oft-frustrating work of conciliation and compromise. He symbolizes qualities that Canadians prize most, and would most hope to have identified with our national character.

His army and flying days in World War I left him with the *nom de guerre* of "Mike," and Mike Pearson he will always be when Canadians speak of the first golden era of our rise to international stature. Pride in the award of the Nobel Prize to Mike Pearson will be felt in all corners of Canada, pride mingled with humble thankfulness that our national growth is founded upon the victories of peace which, as John Milton said, are no less renowned than war.

—*The Toronto Telegram,*
October 15, 1957

What They Died for in Normandy

The glory of war is always more obvious to the directors than the players. Visiting Normandy a few days after the D-day landings, British Prime Minister Winston Churchill wrote to U.S. President Franklin Roosevelt, "I had a jolly day on Monday on the beaches and inland... The marvellous efficiency of the transportation exceeds anything that has ever been known in war... We are working up to a battle that may well be a million a side... How I wish you were here!"

For the men on the ground, it was not such a lark. When the first Canadian assault wave hit Juno Beach at a few minutes after eight on June 6, 1944, many of the Canadians were weak with seasickness after their gruelling trip across the choppy English Channel. It was cold and damp, and the wind drove heavy breakers on to the beach. "The tumbling sea and the treacherous offshore reefs delayed the run-in," writes historian Donald Creighton in *Dominion of the North*; "the armour, which could not be put down as early as the plan required, failed in places to lead the troops in; and the infantry, racing across sand and shingle, found German gun emplacements, which ought to have been silenced, blazing instead with fire."

Some of the invaders drowned in the surf, pulled down by their heavy equipment (one battalion, the Canadian Scottish, was forced to lug heavy bicycles that some inspired war planner had thought would come in handy). Others were killed by mines covered by the tide. Still others were cut down by withering fire from German pillboxes and bunkers, made of four-foot-thick concrete, that had survived the Allied bombardment beforehand. "Even so," writes Professor Creighton, this first Canadian assault wave – the Royal Winnipeg Rifles, Regina Rifles, Queen's Own Rifles, and North Shore (New Brunswick) Regiment – carried everything before them in the superb dash of their attack." When the day was done, the 3rd Canadian Division had gone farther than any other in the first wave of the assault.

How, and why, did they do it? Partly, perhaps, because they had no alternative; not to advance was to die. But partly, as well, because they knew what they were fighting for – and what they were fighting against. D-day, as every soldier on that deadly beach knew, was the opening scene in the final act of the Second World War, the death knell for the cruellest tyranny that Europe had ever seen. It was also, in a sense, the beginning of the modern Canadian nation.

In the First World War, Canada fought as the little brother of Britain, a member of the great imperial family still run, effectively, from London. It entered the Second still a young country, held in scant regard by the rest of the world. But as Prime Minister Jean Chrétien said in his eloquent commemorative address yesterday in Courseulles, France, "we emerged from the war as an adult nation – a major industrial nation and a force for peace in the world."

There are some who say that the nation thus forged no longer stands for anything, that Canada today is nothing more than a formless collection of petty jealousies, self-pitying victims and regional complaints. It isn't so. As the Prime Minister put it, the men who fought in Normandy came from diverse backgrounds, spoke different tongues, practiced different religions, came from all sorts of different places. But they had one thing in common. "They were all part of a young nation. A new kind of nation. Where the ancient hatreds of the past were no match for the promise of the future. Where people believed they could speak different languages, worship in different ways and live in peace."

That is what Canada stands for. That is what Canadians died for.
—*The Globe and Mail,*
June 7, 1994

Canada's Iraq Policy: Inconsistency Ho!

Nobody splits hairs the way Jean Chrétien does. The late F.R. Scott said of former Prime Minister Mackenzie King that he'd do "nothing by halves that cannot be done by quarters." Prime Minister Chrétien calibrated his moves by 8ths and 16ths, then waited until the last moment to say Canada wouldn't go to war against Iraq.

It was the wrong choice. Ottawa wholeheartedly endorsed United Nations Security Council Resolu-tion 1441 last fall, which gave Saddam Hussein a last chance to eliminate all weapons of mass destruction. The Liberal government has pulled back just as the military consequences of Mr. Hussein's failure to abide by the resolution seem about to commence.

The United States didn't think Canada could provide much support on the battlefield, given the state of this country's armed forces. But the Bush administration must still marvel at Mr. Chrétien's announcement.

The Prime Minister didn't unduly condemn an invasion of Iraq, so as not to offend unnecessarily our American and British allies. Nor did he condone it, certainly; our French and German allies can feel reassured. It's just that Canada won't get involved.

Remarkable. The Canadian straddle that has served the Prime Minister well for months continues to a degree even after he has made up his mind. Mr. Chrétien may be less exposed politically than any other major Western leader, but Canada's Iraq policy barely casts a shadow. Neither does the Prime Minister.

Mr. Chrétien was particularly canny to commit 3,000 troops recently to a one-year deployment in Afghanistan. This was welcomed by Washington. It also made it virtually impossible to make a substantial Canadian commitment to an invasion of Iraq.

But what of the resources that Canada already has in the Strait of Hormuz and the Persian Gulf, which lead to Kuwait? Three Canadian ships are there and HMCS *Iroquois* is on its way, soon to be the flagship for the Canadian commanding a multinational fleet.

Washington's view is that the war against terror and the impending war against Iraq are synonymous. Canada insists otherwise: that the Canadian ships are fighting terrorism just as the contingent in Afghanistan will. A similar rationale applies to the 31 members of the Canadian military on exchange programs with the U.S. and British forces. Canada has decided not to pull them out, saying they won't participate in combat.

It's hard not to conclude, though, that Canada is a furtive member of the "coalition of the willing." Canadian military resources now near Iraq may be greater than those of many overt U.S. partners, such as Spain.

Remarkable. Some countries provide rhetorical support without tangible help; Canada does the opposite.

Equally curious is Mr. Chrétien's position that Canada required a second UN resolution, specifically authorizing war, to participate in an invasion. As recently as January, Mr. Chrétien suggested that 1441, which was passed unanimously and threatened "serious consequences" if Mr. Hussein didn't abide by it, might be all that was needed. Foreign Minister Bill Graham agrees that Iraq is a threat to international security, including Canada's. He suggests the United States, by massing troops on Iraq's border, sparked what disarmament Mr. Hussein did carry out. Can-

ada's concern, Mr. Graham told the CBC Monday night, lies with "the choice to use force at this time."

But passage of a second UN resolution required the support of France, which wields a UN veto, and France would not agree to deadlines that smacked of "the logic of war." So Canada's real choice may not have been force now or later, but force now or never. And by requiring a second resolution Canada effectively gave France authority over whether Canadian troops could invade Iraq.

Remarkable. In rejecting U.S. unilateralism, Canada has acquiesced in French unilateralism.

Canada will not sit out, at least officially, the war that could begin as early as tonight. Having made this unfortunate decision through pretzel logic, Mr. Chrétien should be especially willing in the months ahead to commit Canada to the reconstruction effort. This country has great capabilities in building infrastructure, peacekeeping, law-enforcement training and development of federal institutions. Canada can't remain aloof indefinitely, and this postwar involvement would at least fit the Chrétien mould and be politically popular.

—*The Globe and Mail,*
March 19, 2003

Afghanistan 2006

Many Canadians question why Canadian soldiers are fighting and dying in Afghanistan. What's interesting is that those doubts don't seem to be shared by the men and women who are actually doing the fighting and dying.

By all accounts, morale among the troops in Kandahar is high. They support Canada's mission and believe they should persevere despite the dangers. They have seen Afghanistan's devastation up close and want to help its suffering people rebuild.

They understand that the rebuilding can't happen unless the extremists who are trying to wreck it are kept at bay. These are not unthinking cannon fodder or dupes of military propaganda. They are gung-ho soldiers, determined, professional, committed. They have thought hard about what they are doing and they think it is right.

Captain Nichola Goddard was typical. One of the handful of women performing combat roles overseas, she loved her job as a forward observation officer in the artillery and did it with gusto. When she was killed in a firefight this week, her husband dismissed the idea that "we should be backing out just because there's been Canadian casualties. We shouldn't tuck our tails behind our legs and run or anything like that... We've kind of got our foot in the door now to start making a difference. I think we need to follow through and carry on with the mission."

That seems to be how most of Canada's soldiers feel. Canada has a job to do in Afghanistan and they are getting on with it, accepting the risks as an inevitable part of the good, brave, useful work they are doing.

People back home have every right to criticize the mission. That's democracy. There are legitimate questions about how long to stay and how to measure progress. But before they dismiss Afghanistan as a fool's errand, they should listen to the people like Captain Goddard who stand in the front lines. They believe in Canada's mission. They are putting their lives on the line for it every day.

—*The Globe and Mail,*
May 19, 2006

War Memorial Outrage

What, if anything, were they thinking? As we marked Canada Day in part by honouring our veterans, three young men sparked outrage by desecrating the National War Memorial in Ottawa.

Their actions, captured on film, showed a brutal disrespect for veterans on a day when we celebrate the freedom and peace for which more than 116,000 Canadians gave their lives in war and peacekeeping, and which Canadian troops are upholding in Afghanistan today.

Close by Parliament Hill, the War Memorial is hallowed ground, the Tomb of the Unknown Soldier who died during World War I. Just hours before the trio urinated on the monument, it was the scene of as wreath-laying ceremony to mark the 90th anniversary of the Battle of the Somme, where thousands fell.

Prime Minister Stephen Harper's description of the desecration as a "terrible thing" captured the feelings of a nation. Mischief charges are in order. So are fines.

But a wise judge would order these louts to spend some time doing community service at their local Royal Canadian Legion. There they might look a few veterans in the eye and hear, first-hand, of the sacrifices good women and men have made for their country.

—*The Toronto Star,*
July 5, 2006

11
Havoc, Home and Away

The Great Fire

The destructive fire in Ottawa and Hull has put many thousands of unfortunate people on the street, homeless and penniless, entirely dependent for a time upon the bounty of others. And the worst of it is that these people are not only homeless and in want just now, but the factories and mills in which many of them worked being gone, they have lost their means of making a living, and it may be a long time before this means is restored.

It is to be hoped that the owners of the factories destroyed will come out of the fire able to replace their buildings and machinery; but even if that piece of good fortune is left, it will be a long time before the new mills can begin to run.

In view of this terrible calamity it is the duty of all Canadians to give to the unfortunate. The giving can best be done by the various governmental bodies, which represent the people and all the people. The subscription plan is slow, and money is needed at once; it bears heavily upon the generous while the whole people should pay.

We think the City council of Hamilton should meet and make a liberal donation to the sufferers: we are sure such action would be endorsed by the whole people.

The Ontario legislature has already agreed – both government side and opposition – to do something handsome in the way of a donation.

The Dominion parliament, being assembled upon the very ground of the disaster, will be able to appreciate the calamity to its full extent, and will undoubtedly pay generously into the treasury for the fire sufferers.

Let the whole business be done as soon as possible – fifteen thousand homeless and foodless human beings are waiting for help.

The news of the calamity at Ottawa and Hull created a sensation in London, and the *Times*, after dwelling upon the widespread and unmerited misery inflicted upon innocent sufferers, says:

"We cannot allow Canada to bear this burden unaided at a time when she has come to our aid, not merely with her purse, but with the best of her blood. It must be our privilege to do what in us lies for the relief of her suffering children. The war and the Indian famine are heavy claims on the generosity of the British public, but the claim of Canada is not less binding. It is a claim that we should meet freely at any time, but which we shall now meet with joy that we can show ourselves sensible of the service that Canada has done us."

These kind words are just what we might expect from the British press; but we think the Times magnifies the disaster and minimizes the ability of Canada to meet it. Canadians will, of course, be grateful to Britain for her good intentions, as expressed in the *Times*, and for her sympathy for the unfortunate Canadians who have suffered from the fire; but really there is no need for substantial assistance from over the sea. Canada can easily take care of the homeless people of Ottawa and Hull. It will be but a small job for the great and prosperous country Canada is.

—*The Hamilton Spectator, April 27, 1900*

Halifax Will Rise Again!

"HALIFAX WILL RISE AGAIN!… Desolate as the city may appear today, the ruins will soon give place to new and more substantial structures, its business will soon flow in regular channels, and its great misfortune will have become a memory. In the hour of the city's trial it will find solace in the thought that friends have arisen for it everywhere, and it will have reason for thankfulness, in all the future, that through tribulation it came into a clearer and higher knowledge of the good that is in the hearts of men than it had ever before attained."

The above extract from *The Christian Science Monitor*, published in another column of this paper, is indicative of faith in the initiative of the people of Halifax. The city most assuredly will rise again, transcending the Halifax which we knew.

The one only duty of the hour, however, as everyone must clearly recognize, is first, the burying of our dead, the care of the maimed and wounded, feeding the hungry and clothing the naked and providing homes for the homeless and those rendered destitute by the appalling catastrophe of Thursday.

It is no exaggeration to assert that since the outbreak of the great world war no city in the civilized world has enjoyed more general, material comfort and prosperity than Halifax.

Mere boys who were then clerks at the modest pay of six or seven dollars a week, found themselves readily accepted to all positions of men who proceeded overseas, thus drawing a proportionally increased rate of pay.

Girls who had been in service or engaged in factory work became the wives of soldiers drawing military pay and separation allowance, and from the financial standpoint found themselves better off and handling more money than ever in their lives before.

The various theatres and amusement halls, the numerous restaurants and cafes, were thronged and crowded to capacity. The city presented the appearance of prosperity, of affluence and of luxury. WE knew NOTHING of what war REALLY meant. We had no conception of all the grim, cruel tragedy it involved. Safe and proudly secure behind our Virgin ramparts ... THE ONE main object with a great many appeared to be self-advancement, self-gratification and a wholesale indulgence in the pursuit of pleasure. In a general way the grave seriousness of the war was realized, but among a large section of our people the remoteness of the conflict – separated from us by 3,000 miles of ocean – and the FANCIED security of Halifax produced an apathetic indifference to aught save personal welfare and pleasure.

The churches of the city were NOT able to report any depending or real awakening of the religious life of the community. The first wave of religious emotion which arose at the outbreak of the war speedily subsided, and in sober truth it cannot be said that there was that prayerful waiting upon GOD which should characterize a people engaged in a war for liberty and life.

The exceptions to this statement are the homes from which brave sons have gone forth to the war, many of whom have laid down their lives on the field of honour.

The great disaster which has befallen our city, carrying with it death, devastation, and ruin, was, in the decided opinion of many, a deliberate act of the Germans –

and people are entitled to their own opinions. It is an indisputable fact that Germans have resided here during the whole period of this awful war and lived a carefree life of luxury and indolence. Their sympathies are NATURALLY with the Kaiser and their own land beyond the Rhine. Some Germans have been arrested, and for the present are beyond the power to work out any evil designs they might have cherished.

It is A FACT nevertheless that the terrible convulsion of Thursday last, with all its awful attendants of slaughter, and tumult, and tragedy IS the work of the ruthless Hun, for verily the whole world travelleth in pain and peril today BECAUSE of the war, forced on humanity by the imperial war lord of Central Europe.

Halifax today knows the meaning of Gethsemane and the dark foreboding shadow of Golgotha; but the sufferings of our people would baffle all attempt at description if the Huns were here to carry out their policy of "frightfulness" and follow up the ruin of Halifax with the savage barbarity which found full scope at Louvain and other towns and cities in Flanders and in France.

This is no time to think or speak of politics or rival politics – these things must stand aside –

but let us remember that WHAT Halifax has endured and suffered and witnessed has all and more been grandly borne by our brave Canadian soldiers for our three dreadful years of war.

They have seen their dead piled high on shell torn fields, heard the low moaning of their mutilated wounded, and have witnessed their fast thinning line eloquently appealing for much needed reinforcements!

Halifax NOW knows the value of SWIFT relief. The resources of well nigh all a continent were without delay hurried to our assistance and with gratitude profound we received the proffered aid.

But HOW terrible OUR plight if NO reinforcement of our medical and nursing staff, our transportation facilities, or our relief committees had arrived!

NOW we know something of the REAL meaning of war.

—*The Halifax Herald,*
December 12, 1917

The Blast Heard Round the World

On July 16, 1945, the first atomic bomb was set off in the desert in New Mexico. Some effects of the blast are reported to have been felt as far away as Albuquerque, 120 miles distant.

On August 6, 1945, an atomic bomb was dropped on Hiroshima, in Japan. Today, its blast is heard round the world.

The lay imagination, inured to thoughts of V-1 and V-2 rockets, is staggered by the atomic bomb. Anyone reading the accounts of its destructiveness can write his own editorial on the destruction that awaits humanity unless this war ends war forever. It needs no H.G. Wells to picture the awful "shape of things to come" if war returns hereafter. Man, that is born to die in any case, now lives under sentence of sudden, violent death – unless war is really outlawed. The blindest intelligence can understand that much about the atomic bomb.

It is well known that the Nazis were working "feverishly" in the attempt to produce an atomic bomb. One of the first thoughts that flashed through the minds of Canadians as they read President Harry Truman's announcement was, "Thank God that V-E Day came in time to spare London and all Britain from this ultimate weapon of destruction."

With the Nazis and the Japanese for enemies, it has all along been a case of *them* or *us*. Our enemies, the inventors of terror weapons, have all along shown great skill in their perfection and the utmost ruthlessness in using them. Can anyone doubt for one second that the Japanese and the Germans would have used the atomic bomb? The world will echo Mr. Churchill's statement: "By God's mercy, British and American science outpaced all German efforts."

Canadian scientists played a real part with their American and British colleagues, in the forging of this fearful weapon. Every Canadian must feel an added responsibility for preventing war in the future, since Canada is a major source of uranium, the raw material on which this new source of power at present depends. Our national part in this new development, though obviously subordinate to the parts played by the United States and Great Britain must leave Canadians with a sense of awe.

While the mind reels at the destructive possibilities of this weapon which our scientists can appreciate, the layman finds himself standing in wonder as people might have stood if they could have comprehended any of the great epoch-making discoveries and advances of science. It is as if we were standing at the elbow of Isaac Newton, a Copernicus, a Galileo. This may be the story of the century. Laymen cannot hope to grasp the potentialities of atomic energy, harnessed to the good of humanity in peace. We can only await the pronouncements of scientists. Meanwhile, as we grope toward understanding, the lines of John Keats come to mind:

"Then felt I like some watcher of the skies. When a new planet swims into his ken; Or like stout Cortez, when with eagle eyes. He star'd at the Pacific – and all his men Look'd at each other with a wild surmise — silent, upon a peak in Darien."

—*The Winnipeg Tribune, August 7, 1945*

Taking Care of Our Own

The hearts of the Canadian people go out in the warmest sympathy to the people of Winnipeg, Rimouski and Cabano as they suffer from the scourges of flood and fire. Fortunately, the sympathy consists of more than fine words and is taking practical form in material aid to the homeless and distressed.

In the time of such disasters a generous public has to rely to no small degree on provincial and national governments and on great humanitarian organizations like the Canadian Red Cross. These are the agencies in the distribution of public monies and private donations and of supplies contributed from near and far.

The number of families rendered homeless in Winnipeg and Cabano is surprisingly similar. Twelve hundred families quickly registered with the Red Cross in both cases, a number not half the total.

The Red Cross at once outfitted 135 families in Winnipeg and 150 in Rimouski with clothing and bedding in temporary quarters. Arrangements were made for Kenora to provide accommodation for 400 additional flood victims in case of necessity. Altogether, 20,000 persons are temporarily homeless in the Red River district.

Red Cross and other relief workers were on continuous duty for 48 hours. At Rimouski, Red Cross workers, wearing white bands, issued blankets, food and clothing in the hockey arena, which was used as a temporary hostel.

A hundred heaters were rushed to Rimouski from Montreal. Troops dealt with looters.

The Royal Canadian Air Force gave assistance in both cases. It carried up to a half-million potato bags by air to damn the flood waters, as well as 3,000 hip-length boots. The army helped by sending men from the famous Princess Pats to aid the authorities. "Frog men" in weird outfits were sent to Winnipeg by the Royal Canadian Navy. Commissioner Dr. W. Stanbury, head of the national Red Cross, supervised relief work in Winnipeg.

A Rimouski relief fund was started with an anonymous private donation of $30,000. The dominion government intimated that it would treat both disasters as an emergency that warranted the giving of the utmost federal aid. Plainly, the task of relief and rehabilitation is much too great to be carried through exclusively on a local basis.

Cabano is only 60 miles from Rimouski. The number of homeless reaches 1,500. The Red Cross is prominent there, also, in the work of relief, and help is pouring in from all parts of Canada.

The people of the United States were most enthusiastic about the way Toronto cared for the *Noronic* fire disaster victims. This time our own fellow Canadian citizens are in trouble

and everything humanly possible should be done to enable them to face the future with confidence in the sure knowledge not only that somebody cares but that every Canadian cares.

*—The Toronto Daily
Star, May 10, 1950*

(Editor's Note: On May 8, 1950, a spring flood on the Red River in Manitoba destroyed 8 dikes and 4 of 11 bridges in Winnipeg, cresting at 9.24 metres downtown. About 100,000 residents were evacuated. The same week, two fires in Quebec destroyed half the town of Cabano and 319 houses in Rimouski.)

Who Will Help Rwanda?

Last week a reporter asked Major-General Roméo Dallaire, the Canadian who heads the United Nations mission in Kigali, what the world could do to save lives in Rwanda. "Send me troops," he replied.

He has not received them. Three weeks have passed since the United Nations Security Council voted to reinforce General Dallaire's small UN force in Rwanda with 5,500 additional troops, a drop in the bucket for the armies of NATO, the former

East Bloc and beyond. Yet, amid all the millions of men under arms in scores of UN members around the globe, virtually none can be found for Rwanda. Belgium, a former colonial power in Rwanda, lost 10 men in the early days of the war and is determined not to send more. Germany has constitutional reasons why it cannot help. Australia says it will not send troops until their safety can be guaranteed. Britain and France say they are already doing their bit in the former Yugoslavia. The United States, burned by its peacekeeping experiences in Somalia, has no intention of sending American boys to another obscure African war. Everyone seems to have an excellent reason for not helping.

Of course, Canada has come forward, as it usually does, offering 300 communications specialists. Canadian Forces transport planes continue to fly vital supplies into Kigali. In addition, four African countries – Ghana Senegal, Ethiopia and Zimbabwe – have offered a total of 3,600 infantry troops. But the Africans will only send soldiers if others will supply transport, equipment and funding. Result: more than two months after the outbreak of the war, and despite as many as half a million deaths, the international community is doing almost nothing to help the suffering people of Rwanda.

That suffering is by no means over. Since the horrific massacres of April and early May, perpetrated mainly by the Hutu-led military against the Tutsi minority, Tutsi rebels have counterattacked and overrun much of the country, driving tens of thousands of refugees before them. General Dallaire said yesterday that he fears that a "human tidal wave" of more than two million Rwandans may be pushed across the border into neighbouring Burundi, presenting the UN with an enormous new humanitarian challenge.

Without more troops, General Dallaire will surely fail. As it stands, his minuscule contingent of less than 500 is confined to a few guarded compounds in Kigali, too lightly armed to deliver food to refugee camps in the hinterland. Reporters who have visited those camps say that many people are dying of hunger and disease. The Red Cross and other agencies can do little to help them because, without armed escort, it is too dangerous to travel there. The possibility exists that Rwanda, having endured one of the century's worst massacres, may soon experience a second catastrophe: famine.

The world stood by while Rwandans were slaughtered. Will we now stand by while they starve to death?

—*The Globe and Mail,*
June 8, 1994

Death in the Morning

The visceral shock of watching the World Trade Center demolished by terrorists while thousands of people were inside will indelibly mark those who saw it – which is most of the world. In every time zone, people who were waking and turning on the radio, commuting, arriving at work, heading out to lunch, leaving for home, or watching the evening news on television, were witnesses to a crime so devastating that it will likely change the way liberal democratic societies organize and protect themselves for a generation to come.

But before considering what may happen in the future, let us dwell for a moment on the immediate past, on the terrible event that engulfed so many innocents, on the tens or hundreds of thousands of people for whom the attack was not just a numbing though mercifully distant shock, but an immediate tragedy. Some 40,000 people worked in the World Trade Center, and upward of 10,000 are thought to have perished there. A smaller, though terrible number, also died in a parallel attack on Washington.

Only a tiny proportion of those in the New York twin towers and the Pentagon were soldiers who might, by a stretch of terrorist logic, be regarded as legitimate targets. Rather, they were secretaries, paralegals, stockbrokers, bureaucrats, journalists, janitors and security personnel who rushed to try and rescue them – ordinary private people with friends and families whose emotional lives have now been ripped apart.

It is hard to fathom the fact that anyone could rejoice at this, and yet it is so. The terrorist commanders are doubtless celebrating, and in the Middle East yesterday, the enemies of Western civilization danced in the street and cheered the flow of innocent blood, just as they danced and cheered the murder of Israelis in a Jerusalem pizzeria last month. They know that the people they have attacked will never sink to their level; if they did, the party-goers in Damascus, and Cairo and Ramallah would be incinerated.

It is scant comfort in the short term, but is sustaining in the long term, to know that terrorist celebrations are predicated on the fact that the democracies they seek to destroy are their moral superiors. That superiority makes it imperative that the United States and liberal democracies everywhere fight terrorism in all its forms and wherever it lurks.

The last time a large aircraft crashed into a New York City skyscraper was in 1945, when a B-25 bomber accidentally hit the 78th and 79th floors of the Empire State Building. That plane is a relic of an age in which wars were fought against armies, not against office receptionists and airline passengers.

As former Central Intelligence Agency director R. James Woolsey said a few years back: "Following the Cold War, the U.S. is like the knight who has slain the dragon, only to find himself among numerous poisonous snakes." It is long since time that those snakes were crushed.

U.S. intelligence failed yesterday, but the CIA, National Security Agency and others have detailed information about where many terrorists are in hiding. And it is obvious to everyone else who is harbouring and encouraging the killers.

Osama bin Laden is protected by the Taliban in Afghanistan, and in Palestinian-controlled territory, Yasser Arafat has a symbiotic relationship with bombers who are waging a war of destruction against Israel on his behalf. Mr. Arafat, the Taliban and others who nurture terrorists must be punished.

When killers and their commanders are identified, they should be hunted down and destroyed. But similarly, when foreign governments are discovered to be giving aid and succour to terrorists, they too must be hit. They must be hit as hard as possible and as often as necessary to deter them.

When explosions lit the night sky over Kabul eight hours after the New York and Washington attacks, it was briefly presumed the U.S. retaliation had begun. That presumption turned out to be misplaced, but Washington must and will hit back.

Only minutes before the Kabul skyline was set ablaze, Lawrence Eagleburger, former U.S. secretary of state, made the blunt but accurate assessment that people were going to have to be killed in retaliation even if those directly responsible are never identified.

It should not be sufficient defence for state sponsors of terrorism to say that there is no proof of their involvement in a particular murder. If they deliberately operate outside humane, international norms and harbour terrorists, they cannot expect to benefit from those norms.

President George W. Bush promised yesterday that he would hunt the killers down. He is right to do so. He should make a start by destroying those who have created and perpetuated the murderous culture that has now brought mass death to the heart of Western civilization.

September 11 marks perhaps the single-day tragedy in the United States since the Civil War. It should also mark the end of a contemptible and debilitating epoch in which some people living in civilized democracies have made excuses for what has, all along, been inexcusable.

—*The National Post,*
September 12, 2001

12

Workers of the World Unite

The Irrepressible Conflict

The ceaseless conflict between capital and labour has assumed a new phase. It is proposed to reduce the wages of the Division Court clerks, local registrars of the High Court, deputy clerks of the Crown, County Court clerks, Surrogate registrars, registrars of deeds and sheriffs.

The reduction will be felt most severely by the skilled mechanics who do piece work, but whose wages, on an eight-hour a day basis, would amount to 99 cents an hour. Some of the more daring spirits among them are trying to organize a strike. In the event of a strike the Provincial Government, following the usual tactics of employers in such cases, will try to starve them out, and in the meantime to get along after a fashion without them. The strikers will then endeavour to convince the deputies, clerks and copyists that their interests are really identical with those of the superior workmen and that they will be the next to feel the tyranny of Capital as represented by the Provincial Treasurer.

The despot will then doubtless import non-union sheriffs and registrars – (say Tories). These despicable tactics will be met by a complete and vigilant system of pickets, under the direction of Mr. Ryan, and by appealing to the conscience of the Tories. A Tory, when properly approached, will always oppose anything in the shape of a reduction of fees.

If Mowat succeeds in this attempt the persuasive registrar say De Boucherville will be trying it on next, and even Abbott; the Usher of the Black Rod will have his allowance reduced to $100 a genuflexion. Should the attempt to call out deputies, clerks and copyists fail, a powerful appeal will be made to the legal profession, who are also exceedingly sensitive on the subject of fees. They will be asked not to accept certificates of registration or abstracts of title unless they bear a blue stamp, signifying that they are the produce of the labour of union registrars. Indigent debtors, a numerous and powerful class in these hard times, will be encouraged to resist seizures by "rat" bailiffs. This will cause breakages of the peace, and also of much furniture, and will bring the affair into public notice.

The people will also be aroused by indignation meetings and processions, in which men will carry transparencies and banners with strange devices. With a large majority and a big surplus the Ontario Government thinks it can trample with impunity upon the rights of the poor; but the end is not yet.

—*The Toronto Globe,*
March 14, 1892

Punch Clock Absurdity

It seems as if the authorities at city hall were bent on putting their "punch-the-clock" regulations into force. The committee in whose hands the arrangements lie for making the rules operative have decided apparently that certain of the employees shall be exempt from the orders which govern the rest.

The departmental heads, it seems, will not be subjected to this humiliation. In a way that is satisfactory, too, because if these department heads are good and efficient men, as we have no doubt they are, it would be monstrous to aim this blow at their self-respect. But after all a principle which is held to be good for one official should be held to be good for all.

The heads of departments have hours in which they are to be at the city hall just as the subordinates have: they are paid with the public money just as the others are, and it is hard to see why they should be exempt from regulations which are binding upon all the rest. The fact that they are to be exempt, however, will only deepen the humiliation felt by the other employees.

Vancouver's aldermen have been guilty of many absurdities in the past and, no doubt, they will in the future, continue to be guilty of absurdities, at least, while the class of men who are now selected for the municipal council are favoured by the voters. But never have they been guilty of any absurdity quite so pronounced as the wanton display of complete disbelief in the good faith of the city employees implied in the installation of this punch-clock.

If the aldermen think they will get any more work out of the men by such a reflection upon their conscientiousness in the discharge of their duty, we can assure them that they are greatly mistaken. Men do not respond in the way the aldermen seem to think the city hall clerks will respond to such a silly attempt to discipline them. Unless confidence and trust are reposed in employees, it is impossible to get the best work out of them, and to get the best work out of the men at the city hall the aldermen have taken exactly the wrong course.

—*The Vancouver Sun,*
June 30, 1912

The Winnipeg Dispute

It is to be hoped that the authorities will not be guilty of the error of judgment comprised in the sending of troops from Toronto to Winnipeg in order to keep the peace there during the strike, as reported. The Winnipeg strikers show no signs of being unruly. If they are dealt with as reasonable men and given every opportunity to present their side of their disputes with their employers there will be no occasion to import armed soldiers as guardians of the peace.

The Winnipeg strikes are aware that any violence displayed by the men now voluntarily refraining from working would damn their cause in the eyes of the whole country and strike a blow at organized labour that would be felt for years. The responsibility of the unions to keep the peace at this particular time is very great. Any serious disturbance would likely play into the hands of a great restless element that is not at all kindly disposed towards organized labour as a general thing, and which hopes only in this instance to use trades unionism as a means of creating a chaotic condition industrially all over the Dominion.

Our Canadian workers are not Bolshevists, nor are they going to play the Bolshevist game. They are, we think, exercising their legal and moral right in going on strike, and as long as they continue to conduct the strike on orderly and law abiding lines there is no excuse for importing troops, and thus virtually declaring that the strikers are potential law-breakers and a danger to society. That is something the men may resent in a very disagreeable way.

The authorities are quite competent to handle the Winnipeg situation. If matters were to require the presence of troops it would seem to be good policy to employ local men and not soldiers from points far distant. The intervention of troops from a different part of the country will prove the reverse of pacifying. Even the most law abiding element would resent the importation of outside troops in such a case. But we are confident that there will be no necessity for the intervention of either home or outside soldiers in the Winnipeg dispute.

—*The Ottawa Citizen,*
May 20, 1919

Letter Carriers Threaten

A recent Ottawa dispatch reports the letter carriers of Canada as once more threatening to strike. The dispatch states that the letter carriers at present start at a wage of $1,427 a year, and that their demand is for a minimum of $1,700. The public should consider this matter at once; make up their minds with regard to it, and instruct their representatives in parliament accordingly. Letter carrying is not work requiring special qualification. All that is necessary is that a man should be able to read writing, and be reasonably active, physically. It is most emphatically, "unskilled labour." An initial salary of $1,427 provides nearly $4 a day, including Sundays and holidays, for every day in the year. In addition, letter carriers receive all their working clothing, including overcoats, raincoats, boots and head-wear. They are provided with tramway tickets. They are not required to work on statutory holidays, or on Saturday afternoons in summer. They are allowed three weeks' vacation every year. Their regular hours are not nearly as long as those of other postal employees.

The minimum salary of $1,700, which they are now said to be demanding, is in excess of that paid to all but the highest officials of the department. In Halifax, for example, there are clerks in every branch of the postal service, of life-long experience and the best business training, who are receiving less. The salary of the assistant postmaster of Halifax has heretofore seen only $2,000, assistant inspectors begin at $1,800, after years of previous service and special training. Relatively, therefore, the letter carriers are much over-paid. As to their renewed and repeated threats to "strike," they should not be made to understand clearly and finally that if they attempt to carry them out, they will never again receive public employment in Canada. We had more than enough of that sort of thing in connection with the Winnipeg strike of last spring.

A public servant is the servant of ALL the people. He has, in parliament, representing the people, a standing court of appeal with regard to his grievances, real or imaginary. He must have a poor case indeed if he is not content to submit it to such a popular tribunal. At any rate, he must not be allowed to strike, or to profit by it if he does. Not many of the present letter carriers went overseas. They stuck by their places and salaries. If those places and salaries do not suit them now, there are thousands of returned men ready and willing to accept them. Four dollars every day in the year with clothing and other perquisites, would look attractive enough to most unskilled men and more so to men who spent years in the trenches at a "dollar-ten" a day. It is high time to deal definitely with the letter carriers, and put an end to their trouble-making and threats.

—*The Halifax Herald,*
January 28, 1920

Insurance for Jobless

It is evident that if the provinces, at a conference with the Dominion authorities to be held during the approaching parliamentary recess, agree to such a change in the British North America Act as will vest in the Dominion sole authority in the matter of unemployment insurance, such a scheme, of a contributory nature, is likely to be enacted within a few months.

It is a bad time to begin. According to A.A. Heaps, one of the Labour M.P.'s from Winnipeg, 750,000 men and women are tramping the streets of Canadian cities today looking for work.

The principle of unemployment insurance was sympathetically regarded in a report worked out by a committee of the House of Commons under the chairmanship of C.R. MacIntosh, Liberal member from North Battleford, a few years ago during the premiership of Mr. Mackenzie King.

Since then, while first meeting with considerable criticism – mainly being regarded as tantamount to failure to deal with unemployment by a constructive program of public works and kindred projects and as likely to introduce abuses that have crept in under the system in Great Britain – the idea of unemployment insurance has appeared to gain steadily in public favour in Canada, the view growing that it represents a scientific, methodical means of averting distress in times of business and industrial slackness.

No system of unemployment insurance will be perfect and abuses may develop under it. But what kind of a situation have we today? We have the dole in its worst form.

—*The Regina Leader,*
November 17, 1932

Settlement or Strife

The Dominion Day Clash between police and relief-camp strikers in Regina streets serves notice on the Federal Government that the time for choice of one of two developments has arrived. The situation stands today as either portending a series of deplorable catastrophes, or marking the end of thoughtless and ungainful agitation in this country.

As one of the strongholds of democracy, this Dominion cannot afford to give the lives of citizens, whether they be the uniformed officers of the law or restless camp deserters, to hysterical bloodbaths. Separation of the unfortunate unemployed men from the leadership of political brigands seems to be the first necessary step.

Canadian citizens do not deny these marchers an ample measure of sincere sympathy. Nor can they fail to realize that years of unemployment must have created a state of mind which, when influenced by the lawlessness of such agitators as do exist in their ranks, becomes susceptible to unreasoned coaxing and incessant prodding.

It can hardly be argued, in all fairness to the rank and file of the marchers, that such numbers would face the strain of the journey which they made and give themselves so completely into the hands of professional trouble-makers if they did not have some honest grievances to urge them on, magnified as those grievances may be by months of physical inactivity and worry over the future.

Certainly, then, it can be admitted that something must be done to remove the basis of those complaints – some compromise between men and Government after the agitators have been isolated and dealt with. Always in the past there has been a middle

159

course, and, as *The Globe* stated yesterday, the original requests of the marchers carried to Ottawa by the 'delegation of eight' were plainly the 'demands' framed by leaders who knew that no part of them would be possible of gain, and who depended upon the forthcoming refusal to aggravate the strikers more than their own oratorical powers had been able to accomplish."

In the death of Detective Charles Millar of the Regina police force, the strikers have surely learned a terrible lesson, and they cannot, as young men, afford to have their futures, dismal as they may now appear, burdened down by the mob-killing of any one. It is their duty, and in their own interests, to cast aside their leaders voluntarily and come frankly to the Government. It is the Government's duty to give earnest, unbiased ear and help them.

—*The Toronto Globe,*
July 3, 1935

The Forgotten Unemployed

One of the first duties of the newly created Employment and Social Insurance Commission will be to organize a nation-wide survey of unemployment. The Ottawa correspondent of *The Globe* states that "such a canvass of those out of work, the causes for the unemployment, the classes of industry affected and the periods of unemployment has never been undertaken, beyond that of the questionnaire attached to the 1931 census."

This is, of course, a fact recognizable to the scores of thousands of persons who lost their jobs during the past five years and hoped against hope in vain that somebody was doing something to fit them into useful occupations again.

There was some expectation that the census survey would be utilized to study the situation and provide a remedy. The census figures have served a purpose, apparently, in providing answers to questions asked in the House of Commons and finding accommodation in Department pigeonholes. As a means of practical study for a practical objective they are like most other Government statistics.

However astonishing it is that no effort was made to apply this information for assistance of the unemployed, it is more remarkable still that no attempt has been made to revise the record and keep it up to date. This can be done with a voters' list and is considered advisable. The voters are persons on whom the Government believes it necessary to keep a check at all times. The unemployed people are not.

The Unemployment and Social Insurance Commission has nothing to do with looking after unemployment relief, and it remains to be seen whether or not the survey to be made "which will occupy many months" will be limited in application to the specific functions of the Commission. If so, the relief recipient will remain a forgotten man.

The work to be undertaken by this new organization is important, and in years to come will provide relief for men and women who have contributed to an unemployment fund. Still, it is deplorable that no Government has been willing to make an adequate survey of the helpless unemployed of the present time and endeavour to handle their difficulties on a systematic and scientific basis.

—*The Toronto Globe,*
August 5, 1935

"On-to-Ottawa"

Premier Bennett has again explained to the "On-to-Ottawa" trekkers that they cannot tell him anything he does not know. Their seven-point program was ancient history to him, and so, in fact, was their main objective, which was to embarrass the Government and endeavour to attract attention to their cause. They made no progress with the Prime Minister, and, it is safe to say, none with the country at large.

The situation for trekkers and their allies has changed in the last few weeks. Proof that work is available for most able-bodied men has alienated considerable of the public sympathy which previously was extended those having hard luck stories. Men who can

161

tramp hundreds of miles are not suffering from physical weakness. Seven-point trekking and hunger-marching have lost their glamour. The leaders will have to try something else.

In New York the Communist leaders have decided to take the advice of the Comintern in Moscow and inaugurate an intensive "united-front" campaign. This sounds like big business, and is much easier for the leaders than hunger-marching. Possibly it will be the next phase in the "revolution" here also.

—The Toronto Globe,
August 12, 1935

Labour Day, 1981

As Canada marks Labour Day, 1981, it looks back on what was undeniably a turbulent year on the labour front.

Here in New Brunswick, there was a short-lived, first-ever general strike by school teachers, a bitter eight-week walkout by outside civic workers in Saint John and brief police strikes in Saint John and Sackville which raised anew the agonizing question of public protection in the absence of law and order.

There were threatened strikes by hospital nurses and liquor store employees in the province. Fishermen, impatient at delay in legislation to grant collective bargaining rights, demonstrated at the Legislature.

New Brunswick, like the rest of Canada, was hit by the harmful effects of the 42-day postal strike. A cross-country strike by the CBC technicians affected radio programming here as it did in other provinces – although some CBC listeners professed to enjoy the recorded music more than the disrupted regular programming.

Unthinkable as it may have seemed, even baseball was stopped by a labour dispute as players for the Canadian teams joined the other major leaguers in the U.S. in walking out on strike.

The New Brunswick Federation of Labour, which traditionally keeps its presidents in office for long terms, ousted its incumbent president, Philip Booker, after only one year. He was replaced by Larry Hanley, an activist union leader from Saint John.

As Labour Day 1981 approached, a strike by 1,600 grain handlers in central Canada was exacting a heavy price on western farmers. In New Brunswick, a long-running strike continued at a fish plant near St. Andrews and picket lines were still up in a bitter strike by employees at the Bethel Nursing Home in Queens County.

So it has been a tough year just passed on the Labour scene and the year ahead is expected to be difficult, too.

As the economy remained sluggish, unemployment continued to be high. Double-digit inflation pushed up the cost-of-living. Towering interest rates presented a crushing burden for many families, particularly those faced with mortgage renewals at 20-plus percent.

Political leaders were calling for restraint in labour demands, pleading that the cupboard is all but bare – but when a man is hungry, there is little point in telling him he should go on a diet.

These conditions, as Dennis McDermott, president of the Canadian Labour Congress, has pointed out, will intensify the pressure at the bargaining table in the coming year. And Mr. Hanley, president of the New Brunswick Federation of Labour, has served notice the federation will be fighting for various objectives, including protection of strike rights by public sector employees.

All in all, it means that in the year immediately ahead, labour will be like a black bear coming out of hibernation – hungry and mean.

And it will take all of the restraint, ingenuity and resources of both labour and management to reach accord at the bargaining table. This is not necessarily an entirely black picture, but it is a challenging one. On this Labour Day 1981, let us salute labour and wish it well as it enters yet another year of struggle for its members.

—*The Saint John Telegraph Journal, September 7, 1981*

Big Mac Attack

The union movement's tough guys, the International Brotherhood of Teamsters, have taken on McDonald's, the giant of the fast-food industry. The Teamsters have promised war against the restaurant chain, not one of whose 14,000 North American outlets is unionized. They have vowed they will win at any cost.

Someone seems to have taken them literally, planting a make-shift bomb last Friday at a McDonald's restaurant in Rigaud. The bomb scare should serve as a warning to everyone involved in the battle over unionizing the 1,065 Canadian McDonald's outlets to calm down and cool the rhetoric.

There are a number of reasons the union movement is so excited about the prospect of unionizing McDonald's. The employees fit the profile of the kind of worker whom unions are going after. They are young and at the bottom of the wage scale, and they're employed in the expanding service sector, where unions are scarce.

Union membership in Canada has been stagnating for the past 30 years, ranging between 31 and 33 percent of the work force. Thirty years ago, unions got their members from the manufacturing sector, a field that has been in steady decline. Organized labour is looking for fresh blood. As the president of the Quebec Federation of Labour, Clément Godbout, put it so inelegantly, "We can't recruit in the graveyard."

McDonald's restaurants have long been seen in North America as the key to unionizing the fast-food sector on a large scale. They're big and they're seen as the industry standard. For a few months in Quebec, it looked as though there had been a breakthrough.

In February 1997, the Teamsters filed for certification with the Quebec Labour Board on behalf of 62 employees of a McDonald's in Saint-Hubert. A year later, the workers won accreditation. On the other hand, they no longer had their jobs. The owners had closed down the restaurant two weeks earlier, claiming they were losing money. The timing was suspicious and the union complained long and loud.

But under Quebec labour law, the owners were entitled to close their business. The prospect of unionized workers seeking higher wages could hardly have been appealing to a company claiming to be in the red.

There are arguments on both sides of this debate. Unions believe fast-food workers are increasingly exploited on the job. The fast-food industry counters that it must keep costs down to stay profitable and provide those after-school jobs to teenagers.

The union may be within its rights to call for boycotts and investigations, but the rights of business owners must also be respected. What's clear is that labour has no right to try to inflame passions with talk of war and winning at all costs. This is not a war. It's a labour dispute, and both parties should stay strictly within the limits of the law.

—*The Montreal Gazette*,
March 24, 1998

Ensuring Safety on our Farms

It won't be popular among farmers, but the province should act on a recommendation made by a coroner's jury and extend occupational health and safety regulations to agricultural operations. All Island workers, including those working on our farms, deserve such protection.

The recommendation came after the jury heard testimony last week on the death of 16-year-old Alex Webster last July. Evidence revealed that he was working alone in a field when he tried to hook a fully-loaded hay wagon to a tractor. The wagon rolled forward and pinned him against the rear wheel of the tractor. He died of asphyxiation.

The jury made three recommendations: that there be mandatory blocking under free-wheel farm equipment, safety courses for young people hired through a government agency, and removal of regulations exempting farms from occupational health and safety standards.

These are reasonable suggestions. Modern agriculture is like many other sectors today – it's highly technical and highly mechanized. And just as other sectors must comply with regulations that ensure minimum standards of safety in their workplaces, so must our farms. Why should any economic sector be exempt from basic standards required by the province? And in the case where taxpayers' dollars are going toward certain employment programs, such as the one under which Alex Webster was hired, it's government's business to insist on safe work sites and environments.

Having said all this, it's obvious that the above recommendations would mean an extra cost to farmers. Government therefore should work closely with the farm community and perhaps phase in the regulations to give farmers time to adjust. Obviously farmers themselves are aware of what constitutes safe farming practices – the P.E.I.

Federation of Agriculture has a farm safety program – so it's a matter of government and farmers putting their heads together to come up with an agreeable method of extending occupational health and safety regulations to the farm sector.

The point here is not to impose yet another burden on farmers, but to foster a safe working environment on the farm. Current statistics tell us that a dwindling percentage of Canadians live on farms or have a farm background. That means fewer of us have any savvy about the demands of farm labour or any instinct about how to conduct ourselves around farming operations. Occupational health and safety regulations in most provinces now apply to the farm workplace. P.E.I.'s laws and regulations should do the same.

—*The Charlottetown Guardian, March 6, 2002*

13
Balancing the Scales of Justice

Education and Crime

While Kaiser William's somewhat fantastic scheme for teaching religion in the schools is being hotly discussed in Prussia, the people of England are considering a report made by the chief constable of Manchester on the relation of crime and education. He says that never in Manchester was there a time when crimes were so frequently committed by persons of good education as now.

While ordinary thieves stole last year in Manchester property to the value of £6,398, the amount of which firms and persons in trade were defrauded by people of good education, by means of forgeries and like devices, was upwards of £90,000. "Hardly a day passes that letters are not received complaining of 'long firm' frauds, which are rampant in all parts of the country, and all of which require the ingenuity and dexterity which are alone given by good education."

The majority of such cases are hushed up, but the chief constable offers to produce instances of persons in good position having committed such crimes and then absconded, or made restitution, or otherwise obtained condonation for their offences. *The London Times* points out that in Liverpool the number of persons proceeded against summarily and by indictment has increased from 37,421 in 1859 to 52,879 in 1890, an increase of 40 percent, while the number of grave offences, such as burglary and house-breaking, has trebled in the same time. This latter increase is of course out of all proportion to the growth of population in Liverpool.

"From all countries," says *The Times*, "comes the same complaint. The statisticians of France, Germany and Belgium, even those who think that, on the whole, there is a reduction in the army of crime, equally deplore this blot, which appears to spread, upon the face of their civilizations. They warn us with all solemnity that crime is entering a new phase and that the outlook is not better because the perils ahead are different from those of past times. Poverty has its temptations and its corresponding crimes; so also has, it would seem a plethoric state of wealth and material prosperity. There are offences almost peculiar to the starved, miserable and underfed; more than one moralist has bluntly told us that we have nowadays to be more on our guard against the crimes of the overfed."

It is quite possible to construct an argument to prove that education is actually the cause of crime. If a man could not write he could not forge, nor would a boy read pernicious literature if he could read none. The trouble with this argument is that it carries us too far. A blind man is removed from many temptations to wrong-doing and a bed-ridden invalid is not likely to commit crimes of violence. Nobody, therefore, argues that blindness or infirmity is a desirable condition.

There is no blessing which malevolent ingenuity is not capable of turning into a curse. There are, nevertheless, some useful lessons to be learned from the figures, which show that the spread of education has not prevented the increase of crime.

One is the lesson which it seems needful to teach anew to every generation of men, that human ingenuity has never yet devised a panacea for human ills. Carlyle used to thunder against the delusion that such a panacea was to be found in the ballot box. The more enthusiastic advocates of education for the poor expected too much and have been disappointed.

It is quite natural that men who dwell long and earnestly upon one particular mischief should come to regard it as the source of all evil, and its removal as the one thing needful to regenerate the world. One man will argue that the prime evil is the use of intoxicants, and there seems to be no flaw in the reasoning by which he traces back all vice and misery to this gigantic source.

Another will demonstrate with equally unassailable logic that the cause of intemperance and of all other evils is the social injustice which causes poverty and degradation; another points to ignorance; another to the decline of religious belief. They are all in a measure right.

Drunkenness causes poverty and misery, and misery drives men to drink; a decline in religious belief saps the foundations of morality and vicious practices injure the capacity for sound belief. It is possible to trace immorality and poverty back to ignorance. The fact is that those forces of evil act and react upon one another, each appearing now as cause, now as an effect; and the lesson which generation after generation has learned is that all cannot be subdued by striking at one.

The question under discussion is further complicated by the variety of notions as to what education is or should be. One school of educationists maintains that the only thing to be aimed at is to enable the student to earn his living; another plea for the culture and training of every faculty, physical, mental and spiritual.

Every country where a system of public education prevails has had to settle in some way the question of secular as against religious education. The view that education should be religious in the broad sense – that it should make for courage, reverence, self-denial, duty – would probably find general acceptance.

These things are more important than the much-vaunted three R's; but unfortunately the attempt to frame a scheme for that kind of teaching is rendered difficult by the jealousies and contentions of the advocates of various forms of doctrine.

—*The Toronto Globe,*
February 10, 1892

To Check Suicide

The epidemic of suicide is becoming very alarming, and it appears to increase in the same ratio as graphic descriptions of the theatrical tragedies of other cases of suicide are given. The victim is led to believe that there is a kind of heroism, a sort of stoical bravery about such a deed that will make him admired and will give him notoriety.

The proper way to check this idea is, in the first place, to pay out speedy vengeance on those who survive an attempt at their own destruction.

This is not done, for, as a rule, the attempted suicide receives a lecture from the Magistrate and is discharged.

The idea that the deed is nearly as disgraceful as murder, and that the perpetrator is considered a coward and a brute, should be made plain, and this should be done by exacting the full penalty of the law on a survivor, and should even go to the length of requiring that scant reverence be paid to the body of the one who may be successful, and that the remains should be interred in dishonoured graves.

—*The Toronto Evening Star, July 29, 1895*

Carrying Concealed Weapons

The recommendation made to the grand jury in the presentment to Mr. Justice Gregory yesterday morning, that stringent laws be enforced to prevent the promiscuous sale of pocket weapons to foreigners, is one which should receive the prompt and favourable notice of the Victoria authorities. The grand jury, in supporting the suggestion, drew attention to a large number of cases before the court in which weapons had been used.

The carrying of concealed weapons is already an offence in British Columbia, as it is in most other parts of Canada, but the regulation is not strictly enforced and one of the results of the indifference with which it has been hitherto regarded is the large number of stabbings and shootings which occurred in this city during the past winter.

There is no occasion for people to carry concealed weapons in this city, and as a matter of fact not one out of a thousand who is not a foreigner ever thinks of carrying them. But the foreigner, that is, the southern European immigrant, may usually be expected to have some dangerous instrument about him, and it is his habit to make use of it as a rule on very slight provocation. Why should he carry it if he did not purpose using it?

It is consequently a matter of the education of such people as these to a realization of the fact that speedy punishment will follow the carrying of dangerous weapons in this country. That can only be accomplished by fixing penalties and rigidly enforcing them. In Canada we should not tolerate people who carry either knives or pistols.

The native citizen of the country who is found with such weapons on his person should be fined and imprisoned and the foreigner who is guilty should be deported. It is only by a strict enforcement of the law that we can hope for security to person or property at a time when so many hundreds of thousands of aliens are annually pouring into this country.

—*The Vancouver Sun,*
May 16, 1912

A Too Expensive Legal System

The late E.F.B. Johnston, K.C., is credited with having won the acquittal of a score of defendants charged with murder. It would be interesting to know just how many of these defendants were guilty, if any. Because it is a highly questionable service that a lawyer may do to his fellow countrymen in bamboozling a jury into believing that black is white. On the other hand, it is an inestimable service that he renders where he is able to extricate an innocent person from a seeming mass of condemnatory evidence.

This is one of the defects of our legal system – that a skillful lawyer may save the neck or the liberty or the pocketbook of the guilty. Only those who have the necessary amount of capital can employ lawyers of outstanding ability, because they naturally charge the highest fees they may reasonably command. That is true not alone in murder cases, but in every kind of legal difficulty. Were it confined to murder cases, that would be bad enough. But who has not seen traces of where wealth has been able to put forward its best possible case in the courts because it can command – indeed, holds a permanent retainer of – the services of legal experts, while the poor man takes what remains.

To find and to supply a remedy obviously is not easy, but we believe that the situation is one calling for earnest action. Our legal system is greatly in need of simplification. Its manifest unfairness must be removed. It must not be said that money is an influence in the administration of justice, of course, not in the sense that money is used as bribery, but that it can employ services that poverty cannot command.

The courts must be cheapened. Judges not infrequently advise litigants to keep out of court, because they foresee that their whole properties will be swallowed up in court costs. Why should this be so? Citizens are entitled to have their grievances investigated and their disputes settled, and ought not to be compelled to sit under injustice because of the fear that justice can be had only at a price beyond their means.

—*The London Free Press, February 1, 1919*

Too Many Guns

Every time a shooting accident occurs there is an outcry over the laxity of our gun laws. But once the shock of tragedy wears off we return to the old regulations.

Early in 1957, a 15-year-old boy died in a cowboy game played with rifles and live ammunition. But the law, which contains nothing to prevent a 14-year-old from buying a rifle in a sporting goods store, is still on the books.

Now, almost six years later, a coroner's jury urges that the minimum age for buying firearms be raised from 14 to 16 and that police more rigidly enforce the Criminal Code section banning the sale of guns to boys under 14 who don't have a permit from the RCMP. (It's hard to imagine why the RCMP should grant a permit, for any reason, to anybody under 14.)

The jury's recommendation rises out of the case of a 13-year-old who accidentally killed himself with a rifle ordered from a store over the phone. Obviously, the jury also urged that purchases of firearms through phone or mail order be prohibited.

What's the good of these investigations and recommendations if we don't heed them? As grievous as the death of the boy are our apathy and reluctance to change.

There are too many guns too easily obtained around Toronto. Some 150,000 are registered in this area, and this is estimated to be only a small portion of the arsenal in private hands.

We treat the gun as if it is a toy or a harmless instrument for enhancing sport. The plain fact is that it is a death-dealing weapon.

Because of our lackadaisical laws and enforcement procedures, boys continue to lose their lives and criminals have easy access to firearms.

How many tragedies do we have to suffer before the authorities toughen up our gun laws?

—*The Toronto Telegram,
December 6, 1962*

173

Punishment and Crime

Early this morning, in the Don Jail, society exacted the supreme forfeit from two men for the offence they had committed against society. The manner of their death is repugnant, but the community, for its own protection, cannot tolerate the existence of men who have brutally shown their contempt for life.

The formal, almost ritualistic killing of a man by hanging is ugly, but there are occasions when there is no justifiable alternative to the execution of a criminal for the murder he has committed.

In both cases, the men sentenced to death killed either a policeman or an accessory in the service of the law. Both received all the safeguards and the scrupulously careful processes of the law courts. The Supreme Court of Canada denied their appeals, and the cabinet, after reviewing the cases, found no grounds to grant clemency.

No one can say that these men were denied justice according to the law of the land. Yet voices are raised to amend the law, to abolish capital punishment. Murderers, it is said, are still human beings and life imprisonment is enough to satisfy society's rightful demand for protection; to execute them brutalizes every member of the community.

The Telegram cannot agree with this generalization. The first consideration must be the protection of the community, not the welfare of the criminal. The community is given no assurance of protection if policemen or jailers can be shot down with impunity, or if criminals know that a murder in a premeditated, coldly planned crime, as in an armed holdup, will not automatically bring a sentence of death. Since a sentence of life imprisonment is seldom for life, the community can never be certain that the released criminal will not again kill a policeman, or rape and murder a child.

Whether or not capital punishment serves as a deterrent to others contemplating an act of violence is a question that exercises the conscience of the community. In *The Telegram*'s view, the fact that the question is debatable is sufficient reason for retaining capital punishment. There is the possibility that the potential killer may debate the issue himself. No possibly restraining doubts would exist in his mind if the law were to exempt him from execution.

Repugnant as capital punishment may be, society must exact it for certain crimes – for the killing of policemen; for killing while in custody; for killing while committing a felony; for deliberate, callously calculated murder. Society thus pays due regard to the victims of murderers and to its own security.

—*The Toronto Telegram,*
December 11, 1962

Prison Reform

The defeat in the House of Commons of amendments to the bill eliminating capital punishment clears another major hurdle on the way to a more just society. For the second, and probably decisive time, a majority of MPs has said that Canada does not need the noose.

It is noteworthy that Canadian politicians should feel confident enough in the social and legal fabric of their country to vote as they did only days after the United States took a more regressive step.

The U.S. Supreme Court ruled that capital punishment is not necessarily cruel and unusual, and therefore, in certain circumstances, is constitutional. To its credit, the U.S. Supreme Court did rule that for some crimes capital punishment is too extreme.

But for Canada, the continued support of the government's anti-hanging position should not be the end of the issue.

Canada's prisons should be the next target for the government's consideration.

In the name of humanity, the government is bringing about an end to hanging. In the name of humanity it should now turn its attention to what needs to be done to make convicted criminals fit to rejoin the mainstream of Canadian life.

—*The Ottawa Citizen,*
July 9, 1976

Shattering the Silence

"The secrecy is perpetuating the crime." What a wonderful thing for the victim of a crime to say.

On Monday, Justice Archie Campbell of the Ontario Court's General Division lifted a publication ban at the request of four women who were sexually assaulted between 1964 and 1978 by William Donald McNall, who was sentenced to eight years in prison. At last year's trial, the judge imposed a ban on publication of the women's names, "and any information that could disclose" their identities. Because three of the women were the daughters of the accused, the ban also covered his name.

The women asked that the silence imposed by the trial court be overturned. They presented a psychiatrist's report arguing that, in their case, publicity would have a "cathartic effect," allowing the victims to stop blaming themselves and focus instead on the guilt of the perpetrator. They worried that others could be endangered by being kept in the dark about the identity of Mr. McNall and the nature of his crimes. Joy Ladoucer, one of the victims, said that she "hoped that by being open and sharing our story with the press," they would encourage other victims to come forward. "The secrecy is perpetuating the crime," said Ms. Ladoucer. "The victims often feel shame and the criminals feel secure in the knowledge that their names will not be published."

Canadian law gives complainants in trials for incest, gross indecency and sexual assault the right to request that their names not be published, and gives the courts power to impose publication bans even when no such request has been made. For the victims of sexual assault, the crime carries with it a powerful social stigma and internalized shame.

Consequently, it is generally agreed that far fewer victims would come forward if this crime were to be treated like any other offence. On the other hand, if publicity allows victims to know that they are not to blame, enabling them to place the blame squarely on the perpetrator instead, then it is best to let their names be published.

Publicity will undermine, over

time, the unjust stigma that attends these awful events. Not every victim will want this publicity, but for those who voluntarily choose to reject secrecy, one can only express admiration.

—*The Globe and Mail,*
September 23, 1992

Is It Just?

If it was simply a case that only lurid detail was being kept from the public, then it would have been easier to accept the outcome and secrecy surrounding the trial of Karla Homolka.

But as it is, the public is left with the most confusing and disconcerting explanation of her involvement in the slayings of schoolgirls Leslie Mahaffy and Kristen French.

People are understandably upset. Just from information that has found its way into public domain, the sentence of 12 years appears terribly inadequate, especially when you consider that Homolka could be out on parole in four years.

And while The Spectator, like other newspapers, cannot publish evidence from Tuesday's trial because of the court order issued by Judge Francis Kovacs, the fact of the matter is this shocking evidence makes the argument for a stiffer sentence even more compelling. The punishment does not fit the crime.

When it is finally disclosed what went on in this rampage of horrific violence, the public will be even more sickened and outraged. The fact that this travesty took place under the shroud of a publication ban makes it worse.

The Spectator, like other Canadian news organizations was allowed to sit in and hear the evidence, but will be able to report Tuesday's evidence only after the trial of Paul Bernardo, perhaps up to two years from now.

The existence of a deal between the Crown and Homolka was something suggested by lawyer Tim Breen who is representing Paul Bernardo. In arguing against a publication ban, Mr. Breen said that in return for special consideration before the courts, Homolka would testify against her estranged husband.

177

Judge Kovacs said: "The accused gave significant and perhaps invaluable information to the police. There are serious unsolved crimes here and elsewhere. There can be no room for error in the prosecution of the offender, whoever that might be."

Was this deal in the public interest, and in the best interest of justice? Was the police investigation so ineffective that the Crown was forced into bargaining away too much?

What exactly was on the table in the negotiations – a fast trial, lesser charges, the Crown's call for a sentence of 12 years? Was the ban on publication something the Crown offered as an enticement?

The judge makes the determination in these matters, but did the Crown promise to push for a series of cushions to make Homolka's experience before the court as painless as possible? And was this appropriate under the circumstances?

Justice is a time-consuming, difficult and constantly evolving process that often involves difficult choices and sometimes deal making. Our fear is that too much has been compromised in the trial of Karla Homolka. And confidence in our justice system has been shaken.

—*The Hamilton Spectator, July 8, 1993*

Sad Death of Discretion

Canada's smallest province has served up a large victory for common sense. The Supreme Court of Prince Edward Island recently threw out disciplinary proceedings against a doctor who began dating a former patient seven years after he stopped treating her. The doctor was accused of violating a 1998 law that prohibits doctors from acting "in any sort of sexual way" toward patients and, in some cases, ex-patients.

"The legislation is flawed in that it constitutes a blanket prohibition, which is manifestly more than a minimal impair-

ment of [the doctor's] Charter rights," Chief Justice Kenneth MacDonald wrote in his decision. "The legislation lacks balance and is incapable of giving proper justice to different fact situations. Neither the public nor the affected parties benefit from this unbending type of legislation."

The point of the law should not be to prohibit such relationships, but to make humane and realistic provisions for them. A doctor who begins dating a patient should have an obligation in most cases to refer the patient to another doctor. A university professor who dates a graduate student should recuse himself, or herself, from judging that student's thesis.

P.E.I.'s law regarding doctor-patient relations is part of a wider pattern. In recent years, governments have embraced "zero-tolerance" policies in the fight against crime, sexual abuse, drugs and other social problems. Thanks to zero tolerance laws against domestic abuse, men have been charged for dousing their wives with fruit juice or throwing dish towels. In the United States, the zero-tolerance war on drugs has resulted in farms and other businesses being seized after a small amount of marijuana is found on the premises. In jurisdictions that have embraced three-strikes sentencing guidelines, criminals with prior criminal convictions have been sent to jail for decades for the crime of stealing a piece of candy. On campuses and in workplaces, the pressure to deal severely with allegations of sexual or racial harassment has caused careers to be ruined because of isolated comments and gestures taken out of context.

It is understandable why legislatures and professional organizations are tempted to institute zero tolerance policies – and why the broad public often initially supports such initiatives. These policies are a product of legitimate frustration at the sight of lax punishment dispensed to criminals and genuinely malfeasant professionals. When people come to mistrust the discretion of judges and bodies that monitor profession conduct, it is inevitable they will agitate to relieve them of their discretionary powers. The best way to avoid the creation of misguided zero tolerance policies, therefore, is for those with discretion to exercise it responsibly.

—*The National Post,*
September 1, 2001

Doing Justice

Saskatchewan has finally launched a public inquiry into the wrongful conviction of David Milgaard for the brutal rape-murder of Gail Miller almost 35 years ago. Mr. Milgaard sat for almost 23 years in prison and then waited longer for a signal from justice officials they recognized they had done a terrible wrong. Now, those officials and police authorities will have their roles reviewed.

This is outrageously overdue. The Supreme Court of Canada quashed Mr. Milgaard's conviction in 1992 after reviewing the evidence against him. In 1997, DNA evidence – the great redeemer of far too many innocents who land in prison due to others' misdeeds – cleared him, and pointed to Larry Fisher, who now is serving time for the murder. Mr. Fisher had committed a string of rapes in the same area within months of Ms. Miller's death.

Saskatchewan authorities must explain why Mr. Fisher was not more fully pursued after Mr. Milgaard's conviction in 1970. They should be made to explain their use of informants whose criminal charges were waived in exchange for their testimony. Why, as well, was the police statement of a woman who said she witnessed Mr. Milgaard kill Ms. Miller used, even after she testi-

fied she could not remember the incident. Perhaps Saskatchewan prosecutor Serge Kujawa can be asked to account for a comment David's mother, Joyce Milgaard, attributed to him in her 1999 book: "It doesn't matter if Milgaard is innocent... The whole judicial system is at issue – it's worth more than one person."

Mr. Kujawa is wrong. The system is not worth more than the conviction of an innocent person. Such a doctrine permits arrogance to breed among those with power, and the sacrifice of the innocent at the altar of that power. It erodes the purpose of law: to protect people and maintain order.

The injustices done to David Milgaard, then a mere 16-year-old Winnipegger travelling with friends, are neither novel nor unexamined. Such police and prosecution tactics have been the focus of numerous inquiries into wrongly convicted persons.

In Canada, the list of names is well-known – Thomas Sophonow, Stephen Truscott, David Marshall, Guy Paul Morin – and growing.

Saskatchewan Justice Minister Frank Quennell said Friday it is likely many of those involved in the case may no longer be available. Why it has taken so long to call an inquiry might be an appropriate question for review.

The inquiry may be limited by the time lapsed, but to not have the inquiry is akin to sweeping a gross miscarriage under the carpet. That would permit some to believe the judicial system is worse more than the innocence of a single person.

—*The Winnipeg Free Press, February 23, 2004*

14
Sport

The Future of Lacrosse

From the time that semi-professionalism made its appearance in lacrosse the game began to decay. A few years ago the leading teams were composed of players who appeared on the field out of love for the sport and the game was popular. Then when competition reached its height many of the teams in the senior league bought up the best players by finding them desirable situations in return for their services on the field and the game began to lose favour.

The first step being taken, it was only a matter of time before the second would be recorded, and it appears it is about to be made. The story is now public property that the Capitals and the Shamrocks are to take money for an exhibition game in Toronto.

This can have but one effect. Lacrosse will cease to be a solely amateur game in name as it has long ceased to be one in fact.

The Torontos always resolutely resisted the introduction of this professionalism and the result was that for some years they came second in nearly all their matches. They may have lost glory in declining to buy up players, but they have gained honour in resolutely struggling against the movement which has finally degraded our national game into professionalism.

It is to be hoped the thing has worked its own cure and that in the near future we will again have a genuine amateur sport in which the clean classes of our athletes may participate.

—*The Toronto Evening Star, August 7, 1895*

Bluenose: "Her Honours Gathered, Her Duty Done"

One additional word about Bluenose. There has always been the absurd fiction among people who knew nothing about such things that this great champion was a "freak." Never was their a more wretched libel on a magnificent piece of craftsmanship.

Bluenose was no freak. She did what she was designed to do. She came from the board of our own W.J. Roue, internationally recognized as one of the foremost of naval architects of our time; she justified his expectations, vindicated his skill and genius and the work of his hands and brain.

One thinks today of the tribute of one of the most highly-rated of authorities in this field: "There has been a great deal of clap-trap talked about this beautiful vessel. There is no mystery or secret to her speed or the excellence of her performance. She is simply a splendid adaptation of the well-known principles applying to naval architecture." That authority pointed to *Bluenose's* "beautiful entrance" and "long, clean run." As, indeed, he might, for she was the embodiment of all naval architects strive for in speed-under-sail: "Easy entrance, clean departure and consistent distribution of displacement."

Bluenose was big as fishing schooners go, able, weatherly. And she had speed. Plenty of speed? No vessel in her class had as much.

She was a working fishing schooner – and she landed a lot of fish. And not only did she have the speed that was put into her lines, but she had *power*, as well. She could carry sail when most of them couldn't; and with the strength and power that was in her, she came through ordeals that sent many another fishing fleet-mate to her doom. She "took an awful beating" in a gale in Sable Island waters... but she emerged triumphant, with disaster all about her and vessel after vessel going under in that terrific fury of wind and sea. It was not the only time *Bluenose* literally "clawed off a lee shore."

Bluenose was a link with a past of clouds of canvas on towering spars. During her racing career her only motive power was sail. She carried the traditional "four lowers," topsails and fisherman's staysail. She was, in fact, one of a great company of "salt bankers" that fished out of this province in those times and has fished out of Nova Scotia for many long years before.

Now they are gone, practically all of them. We are in a newer era of diesels and oil. But in the outfitting centres along the Lunenburg waterfront they still talk – nostalgically – about those "good old times" of "sail-dragging." And wherever a few are gathered together there to renew old associations and recall old days, somewhere in the reminiscences *Bluenose* finds her proud place.

What a pity it is that she ever left this province! Perhaps the war had something to do with it: Canada was thinking of bigger things. The Navy was urged to take her over as a training-ship when the wooden tern-schooner *Venture* was built. But it didn't work out that way... and in no way calculated to keep *Bluenose* here in her home waters or in some snug berth as a monument to a great past and to her own unrivalled performances.

—*The Halifax Herald,
February 1, 1946*

(*Editor's Note: The schooner* Bluenose, *launched in 1921, won many International Fisherman's Trophies. Designed for fishing as well as racing,* Bluenose *later hauled freight in the Caribbean until Jan. 28 when she hit a reef and sank. A likeness of* Bluenose *appears on our 10-cent coin.*)

The Old Western Spirit Still Lives

Calgary has reason for rejoicing. Not just because the Stampeders won the Grey Cup, nor because the local team confounded the Wise Men of the East. But because both the team and its supporters, who travelled in hundreds all the way to Toronto to lend moral support, demonstrated that the old Western spirit isn't dead. Not by a jugful!

This is not to minimize the grand playing of a grand team. The Stamps used brain as well as brawn. They were a younger, less experienced team. They could easily have succumbed to stage fright. They could have been too greatly impressed by the mountain of beef on the other side. But they weren't. They played a cool-headed, almost faultless game, and because they couldn't outweigh the burly Rough Riders, they outsmarted them.

The presence of 500 wild-eyed Calgarians in the stands had something to do with it. Of that we are certain. Their enthusiasm was at fever pitch, and they infected the Torontonians with it. The applause that followed every Calgary gain showed unmistakably where the spectators' hearts were.

We think it was a good thing for Canadian sport that a Western team did win, and against considerable odds. Sport has become almost an Eastern monopoly. The East has many more resources to draw on than the West, more manpower, more money to back teams. But numbers and cash don't always make championship teams. There is always the possibility that the other side may have the determination to win and the skill to back it up. That's the way

it was with the Stamps.

It was a good thing for staid Toronto, too. When a Toronto mayor clamps a 10-gallon hat on his sedate noggin and eats flapjacks with his fingers at the business end of a chuckwagon, there is hope for even the most inhibited Torontonian. It may be a long time before Toronto gets back to normal. Certainly it will be a long time before it forgets the Calgary invasion.

It was appropriate that Calgary should declare a civic holiday on Wednesday. That will give thousands of Calgarians an opportunity to get down to the depot and show the Stamps how much they appreciate their magnificent showing. We have no doubt they will be there in force.

But, as we say, gratification isn't due to the winning of a series alone. The Stamps played cleanly and well throughout the season. They will leave a bright mark on the Canadian sports record. And now for the Allan Cup.

—*The Calgary Herald,*
November 29, 1948

The Champion

It was great: Canadians could cheer proudly for once in rather cheerless years.

Northern Dancer, Mr. E.P. Taylor's champion horse, conquered the field magnificently in the running of the Queen's Plate. He won by seven lengths in a field that offered the best challengers competing in our racing tracks.

But Northern Dancer had proved himself before by winning the Flamingo Stakes, the Florida Derby, the Kentucky Derby and the Preakness.

He had lost the Belmont Stakes; but it was not for want of heart in this small but game racer. Rather it was the result of circumstance that could frustrate any champion – a matter of timing and position. Mr. Taylor was as gracious in defeat as he is modest in victory. He has praised the trainers and the rider who brought glory to his entry and showed no recrimination when his champion was defeated for the Belmont.

The hat trick in classic racing is the triple crown of the Derby, the Preakness and the Belmont Stakes. Northern Dancer did not quite make it.

But who cares?

He succeed in two of the major American classics and he won the biggest track contest in Canada, walking away from his challengers.

Mr. and Mrs. E.P. Taylor had little to gain and everything to lose by bringing Northern Dancer to Toronto to run. The decision to run him here after his earlier trials was in the highest tradition of the sport of kings.

It allowed Canadians to see the best horse ever bred in Canada run in Canada's most important and North America's oldest annual horse race.

The race was a runaway; but it was Woodbine's most memorable moment.

Northern Dancer justified his name. As Shakespeare wrote in *Richard II*, a dance is "a delightful measure." Mr. Taylor's horse performed in delightful measure.

—*The Toronto Telegram,*
June 22, 1964

(*Editor's Note: The first Canadian horse to win the Kentucky Derby, Northern Dancer was elected to Canada's Sports Hall of Fame in 1965.*)

That's our Nancy

Take one very determined, champion skier, give her a tough year sprinkled with agonizingly near wins and setbacks, keep victory just out of reach day after day as the Winter Olympics open and approach their climax. Then watch her, steeled and confident, sweeping to a final smashing victory in the giant slalom at Grenoble.

Give her her second consecutive world title, the first combined gold and silver medals ever captured by a Canadian skier, acclaim her as indisputably the world's top woman skier, and call her Nancy Greene.

—*The Ottawa Citizen,*
February 16, 1968

Team Canada Win brings National Joy

The Victory by Team Canada in its eighth game with the Soviet Union's national team undoubtedly was the most spirit-lifting sports event in Canadian history.

Patriotism and national feeling were intense throughout the eight-game series which saw Canada gain ultimate victory despite losses in the early games. But Canadian reaction, both in Moscow and around the millions of television sets left no doubt that Canada was behind Team Canada all the way, and except for the odd boo in Vancouver, all the time.

The patriotism that contributed so much to the excitement of the series contained a good mixture of politics as well. The entire process of arranging the series to prove that Canada has one area of superiority to which no superpower can lay claim, the task of assembling a team from the best talent Canada could offer only to find the national will overruled by U.S. NHL team owners, and the final debacle over which referees would officiate at the last game is evidence that more than just sportsmanship was involved.

188

Did the series really prove Canada's hockey supremacy?

No, because, as most sports analysts agreed (after the premature euphoric predictions that Canada would win eight straight) the games could have gone either way.

Rather, both sides had the opportunities to pit their ideological differences, as translated into hockey, against each other with the result that neither side showed an overwhelming superiority. The Soviet collectivist style, pitted against the Canadian individualistic style, proved to be an almost even match.

Not only did Team Canada's victory save national pride, it probably also salvaged the future of the NHL in Canada. Had Team Canada lost, ticket sales to regular NHL games would have suffered, for who in Canada would then believe the NHL to be anything but a second-rate league?

One other conclusion to be drawn from this international hockey tournament is that it was a series worthy of being repeated. A rematch with the Soviet Union's team and Team Canada – next time with Canada's very best players, regardless of their league – should be the natural outcome of this series.

O Canada!

—*The Windsor Star,*
September 29, 1972

Goodbye Wayne Gretzky

The City of Champions has lost its quintessential champion.

The shocking trade of Edmonton Oilers' superstar Wayne Gretzky to the Los Angeles Kings is a substantial loss to this city.

To thousands of Edmontonians, Gretzky is more than a sports star. He is part of this city's personality. Edmontonians have a proprietary interest in him that goes beyond mere fan adulation.

He was one of this city's prize assets, a goodwill ambassador, someone who raised Edmonton's profile higher than any publicity campaign could hope to.

Even in places as far away as Italy, people said "Gretzky" when tourists mentioned "Edmonton."

For a city whose psyche is rooted in the culture of championship, of being the best in every endeavour, Gretzky's departure is no ordinary trade.

The trade may be a big plus for professional hockey on this continent, but the loss to Edmontonians cannot be measured – certainly not in dollars.

No doubt Oilers' owner Peter Pocklington likes to make a deal. And no doubt he has just made the biggest deal in hockey history.

It is true that Edmonton was a place on the map – not as well known, perhaps, but existing all the same – before Wayne Gretzky arrived here in 1978.

It's also true that Gretzky scored his first goal in professional hockey *against* the Oilers, before Pocklington bought him for $850,000 from the Indianapolis Racers of the old World Hockey Association. Hockey is a business, as will be said often enough today, and its players are the commodities.

All of this may be true, but there is still something that sticks in the throat as Edmontonians attempt to swallow the news that Gretzky is finished playing in an Edmonton uniform. The city through the years shared from the heart in Oilers' wins and losses, and always Gretzky was at the centre of those feelings. He wasn't just a hockey star, but this city's very own hockey star. The greatest player in the world, but also *our* player. That affair of the heart, mixed up somehow with the city's feelings of pride and rendered easy because Gretzky himself is so naturally accommodating, really blossomed this summer with his wedding to Janet Jones – a royal wedding if ever there was one.

It is worthy remembering that the Oilers have changed substantially since their playoff loss to the Calgary Flames three years ago. Stars like Paul Coffey, Kent Nilsson and Andy Moog have departed, but the Oilers learned to win again as a team – not as a collection of stars. They will need a lot of teamwork now that their greatest star has gone down the road.

Right or wrong, Pocklington's name won't be spoken kindly today by many Edmonton hockey fans. Perhaps Gretzky insisted upon moving to Los Angeles where his wife is pursuing an acting career. Perhaps Pocklington felt the money in the deal was persuasion enough for dealing away hockey's greatest player.

One thing is certain. Gretzky's name in neon will sell hockey in Los Angeles where the sport has struggled. He alone will be enough to turn hockey into another dream in a city that sells dreams for a living.

This city, where hockey is more the stuff of reality, will sorely miss him. No one will hesitate to wish him good luck and to give thanks for the countless hockey memories accumulated on a thousand winter nights.

—*The Edmonton Journal,*
August 10, 1988

Champion Jays Make History

A Canadian astronaut up in orbit whooping it up. A depressed prime minister uplifted on the eve of what seems a populist impeachment. French and English Canadians, Westerners and Easterners, black and white, all united in their collective ecstasy.

It was baseball at its best.

And the best in baseball are our magnificent Blue Jays.

It took seven gutsy pitchers 11 nail-biting innings to prove it, but who would have wished for less. The coveted World Series trophy is not a prize to win the easy way.

But now it's ours. It belongs to Toronto and to the millions of Jays fans cheering from Vancouver to St. John's.

Yesterday these birds flew back north for winter, reversing the Americans at their own game.

The hero of the moment, of course, was Dave Winfield whose 11th inning double drove in the winning run.

You couldn't have asked for a more dramatic, or poetic ending – the oldest player producing the biggest hit of his illustrious career.

Or was the hero Roberto Alomar for that brilliant golden glove snag in the fourth inning?

Or Candy Maldonado for sending one over the wall?

Or was it David Cone, Todd Stottlemyre, David Wells, Duane Ward, Tom Henke, Jimmy Key or Mike Timlin who took turns on the mound Saturday night.

Or Joe Carter, who throughout the series displayed the same deftness at three different positions in the field?

Or Kelly Gruber who worked his defensive magic right after scoring with his chin in game four?

Or Juan Guzman for his pitching in game three? Or Devon White for his spectacular leap in the same game to pick a speck off the centre-field wall?

Or was the hero Pat Borders who won the MVP award for his control of the pitchers – both ours and theirs?

Heck, all the Jays are heroes. For six games, the entire team just kept coming through.

The victory, after three American League East divisional titles, marks the crowning glory of a team born just 16 years ago on a snowy, windswept day at the Ex.

The Jays helped build the SkyDome, the world's best covered stadium with the world's biggest video screen.

They created attendance records, 4 million in each of the last two seasons. They boast the league's highest payroll – $45 million. They make history with Cito Gaston becoming the first black to manage a team in the World Series. And finally, by chopping the Braves, they ease the pain of Toronto losing out on the 1996 Olympics to Atlanta.

As delirious Torontonians join the Jays parade today, and the entire country celebrates, we have another wish: that some of this magic rubs off on the Maple Leafs.

—*The Toronto Star,*
October 26, 1992

Weekend of Champions

For a few glorious hours on the weekend, Canadians could forget about Iraq and SARS and celebrate some remarkable sporting achievements.

Alberta's Randy Ferbey and his rink reaffirmed Canada's long-time excellence in world curling. The Edmonton Oilers, Ottawa Senators and Vancouver Canucks came back from tough defeats in the NHL playoffs. Toronto's Paul Tracy became the first race-car driver to go undefeated in the first three races of a season on the CART circuit.

And Mike Weir made golfing history, becoming the first Canadian to win the Masters, the world's most coveted golf title.

Hockey is Canada's national diversion of choice, and its stars are our most beloved heroes. But for sheer exhilaration, nothing could match the historic performance on Sunday by Mr. Weir, the pride of Bright's Grove, Ontario.

In conquering an elite field of the world's best golfers on one of the world's toughest courses, Mr. Weir catapulted himself into the Canadian athletic pantheon, joining the likes of track stars Donovan Bailey, speed skater Catriona LeMay Doan, skier Nancy Greene, rower Ned Hanlon (and not to forget racehorse Northern Dancer) among those who've excelled in individual sports.

Few have looked less like an athlete than Mr. Weir, whose slightness of build convinced him at an early age that his future lay in golf rather than hockey, his first love. Yet there is no doubt he is a world-class athlete of considerable skill, courage and determination.

Indeed, Mr. Weir exemplifies some of the best qualities for which Canadians are known. He's modest, hard working (it took him years of toil in golf's backwaters to become an overnight success), gracious, calm under pressure and tough when it matters.

As the first Canadian to win one of golf's major tournaments and the first left-handed player to win the Masters, Mr. Weir is sure to become a shining example for young Canadians and young lefties everywhere.

He has already given us a sporting weekend we won't soon forget.
—*The Globe and Mail,*
April 15, 2003

Bringing the Cup Back Home

Is there anyone on Prince Edward Island these days who hasn't been talking about Brad Richards and the Stanley Cup? Probably not. How often does an Island native get to bring home the coveted National Hockey League treasure, along with the Conn Smythe Trophy for being the most valuable player in the playoffs?

We need not apologize for celebrating. And all of Prince Edward Island did that Tuesday as thousands of family, friends and fans converged on the small, eastern community of Murray Harbour to get a glimpse of The Cup and help the hometown hero savour his moment with it.

But there was more to this grand party than watching the popular Tampa Bay centre hoist the cup to the applause of onlookers. This was a communal celebration, a mini-mutual-admiration society. The people of Murray Harbour and all of Prince Edward Island may be fond of their native son – but no more than the native son is fond of them. As Richards himself said in a letter to the editor to this newspaper: "I especially want to thank everyone from Murray Harbour and Murray River, people who have supported me my entire life and who always make it so special to come home. You were there for me long before any of my recent hockey success was even thought possible. I mean it every single time I say I am proud to be from Murray Harbour and Prince Edward Island."

Much has been said about Richards' hockey prowess – his work ethic, his play-making abilities, his leadership skills and his gentlemanly conduct on the ice,

which earned him the Lady Byng Trophy. But the 24-year-old's sudden rise to stardom has caused many to take a closer look at who he is off the ice – a sensible down-to-earth sort whose fame, success or fortune don't appear to have clouded his priorities. Family, friends and community are obviously near and dear to him. So are those who carry special burdens in life – children with autism and cancer, many of whom are the beneficiaries of his generous and willing support.

Success on the ice may earn an athlete his share of fans, but his performance off the ice, in the public arena, is what earns their affection. Judging from the throngs that turned out Tuesday, the pride of Murray Harbour has secured a spot in Islanders' hearts.

—The Charlottetown Guardian, August 4, 2004

15
The Great Outdoors

Tree Planting

The season for planting is at hand, and everyone should look around his premises to see if they cannot be beautified by a few trees, by a plot of grass, or by flowers. Nothing adds so much to the beauty and comfort of a home as trees, shrubs and vines. During the next few weeks the little gardens in front of Regina houses ought to be improved by the setting out of trees and the conversion of untidy plots of land into pretty gardens. Very few can plead poverty as an excuse for failure to plant a tree or two in front of their houses. They cost but little and pay handsomely as an investment. A tree that costs a dollar today will add 20 dollars in value to a property a few years hence. There are both money and beauty in trees. If for no other reason, property owners should plant trees because it will pay them to do so in a near future. The example of Winnipeg is proof of this.

—*The Regina Leader, May 2, 1901*

In Defiance of Authority

The reducing by two thousand of the overgrown herd of buffaloes, owned by the federal government, in Alberta has been postponed until about the middle of the month. In the meantime the killing of a number of these animals by riflemen, while Cree Indians pretended to be slaughtering them with bows and arrows, has taken place for the benefit of the movies. It was against this that protests were made, not, as the superintendent of Wainwright park would make it appear, against reducing the herd.

Among the protests sent from many directions was one in the form of a lengthy telegram to Hon. W.S. Fielding, from the Third Church of Christ, Scientist, of Toronto, in which it was stated: "Our objection is not to the killing of buffalo but to the filming of the incident for commercial purposes. Depicting such a scene would be sensational and harmful to the morals of theatre audiences. It would also be a bad advertisement for Canada. We strongly urge cancellation of the moving picture contract before it is too late."

In reply to this message the following telegraphic reply, dated Ottawa, Oct. 16, was received:

"Department assures me filming of the killing of buffaloes was never thought of. Permission has been given for the taking of pictures of buffaloes. But I am assured there is no connection whatever between the two events." – W.S. Fielding

Mr. Fielding's statement was explicit. The slaughter of buffaloes to make a movie sensation "was never thought of," no permission for the doing of it had been given. In view of this assurance from the department it was assumed that the thing could not happen. Yet it did happen. The movie film of a buffalo hunt by Cree Indians with bows and arrows in the wilds of Canada is now on its way to the picture theatres everywhere. These buffaloes were killed two or three weeks before the date set by the government for the reducing of the herd.

It seems quite clear that the movie people staged this performance without the knowledge of Mr. Fielding, without permission of the department at Ottawa, and in spite of protests from all parts of the country. No doubt an official enquiry is already being made as to where the responsibility rests for this insubordination to authority.

—*The Toronto Evening Star, November 2, 1923*

Unchanging Weather

An address on the weather before the Regina branch of the Canadian Society of Technical Agriculturists by P.C. Perry, divisional engineer of the Canadian National Railways, suggests that coonskin coats may continue an institution in prairie Canada for yet many a year and oft.

Mr. Perry inclines to the view that we are getting the same rigorous winters as the first white men on these plains experienced and that they are apt to be the same 200 or even 2,000 years hence. In other words, he does not think our climate is changing, as some folks sagely opine when a nice soft spell hits us on occasion.

This is comforting news or otherwise, just as one may view it. There may be those who think that the weather we have been getting in these parts the last few days, for instance, has been just a little too penetrating altogether. On the other hand, there are those who grin colossally in the teeth of it and say it's just right.

But if Mr. Perry's dictum is right, all of us can have the satisfaction of knowing that pioneer generations out this way had nothing on us in the elements they battled – that we, like they, are capable of standing the same climatic gaff that made for muscle and whalebone in days gone by.

—*The Regina Leader, December 12, 1932*

Great Dog

These are the "dog days." After yesterday's intense heat, with temperatures in the 90s, high point in a period of hot, humid and enervating weather, there is no need of labouring the point. And yet if it is the dog days which have been afflicting us, we might as well know what it is all about. The origin of the phrase "dog days" is not connected with the fact that canines feel the heat and may be more lazy or irritable in midsummer. The words come from the constellation "Great Dog," which includes Sirius, brightest star in the heavens. The Greek word from which Sirius comes meant "scorching." When Sirius rose with the sun as it did at this period of the year, it heralded the hot and sultry season. The Greek poet Hesiod sang, "Sirius parches head and knees," and Homer called it the "evil star."

There is no doubt about the knees and head and every other exposed part of the male or female form being scorched these days and there is also a scorching temporarily of spirits and energy. "Evil," however, it can hardly be called because, when a cooler spell comes, as is already apparent today, and after the exhaustion wears off, there is a rebirth of vitality, surprising and exhilarating. And the "dog days" have their place in the ripening of the crops and in the beneficent cycle of the seasons. Moreover the inevitable slowing down of activity in midsummer is merely a preparation for revitalized energy and "bounce" in autumn days, when full-pressure work is resumed.

—*The Toronto Daily Star, August 3, 1945*

Will Five Wrongs Make a Right?

Pity those poor men out at Dorval. Toiling for the Central Analysis Office of the Meteorological Division of the Air Services Branch of the Department of Transport, they are presently required to supply forecasts of the weather for 36 hours ahead. Now from Ottawa comes the news that, starting next summer, their stint will be to foretell weather conditions for five full days.

Labouring against the vagaries of a weather map, which seems to be in a continuing state of change over this hemisphere, the present staff of that office often is found far afield. And they are in an unfortunate position. Once they have said it, they are stuck with it. It is there in black and white. They are denied escape, such as is often resorted to by politicians and others, by claims that they have been misquoted.

The weather is acknowledged to be the most popular topic of conversation. Forecasts which go astray or backfire make discussion of that subject even more prominent and certainly more vehement.

Perhaps it is not quite fair to hold the men at the Dorval office to blame. They no doubt do the best they can with the tools they have to work with, on what the Good Lord sends them in the way of weather. Perhaps

the time has come to provide them with some new and improved gadgets for use in their work.

Certainly mere force of numbers in the personnel of the office can hardly be expected to make things much different. The staff is to be increased from about 25 to approximately 85. But that promises to do little more than increase the number of red faces by about 60 when the forecasts miscue.

The margin of error is going to be greatly magnified. But perhaps if the weather were handed out in five-day lots without naming specific days, the public could fit them more satisfactorily.

The convenience of those planning picnics has been mentioned as one of the boons to the public for which this extended service is designed. Ah, well, picnickers probably cannot get any wetter on the fifth day than on the first day of the forecast. And if that happens they may derive what consolation they can from the knowledge that the men at Dorval aren't having any picnic either.

—*The Montreal Gazette,*
October 29, 1952

Smog over Metro

Smoke and fog combine to form poisonous smog. It is taking a deadly toll in London. In Toronto, magistrates take a charitable view of air pollution. The easy fines they impose imply failure to recognize that air pollution is more than a nuisance. It is a menace.

Air pollution is a contributory cause of cancer, heart disease, chronic bronchitis and diseases of the stomach, blood, eyes, throat and other organs.

For hundreds of years the common law has recognized the right of the individual to clean air. In the 13th century the penalty for polluting the air was death. In the 20th century our courts impose fines of a few dollars. In September, the lowest fine was $5, the highest $100. The latest report, for October, shows 20 convictions, four of them repeats, with the highest fine being $100.

Capital punishment would appear to be somewhat drastic in this day and age, but the courts have swung to the other extreme of excessive leniency. The occasional fine is no deterrent to firms who find it cheaper to pay $20 or $100 rather than install expensive smoke abating equipment.

Magistrates are not laying down the law severely enough. The present scale of fines permits a levy up to $50 for the first offence, up to $100 for the second, up to $300 for the third. Yet penalties of only $5 have been imposed. A new scale will shortly come into force, providing fines up to $400 for the first offence and up to $300 for subsequent violations.

If magistrates imposed the maximum fine, and imposed it for every offence, violators would be less inclined to take a casual view of the law. They would soon find that it would be cheaper, and make for better public relations, to install the necessary equipment.

This alone, however, will not clean Metro Toronto's air. Metro's air pollution control still functions under a bylaw passed in 1957, and this bylaw refers to smoke and its by-products. There are other contaminants – substances, materials, odours and fumes emitted to the atmosphere from other than combustion from manufacturing operations.

The present limitations are too restrictive for a highly industrialized area such as Metro Toronto. This is realized by the Works Department and it is preparing an application to the Legislature for broader, more comprehensive powers.

Granted these powers, and with magistrates cracking down on offenders, Metro Toronto will have cleaner air to breathe.

—*The Toronto Telegram,*
December 7, 1962

On Wings Of Sound

The news is mournful: no baby birds have been reported among the 30-odd whooping cranes at Aransas National Wildlife Refuge on the Texas coast.

And the future of the whooper again hangs in the balance.

Ever since 1938, when the decimation of these birds was first noticed, the battle to preserve them has been going on.
It hasn't been easy.

Nature, dedicated to Darwin's survival law, hasn't always cooperated. It is believed that the absence of young in the birds' winter home in Texas this year is due to the destruction of the eggs last summer by high water flooding at Wood Buffalo National

Park, Northwest Territories.

There are always the hazards of the 2,400-mile migration route from the Canadian North to the Gulf of Mexico.

This species of crane has some powerful allies. When the U.S. Defense Department planned to turn the Aransas marsh into a bombing range, Canada protested in a formal diplomatic note. And when a new railway line threatened to run right through the whoopers' summer home, anguished American and Canadian voices were heard in Ottawa and that railway was rerouted.

Jim Baillie, Telegram wildlife columnist, estimates that there are about 40 whooping cranes in existence, including those in captivity – each a long-necked symphony of motion and sound, snow-white except for jet-black wing tips and a crimson head.

Why all this anxiety about a bird with a five-foot windpipe from which comes a call like an Indian war whoop? Because its disappearance would mean that something beautiful has been lost to the world.

There is a hopeful sign in this – that men should be concerned about the rise and fall of a joyous bird even as they are preoccupied with the ups and downs of the cold war.

—*The Toronto Telegram,*
December 12, 1962

Nuclear Waste

About five years ago, science fiction circles were buzzing with the notion that it would be possible to take our nuclear garbage and launch it into the far reaches of space. It was thought to be a simple and useful idea until someone pointed out that from time to time space launchings have failed, and it was possible that a rocket ship full of radioactive trash would rain back down on our heads.

Now someone has modified the idea and wants to use a different and theoretically safer launch technique. The problem with the new idea is that it is counting on frontier science to handle something with potentially dreadful consequences. The past few decades have taught us with unnerving regularity that frontier science can lead us into unpre-dictable territory, and the best of intentions can run awry.

There is a principle of ecology that waste is the term given to unharvested resources, and in any healthy ecosystem all waste must be harvested eventually. Various long-term deep storage ideas have been proposed, but they still leave some experts worried that we may one day face a harvest we don't want. Waste disposal is at the heart of the nuclear problem and the subject of intensive brainstorming. So far, we are still sweeping the garbage under the rug.

—*The Montreal Star,*
September 21, 1979

Golden Day

There comes a day in mid-September when mellow, golden beauty rests like a benediction on fields and meadows. The soft light and a pale blue, cloudless sky blend with the greens and amber browns of the countryside. Wherever one looks he sees a tinge of gold.

If the meadows are still green and the fields covered with rowan, the slanting rays of the ninth month sun change the green to green-gold. As one looks at the grasses, he is sure that the Master Alchemist has passed a magic wand over the landscape.

There are shades of gold in the ripe goldenrod spikes. Down in the swales and swamps, slender leaves of the cattails gleam with a rich gold-brown hue. If the atmospheric haze is favourable, one can see many shades of gold in the needle leaves of pines, spruces, firs and tamaracks.

A golden day is a rich experience in living. There is no movement of air to stir the foliage or bend the amber-hued grasses on the pasture hillside. Apples hang like jewels on the branches and red tomatoes gleam in the garden.

The voices that one usually hears to herald the autumn are silenced for the day. All the land lies waiting, and the murmuring of a woodland brook is muted in the brooding September air.

There are only a few golden days in the interlude while Summer slides into Autumn. We know the voices of changes are tuning up in the northland, and that soon chill, sharp-edged winds will sandpaper the land. But when a golden day comes, it is good for a many to walk his acres and drink of the beauty that satisfies a deep thirst.

—*The Saint John*
Telegraph Journal,
September 14, 1981

No Time for Atmospheric Idleness

There was some disturbing new evidence this week of our atmosphere changing for the worse.

It comes in the form of scientific data, based on international study, pointing to the presence of a wandering and on-and-off-again ozone hole over the northern reaches of the planet. In recent weeks, the hole has been located over Baffin Island in the Canadian Arctic. The "hole" is suspected of having been caused by ozone depletion brought on by release of chemicals, notably chlorofluorocarbons (CFCs), which break down the ozone layer serving as a filter to sift out ultraviolet radiation which can harm plant, human and animal life. Commenting on the latest revelations, Alex Chisholm, an atmospheric scientist with Environment Canada, noted, "We've lived with it for a number of years and it hasn't caused immense harm. But I think we should regard it as a sign that there is something wrong with the atmosphere and deal with it accordingly."

The investigation into Arctic ozone depletion has been conducted by an international scientific team drawn from the United States, the Soviet Union, Canada and Europe. If there are encouraging signs of the multinational cooperation in defining the problem, the hope now must be that there is an equal measure of international harmony in forging a solution.

There are some indications of that happening, such as through the international protocol drawn up in Montreal in 1987 to phase out CFCs, compounds that have a range of uses, including in aerosol propellants, refrigerator coolants and Styrofoam containers.

The latest evidence of a hole in the ozone layer matching one in the Antarctic should be sufficient to push matters beyond diplomatic niceties. The time may have come to borrow a leaf from von Clausewitz by moving from diplomacy and political posturing to a war footing. If the ozone hole were a military threat, how long would we dilly-dally? One suspects, not long.

But still, we appear to indulge in atmospheric appeasement. Armies may be difficult enough to turn around, but it is all the harder to halt and reverse environmental change.

The international scientific co-operation evident in identifying the problem should form the foundation for a "wartime" alliance to come to grips with changes in atmosphere.

Just as fighting a war requires national and supranational efforts, so there is a need for local and individual contribution. (Regina City Council is on track in seeking advice on how it can curb use of products using CFCs.)

As consumers, we can contribute to the war effort by challenging or not dealing with businesses or organizations that continue to employ products that rely on CFCs.

The dangers of overreacting in the fact of the latest news from the ozone front pale compared with the consequences of raising our hands in defeat and of doing too little, too late.

—*The Regina Leader-Post, February 16, 1989*

Another Cod Disaster in the Making?

After four years the cod fishery opened in Placentia Bay to the same old problems that have plagued the industry for decades.

Fishermen snapped up their quotas in three short days, blocked the fish plants that were geared up for cod, leaving many tonnes of fish with no place to go. If anything demonstrates the failure of overall federal fisheries policy more than this fiasco, we haven't seen it yet.

The problem is simple – the fishermen, faced with a small quota, maxed out their fishing effort at the start of the open season, caught the quota quickly and then were faced with the problem of trying to sell fish into blocked plants.

Even though most fishermen know this method of fishing is suicidal in the long run, they have no choice but to run as fast as they can in a race that everyone loses. Holding back individually and spreading the effort over weeks would only result in the individual fisherman losing badly.

The solution to this mayhem may be just as simple, but will require a total change in the way quotas are allocated to fishermen. Instead of a global quota that rewards rapid, rapacious harvesting, the individual fishermen must

205

be allocated boat quotas that will allow them to catch fish over a much longer period of time with less gear and with a more moderate, but sustained effort. That way the fishing effort can be coordinated with the processing effort.

In countries like Iceland, Norway and New Zealand, the fishery is already run on an individual property rights basis. And in those countries the fishery actually creates wealth.

And if the quota is transferable, the fishermen will have a built-in incentive to guard the resource as much as possible. After all, a transferable quota is meaningless if there are no fish to catch.

For this change to occur, the federal government has to completely redesign its quota system. Allowing global quotas may satisfy some mythical equity provision, but in the long run it is a recipe for

disaster. Allotting individual quotas will be extremely difficult, and the system will have to allow for new entrants to the cod fishery, but these problems notwithstanding, something must be done if the fishing industry is not to open to more chaos in the future.

If anything, the current moratorium is a blessing in disguise for it allows DFO to completely redesign the fishery of the future at a time when many of the participants are sitting on the sidelines. Over the next year the department must start on a method of fish allocation that ends the "everyone-race-out-to-get-as-much-fish-as-we-can" system.

Continuing with the present system is just a recipe for another fisheries disaster.

—*The St. John's Evening Telegram, July 12, 1997*

Kyoto Deal Fragile

That any deal at all emerged from the Kyoto summit is a kind of miracle, given the national agendas pitted against each other.

But the Kyoto deal on mandatory targets for greenhouse gas emissions is flawed

and very fragile.

It is testament mainly to the organizers' determination to get some kind of agreement, so the summit would not be seen as a failure. Whether this latest deal, which is supposed to be legally binding, will be any more meaningful than the pious commitments made in Rio five years ago, remains to be seen.

To say that is not to dismiss the problem. There is enough evidence that global warming may cause havoc, and much more that the pollution sources cited aren't good for us in other ways, to warrant a major global commitment to reducing emissions.

But the fact is that when 160 nations are brought together to act in concert to ward off a threat to the planet, national agendas are bound to emerge.

This is particularly true of Canada, a big user and producer of fossil fuels.

As so often happens with deals hammered out in long, intense bargaining, Canada has agreed to a much larger emissions cut than it intended.

It agreed to reduce emissions six percent below its 1990 levels. Given the 13-percent rise in emissions since 1990, that means 19 percent or more in total. We are to do this in the next 15 years.

We will get credits for our forests, which absorb carbon dioxide. Unfortunately, Alberta and British Columbia are busy cutting down their forests.

We will not get credits for shipping clean natural gas fuel to the United States. We can buy credits from other developed nations that have overshot their emissions targets, and gain credits for providing energy-efficient technologies to developing nations.

Reducing emissions as promised is an incredibly tall order.

Why did Ottawa agree? Because to refuse would have been embarrassing, would make us look like the world's hold-out polluters.

Now the Kyoto deal goes back to each individual nation for ratification and implementation. That is when the rubber will hit the road.

Before the federal government ratifies the Kyoto deal, it should give Canadians a clear idea of how it's going to meet that challenging target.

To date, it appears to have no idea at all. The Chrétien team stumbled into Kyoto with an emissions position cooked up at the last minute. In no way has it marshalled national public opinion behind its position – it has left the field to those who mutter darkly about carbon taxes and pretend that global air pollution doesn't matter.

And it does not inspire confidence that the Kyoto deal was reached by bleary-eyed bargainers stressed out from a ridiculous process akin to how employers and unions decide on minor contract details, rather than by calm and thoughtful give-and-take.

Still, Canada is obliged to do its part in this gigantic effort to curb greenhouse gases. So is Alberta, which feels particularly vulnerable because of its fossil fuel-based economy and its lack of hydroelectric power.

But Canada's approach has to be carefully planned. It can't cause such serious harm to the economy that it greatly increases unemployment. It has to involve not just economic sacrifice but innovation, and incentives to encourage energy efficiency – be it wind power or public transit.

Alberta's government should be an active player in this. It is not good enough to be the naysayer who refuses to change anything. This is a province that produce 90 percent of its electricity by burning coal; it has work to do.

Unquestionably, the push to curb fossil fuel use poses a serious challenge to a province so dependent on fossil fuels. But fossil fuels aren't Alberta's only resource.

This province has highly educated and energetic people. There is no reason it can't be a leader in developing new energy-efficient technologies.

Greenhouse gas emissions will only be reduced on Earth if all parts of the planet do their part. That includes not just Canada but developing nations like China and India, which have refused to agree to reduced emissions.

They have a good argument: the current pollution problem was primarily caused by the industrialized world. But if the Kyoto deal doesn't include the world's two most populous nations, it cannot claim to be a global solution to the greenhouse gas problem.

Kyoto was a near-failure for an obvious reason: national self-sacrifice to achieve a planetary goal is not something human beings have done before.

Nonetheless, the issue of greenhouse gases won't go away. Canada must prepare for change, and do so in a careful, creative way.

—*The Edmonton Journal,*
December 12, 1997

16
Across This Great Land

The Baggage Smasher

It is about time that the railway authorities made a move in the direction of suppressing the baggage smasher who ever since he came into the world has carried on his work of destruction unmolested.

The reckless baggage smasher tosses a delicate trunk from a car to the platform as he would a chunk of scrap iron and simply smiles when the receptacle collapses with the shock.

There is really no excuse for such a reckless destruction of private property, as the baggage man has, or should have, sufficient time in which to perform his duties properly and with a due consideration for the safety of the goods he handles. This reckless handling of baggage is an annoyance and a loss to the public, and a standing reproach to the railway companies. The ordinary citizen feels disinclined to sue for damage to a $5 trunk when it would cost hundreds to fight it out.

—*The Toronto Evening Star, August 7, 1895*

Calgary's Possibilities

Rev. Father Devine, S.J., who has written for the *Western World* an account of his trip "Across Canada by Rail" makes the following reference to Calgary and its possible future:

Calgary is also a prairie town, rapidly advancing in population, and assuming importance as a railway centre. We shall hear more of this town when an Alaskan-Siberian Railway is opened to the world; for it is from Calgary that the Canadian Pacific branches to the north through the province of Alberta. When traffic warrants the expenditure, the rails will be pushed through Athabasca to the Arctic Circle, and if necessary, to the very Yukon. It may sound extravagant at the present time to mention an Alaskan railway route to Europe, but who knows what the next century may bring forth? The great Russian railway across Siberia will offer an all rail route from Paris to the Pacific Ocean. The approach of the trans-Siberian roads to the coast of the Pacific will undoubtedly stimulate twentieth century magnates to lay steel through Alaska. The engineering difficulties are great, but are they insurmountable? Behring Strait could be crossed by some powerful system of railway ferriage. And here we have mapped out for us a railway route from New York to Paris, one that would throw M. Jules Verne's calculations of an Around the World trip into the shade. An American paper estimates that the time from New York to the Pacific coast would be 5 days; 6 thence to Behring Strait; 14 from the Strait to London; 6 from London to New York. So that Mr. Fogg would not have the slightest difficulty in circling the globe in 31 days. Were he to take the Canadian Pacific route he could do it in 29.

—*The Calgary Daily Herald, January 15, 1898*

Danger from the Bicyclist

On last Saturday evening a young lady crossing James street, near the Hotel Royal, was run over by a bicyclist. She was badly bruised, her gown torn, and a silk umbrella ruined. The bicycle rider made a quick turn out of Rebecca street, and without warning the young lady was dashed to the hard pavement.

More than a year ago an elderly lady was run over by a bicycle, and she has been an invalid ever since. Last summer a young lady was thrown down by a bicycle, the wheel passed over her body and injured her so badly that she had to spend six weeks in the hospital.

The columns of the Spectator bear constant testimony, in the reports of accidents, that reckless bicycle riders are responsible for the injury of many persons during the season. There does not seem to be any necessity for bicycle riders going scorching through the crowded streets of the city.

The humble individual who has to walk has certainly some rights on the public thoroughfares that irresponsible scorchers are bound to respect. The people who are injured have no recourse to collect damages, and as they are now totally at the mercy of the bicyclists the agents of the law should step in and compel a decent regard for the rights of those who must walk.

The majority of the bicycle riders are careful, but there is a class of scorchers who bring reproach on the whole wheeling fraternity. A few arrests for fast riding might have a healthy effect, for there is no doubt that the police magistrate would make the fine a substantial one.

Every bicycle should have a bell, that people crossing the streets could be warned of the rider's approach; and at night it should be a finable offence for any rider to be on the street with his wheel without having a lighted lamp on the front of it. Hack drivers are fined for not having their lamps lighted at night. Persons crossing a street can hear the approach of the horses and carriage. The bicycle rider slips up on one so quietly that there is always danger of collisions even with the most careful of riders.

—*The Hamilton Spectator, April 23, 1900*

A Giant Canal Scheme

The Associated Boards of Trade of Ontario have unanimously agreed to urge the building of a system of canals that will give ocean boats access to the Great Lakes. The estimated cost of these canals is $100,000,000. To meet the interest and sinking fund charges upon this large sum of money, it is urged that transportation would be cheapened to the extent of millions of dollars annually, while the canals would develop electric power worth at least $26,000,000.

Canada is essentially an agricultural country, and to the extent that our farmers are able to get their product to market cheaply will this basic industry grow and prosper. Ocean freighters that would tie up at Port Arthur and there take cargoes of Western wheat and other grains, besides live stock and meat products, would be a boon to the West not easily to be computed in dollars. Ontario farmers would profit in the same way. Our manufacturers would have their position greatly enhanced also. Ships loaded with Canadian products at an Ontario port would sail direct to the port of delivery.

The further development of cheap hydro-electric power in this province is inevitable. The power commission is working constantly to this end, and the day approaches when the quantity of power now developed will seem small indeed. Our factories will have raw materials delivered at their doors from all parts of the world by means of cheap water transportation, their wheels will be turned by the cheapest power known, and their finished product will be shipped out also by water, with little or no railroad haul to add to the costs. As a manufacturing country, Ontario has a large promise.

The construction of the proposed canal should be assisted in a considerable degree by the United States, all of whose Great Lake ports would be equally benefiting with our own. This assistance might take the form of a direct contribution or tolls, or both.

—*The London Free Press, March 31, 1919*

Suggestions for Establishing Aerodromes

For the assistance of municipalities wishing to lay out and equip municipal flying fields so that they will be practical from an airman's point of view, we give below an outline of the various types of landing fields, compiled under the direction of Lt. Kenneth C. Leggett.

In addition to the runway markers shown in the sketches, there should be a large T made of 14-inch lumber, the long section about 12 feet, and the short section about 8 feet in length. This T should be painted white and placed on the ground with the top of the T in the direction of the prevailing wind.

This can be easily seen from an altitude of 6,000 feet, and will show the aviator the proper point to place his ship on the ground with a clear runway in front of him.

Up-to-date communities are now establishing flying fields so that they may be in position to get the benefit of a regular stop in the Aerial Mail Service and to take care of air tourists who are increasing in numbers every day.

With these and many other subjects which confront commercial aviation we are constantly working.

But the development of this big new industry cannot be successfully carried out by a few. It must receive the approval and support of the public before it can take its place, along with other accomplishments of man, in civilization.

—*The Halifax Herald,
February 28, 1920*

Getting Out of Town

There is a downtown area in Toronto from which at certain hours of the evening tens of thousands of people pour out into the streets and seek street cars in which to get home. The density of the downtown population increases every year. There is scarcely a roof in the area of which we speak that has not under it a steadily increasing number of workers, clerks, office hands. The desks of the clerks are forever being moved closer together so that space for more clerks may be made. Rooms and hallways are brought into service that were not utilized before.

The street car service at times cannot possibly carry away the crowds that await them. There is need for more street cars, but the tracks can scarcely carry more. In order to expedite the departure of tens of thousands of people from the downtown area in which the number of people is forever on the increase, it may become necessary to improve the free-way for street cars by preventing automobiles delaying them at street intersections. It may also become necessary, in serving the interests of the many, to impose inconveniences on the few.

At the most crowded hours of the late afternoon, a glance along King Street will show on each side of the roadway long lines of standing motors. Each of these motors is a one-man vehicle. Each car has been brought down to take its owner home, and stands by the curb awaiting his convenience. It may not wait long, but when it moves out another takes its place. That these one-man conveniences greatly impede public convenience in the matter of transportation nobody can deny. Through two lines of standing motors, the street cars run, and all moving traffic is forced to use the car-trackage, following one street car and preceding the next one.

Whenever a street car crosses an intersection a train of motors is in its wake. A 60-foot street car has a train of motors a hundred yards long behind it, and before the semaphore of the traffic officer signals "Stop" the whole procession must pass, and the street car that is signalled to "Go" is delayed by so much.

Motor cars on the move away from the downtown area are relieving that area of congestion,

214

but in endeavouring to get away they are impeded by the standing motors which occupy one-quarter of the street allowance on one side and one-quarter on the other side of the roadway.

Sooner or later Toronto will have to open up her streets downtown and keep them open to moving traffic only – such streets as Yonge, King and Queen – within specified limits. It will be most annoying for a while to many. But the interests of the great multitudes of people must be regarded as supreme.

—*The Toronto Evening Star, November 28, 1923*

The New Air Service

In one sense it is fortunate that untoward weather conditions should confront the flyers engaged in inaugurating the Trans-Canada Air Lines service between Winnipeg and Vancouver because similar conditions may be expected to recur from time to time after the service is opened to the public. Experience counts heavily in operation of airplanes under any and all circumstances.

The most intense care has been devoted to preparation of the new air system, and the pilots will have the benefit of beam wireless and other modern aids to flying. A half dozen years ago when a regular mail service was maintained between Calgary and Winnipeg, the flyers had little to guide them except their compass and a few beacons set long distances apart on the prairies. Today flying has become a science, and even regular trips across the Rockies in all kinds of weather present little difficulty to an experienced pilot.

There will be both day and night flights when the new system is inaugurated. Regular air mail service will be established possibly within a month, while the opening of the air line to passenger service may be delayed for an even longer period.

—*The Calgary Herald, March 5, 1938*

Driving Tests a Good Idea

In his press interview on Friday, Premier Maurice Duplessis said that the Quebec government is actively considering the possibility of imposing a driving test, before the granting of licences.

If such action is taken, it should prove very constructive. The toll of deaths on the highways grows always more appalling. And in most cases poor driving is the cause. Some people have been driving cars without any real understanding of what the dangers and regulations are.

It must always be borne in mind that anyone who takes a car upon the highway is taking into his hands the power of life and death. An automobile can become a lethal weapon. It is a serious public responsibility.

The present system of granting licences is not likely to do much to cut the rate of accidents. A person is licenced to drive a car if he thinks he can do it, and is willing to pay the fee. All this is rather like the man of whom Sam Weller spoke in Charles Dickens' Pickwick Papers. This man was asked if he could play the fiddle. He said he couldn't say. He had never tried.

By the way some people drive these days you would think they were very like that man. They don't really know whether they can drive or not, and so they try. And they are in danger of landing themselves and others in the ditch, the hospital or the morgue.

Surely there is nothing excessive in requiring those who wish to drive a car to prove that they are able to do it. Perhaps the result would be that more people who are driving cars will be able to drive them.

—*The Montreal Gazette,*
October 6, 1952

Flying Saucers, Chunks of Sputniks, and Radio-Active Fallout

Whirling sputniks which are not consumed by friction but come back to earth in the shape of hulking chunks are a hazard to man, and there ought to be a law – an international law – to control them. That is, future sputniks should be controlled to the point where they can be brought down safely. Andrew G. Haley, president of the International Astronautical Federation, general counsel of the American Rocket Society, told members of the Canadian Bar Association, meeting in Toronto, that with the prospect of 70 or 80 sputniks soon whirling about this earth, falling fragments will menace man.

Man has always been bombarded from the outside. For untold millions of years he has successfully dodged meteorites, lightning, and even large meteors. He is the victim of wind, storm and hail; yet he survives. At present he is confronted by three new hazards: flying saucers, chunks of sputniks, and radio-active fallout. Anyone else would be daunted and dive away in a cave, but not man.

Time and fortune have inured man to about everything that imagination can vision, everything except final annihilation, and even the current threat of this fails to affright him. We look at the shining trail of a sputnik and watch it pass into the far horizon; it never occurs to us that it would dare to fall on us. On someone else, maybe, but certainly not on us. We are made that way.

According to Mr. Haley a lump of sputnik metal can very well fall on any of us, anywhere, and it is only by good luck that Sputnik Three did not fall in the centre of a large city. If, however, we are to depend on international agreement over a gadget which has such military values, we may have to wait a long time.

—*The London Free Press*
September 15, 1958

217

Cabinet Makes Wise Decision on Avro Air Defence

Prime Minister John Diefenbaker and his cabinet have made a wise and courageous decision in cancelling plans for the $2 billion Avro Arrow jet fighter project. No other peacetime government has ever faced so complex and costly a question. As it is, the development of this supersonic fighter will have cost the Canadian taxpayers $403 million by next March for only 37 prototype planes.

While Mr. Diefenbaker said the Arrow project will be reviewed again in March, there is little doubt that this is simply giving the A.V. Roe Company a six-month tapering-off period. Canada has definitely moved into the missile era and we simply cannot afford a full complement of both manned fighters and missiles.

This decision was reached in the light of the best advice, and Canada is following the example set by both the United States and Great Britain. Certainly there will be layoffs in the aircraft and feeder industries, as there will be in Great Britain where 100,000 jobs will become redundant as a result of a sharp cutback in orders for fighter and bomber aircraft. The cabinet action is no reflection on the capabilities of the Arrow and the Canadian engineers who designed and built it, and it is to be hoped that these skills will not be lost to other phases of Canada's defence effort. But the Government has recognized that manned aircraft are obsolescent in the age of the missile. For one-third of the Arrow development cost we will get two Bomarc guided missile squadrons to guard against enemy aircraft.

No nation can afford to arm itself against every possible threat. All defence is a compromise between the militarily desirable and the economically feasible. Canada's defence is linked inextricably with that of the United States, which is arming itself with defensive and offensive missiles as quickly as these can be produced. Canada, to the extent it can afford, is trying to keep in step.

—*The London Free Press, September 25, 1958*

Trans-Canada Not Enough

The Trans-Canada Highway seems to be simply a matter of interpretation. Two official openings have been held in its honour, yet the premier of Newfoundland says it will take at least $50 million to complete the section of the highway through that province.

But whether the primary highway system indeed exists from Atlantic to Pacific at this time is begging the issue. It is possible to travel from one end of the Dominion to the other on excellent roads and the feat ranks alongside those which gave Canada two trans-continental railway systems.

But an excellent highway system itself is not enough. Irrevocably linked with good roads are the other conveniences which must be provided for the traveller and tourist.

In this respect, the government has been remiss throughout the Rockies, and especially over the Rogers Pass section of the Trans-Canada.

There is one stretch of 92 miles in which the motorist is provided with nothing in the way of refuelling or repair services.

Furthermore, no restaurant services are available. This is most disturbing, despite the fact that the first motel, restaurant and service station is promised for Glacier National Park by next summer.

There are many reports, too, of restaurants and cafes elsewhere along the highway being unable to cope with the influx of tourists, a situation which was easily predictable. Long queues for food and gasoline are hardly calculated to enchant the tourists, and it was largely for them that the highway through the Rogers Pass was built.

Facilities providing food, gasoline and shelter should have been encouraged to proceed in conjunction with the construction of the highway. There is no need for the route to become a commercial wonderland – in fact, this should be avoided at all costs, but at least a minimum of facilities should exist.

The travelling public has come to demand a certain standard of service.

If the government is to be in the road construction business, it should allow others to provide the necessary perimeter services.

—*The Calgary Herald,*
September 5, 1962

Walking Weather

We hope you have not forgotten the art of walking. Walking is a form of locomotion in which one limb is pushed forward and the foot set down, and immediately the other limb is propelled forward. This means that the body goes ahead in a reasonably steady motion.

It may be that the advocates of walking are crusading into a lost cause. Small cars and bicycles are on the increase, and we are informed that in populous cities and suburbs there are cars available on a commercial basis, known as taxis.

It would be good for all men to get away from the crowds and tensions of beehive living these blue-sky, white-cloud days, and find a woodland, hillside or upland ridge where one can walk in peace.

There is an art to walking for pleasure. Alone or with a companion – who does not think it is necessary to talk all the time – one can choose his own pace. There is time to inhale the crisp, clean air, smell the fragrance of drying grasses, pick a few checkerberries and explore the bark patterns of trees.

We are told that in other lands, walking is a favourite form of recreation. We hope that as we learn to live in a world of speed and tension, that walking will become more popular. For the man who learns to walk and harvest some of Nature's verities knows that the harvest he gathers adds meaning to his life.

—*The Saint John*
Telegraph Journal,
September 21, 1981

Vanishing Railways

Remember the small, soot-stained depot beside the railroad tracks at the edge of the village? Remember the old steam engine that pulled the accommodation with its two or three passenger cars and one baggage car?

It was just a branch line that ran from the city through the valley and among the hills, an artery that connected small towns and villages with the heart of a population centre.

Many Canadians remember the long-drawn, high-pitched lonesome-sounding whistle of the engine. Ole 57 came chugging along between hills, over trestles and built-up roadbed. Far down the line at Wilder's Crossing, the whistle blew, two long and two short.

In small grey depots men and boys waited for the train with its cream jugs, milk cans, egg cases and hen crates. The whistle of steam engines is part of the unfinished symphony of a great nation's growth. Branch lines spread in the wake of the great east-west rail connection. They ran through pine woodlands; they twisted in and out among the mountains; they snaked through the Maritimes. That far-carrying whistle floated over the plains, echoed among the hills, and spread through the evergreen flats.

Branch lines have virtually vanished. Branch lines with their trains and depots have gone over the horizon, and now a lot of passenger service seems destined to follow them into oblivion.

It would be good if once again a man could stand by the depot and watch Old 57 come around the bend with bell clanging, steam hissing and hear the clatter of metal as the brakes were applied. And part of the history of branch lines would be the resolutions of boys who have watched the train disappear up the track, and have vowed that some day they would be on that train, riding away to life's high adventures.

—*The Saint John Telegraph Journal,* *October 5, 1981*

17

Good Old Days of Flu, Cholera, and Hasty Burials

The Grip

In none of the previous visits of the mysterious and unwelcome visitor which for lack of a better name we call "la grippe," or Anglicize into "the grip," have its effects been quite so widespread or created quite so much consternation. In 1889, when the disease reappeared after a long interval of absence, it was regarded lightly enough until the devastation that followed in its wake began to be perceived. In 1890, the world shuddered when its reappearance was announced, and now in 1891-92, for the third time within three years, when it again holds us in its fatal grasp, medical men stand dazed and confounded before this arch enemy of human life.

Meantime it is doing havoc in every land. In England the heir to the throne has gone down before it, and men eminent in every walk of life, besides countless thousands of those whose troubles are mentioned only in a general way in the news that comes across the ocean, have had to battle with the dreaded scourge, too oft in vain.

The death rate in London is excessive, and in other parts of Great Britain it is alarmingly large. In Rome the grip has invad-

223

ed the College of Cardinals, with fatal results, and all over Upper Italy the population is suffering and yielding hundreds to the graveyards. Schools are closed and hospitals crowded. In France and Germany the disease is raging furiously. In Constantinople scarcely a house has been left unvisited. In Egypt the Khedive's life has been cut short. In Algeria the death rate is three times the normal. Everywhere in the old world it is the same melancholy story.

On this side of the Atlantic, the upper half of the continent at least is being devastated equally with Europe. The past Christmas was a green one, and the large amount of sickness then prevalent recalled the old saying that "a green Christmas makes a fat churchyard." It was never more truly exemplified. It was hoped, however, that with the disappearance of the unseasonable weather the sickness would disappear, but the frost and snow have come and the epidemic continues.

Children and the aged appear to be more susceptible than others to the disease, while women succumb more easily than men; at the same time the grip attacks people indiscriminately, regardless of age or sex.

The grip is no new disease. Physicians trace it back to the day of Hippocrates, and an epidemic among the Athenian army, while in Sicily (415 B.C.), is supposed to have been the grip. From that time to this it has been a frequent epidemic in various parts of the world. It has occasionally before occurred in both hemispheres at the same time, but more usually it appears successively at different places, being seen at some point or other for two or three years and then disappearing.

The most terrible feature of the malady is that it predisposes to pneumonia, from which, indeed, far more fatalities have occurred than from the grip itself, but when it leads to no worse disease it leaves very debilitating effects. There appears to be no specific remedy; none, at least, has been so far discovered. It is the most discussed subject of the day among physicians of all countries, but there is no agreement as to the best mode of treatment.

The British and German peoples appear to be the most active in devising measures against the grip. In Germany medical scientists are making vigorous search for the microbe organism to which they believe the grip is due, with small reward as yet for their labours. In England the disease has reached so acute a stage that it is now proposed that influenza shall be classed by Parliament with diphtheria, smallpox and such other maladies, and that the local authorities be required to treat it in a similar manner.

Meantime prevention is better than cure, and while it may not be possible to certainly ward off the grip, an attack may be made less likely and may be parried more successfully by an observance of the following suggestions of a famous New York physician, Dr. Cyrus Edson, suggestions which should be particularly followed by persons convalescing from other ailments, by those suffering from chronic diseases, and by old persons.

Wear warm clothing next to the person. Adopt a plain, nourishing diet and take your meals regularly. Avoid late hours. Keep indoors as much as possible, especially at night. Shun crowded places, public meetings, etc. When in the open air keep in motion. Avoid wetting the feet. On entering the house remove overcoat or wraps at once. Keep away from those suffering from the disease. In a word, avoid exposure and excess, adopt regular habits and live well. On the first symptom of the disease do not attempt to treat yourself, but send at once for a physician.

—*The Toronto Globe,*
January 16, 1892

Preventable Disease in Toronto

Now that the typhoid outbreak has been almost entirely stamped out for the time and the diphtheria scare is over, it may be of advantage to sit down and discover to what extent these preventable diseases have added to the rate of sickness and suffering in Toronto during the past few years.

And this is the more necessary because there is a disposition in certain quarters, in spite of the terrible lessons of the past year, to regard sanitary science as a good deal of a fad, to talk of the garbage crematory as a useless appendage, and to fight to the last ditch for the continuance of privy pits and kindred abominations in the city. Even a member of the Board of Health the other day had the hardihood to tell the medical health officer that his efforts to stamp out contagious and infectious diseases seemed only to foster them.

The fact is that so long as disease-breeding conditions exist in Toronto so long will disease flourish, whether the Local Board of Health employs many or few officers. Eminent scientists have not been slow to account for similar outbreaks to those through which Toronto has recently passed. The garbage dump has flourished elsewhere, the soil of other cities has been impregnated with the filth germs from pits similar to those in our city, and the result has been invariably a harvest of sickness and death.

A community can no more remain healthy under wrong and vicious conditions than can an individual. It is true that in a measure the outbreak may be accounted for by the digging out of cellars, the removal of soil and the levelling of obstructions consequent upon the great building operations of the past few years, while the cedar block pavements on our principal streets undoubtedly become breeding grounds of pestilence, retaining as they do all manner of *liquis excreta*. But, after all, the dumping of garbage and the retention of outside pits must be set down as the most probable causes of the outbreak which the Local Board of Health returns for the past five years show to have been the most serious.

The steady and alarming increase of over 150 percent in zymotic diseases during the past five years is a fact that cannot be explained upon any other theory that sanitary conditions in the city are exceedingly imperfect. Dr. Allen himself says that there is no other great civilised city with such a large and steady percentage of zymotic disease. The totals show that over 1 in 90 of the population suffered last year from this cause. From a purely mercenary point of view this should be stopped.

The money loss is enormous, not only by doctors', nurses' and undertakers' bills, but indirectly through the loss of labour on the part of breadwinners detained at home through sickness in their family. The members of the Board of Health show a disposition to let things drift instead of trying to get at the root of the trouble. We trust this course will not be persisted in.

The present is a far better time to extend the crematory system, and to make arrangements for the gradual extinction of out-door closets than will be offered next summer, when unless vigorous action is not taken we may look for a renewal of typhoid and diphtheria. They are no friends of Toronto who thoughtlessly stand in the way of sanitary reform, and brand as disloyal to the city's interest those who state the facts as shown by official records and demand the removal of the plague spots.

—*The Toronto Globe,*
February 24, 1892

Danger!

The city of Calgary is full of visitors and now that the snow has nearly gone many back yards and lanes are revealed in a filthy state, ready to breed disease as soon as warmed up by the increasing heat of the sun's rays.

Responsibility for the spread of disease will rest in two quarters: on the shoulders of private citizens and on the police and civic authorities. Private householders, hotel and boarding housekeepers will see that cleanliness is a duty they owe not only to the other occupants of their premises but to themselves. But in an important matter of this kind there must be a universal cleansing and the sanitary department should be taxed to the utmost during the next few weeks. Not to employ additional scavengers for a week or two would be a short sighted policy.

Calgary cannot afford at this time above all others to invite an epidemic. She has too much at stake. Thousands of people will be here this spring and summer. The eyes of the whole world are on us. It behooves our city fathers and officials to do even more than their duty during this month and we believe the public has sufficient confidence in them to be assured they will prove equal to their grave responsibilities.

—*The Calgary Daily*
Herald, April 5, 1898

Are People Buried Alive?

The Society of Medical Jurisprudence in New York asks the health board of that city to make such a thing as being buried alive impossible, and the health board had the matter under serious consideration at its meeting on last Wednesday. Every now and then comes up the question of premature burials, and it is thoroughly threshed over in medical journals as well as the newspapers, and when the timid are well frightened, and all kinds of tests are applied to prove that the mortal coil has actually been shuffled off, then the question is allowed to rest for a while, to be resurrected at some opportune moment.

The New York Society of Medical Jurisprudence has a committee on Apparent Death, and at one of its meetings the committee prepared some suggestions for altering the mortuary blank, in which it is suggested that "only authorized practitioners of medicine should decide whether a person is dead or not." The new death certificates are to be changed so as to "contain the declaration that the physician has personally examined the body." A further recommendation to the health board is a clincher in the way of proof, which might not be a bad thing for the medical fraternity in other places besides New York to adopt.

We further recommend that the chief signs of death be enumerated in the blank, and that the physician shall indicate the presence or absence of each with "Yes" or "No." The questions which we would suggest to ask would be:

Has the respiration stopped permanently? Has the pulsation of the heart stopped permanently? Do the dependent portions of the body show a purple discoloration? Is rigor mortis present? Are the corneas dull? Are the pupils dilated? Are there unmistakable signs of putrefaction?

As all sorts of tests are occasionally resorted to by anxious friends it is further suggested to "make it illegal to do anything to the body of the supposed dead which, if he were alive, would cause him pain or injure him before the certificate of death is signed by the physician." Objection is also made to "treating the supposed dead by exposing them to cold or injecting poisonous fluids into their veins before their death has been ascertained and certified to by the proper authority."

It goes without saying that in cases of epidemics of cholera and other contagious diseases there is danger that now and then the supposed dead is buried, as a precautionary measure, when life may not be extinct. During the cholera epidemic in Hamilton in 1854, when the death rate was as high as 80 and 90 in a day, it was often thought that some were buried who were only in a trance. The pall of death hung over the city, and whenever the disease entered a household the whole neighbourhood became excited and alarmed. Time was barely given for the body to cool off before it was encased in a coffin and hurried off to the cemetery.

As an illustration of the terror people had of the cholera, the city editor of the *Hamilton Banner* lost his head when the disease invaded his household. He was naturally a very excitable man and he had written so much about the prevailing epidemic that he thought of nothing else.

Day after day he wrote columns urging cleanliness in the streets and about the homes. The *Banner* office was then in the alley between King and King William streets, and the alley was, as it is now, so filthy that in the hot, rainy weather a stench arose from it enough to poison the atmosphere of the whole city.

One morning when he returned home from work – his labours on a morning paper keeping him up till near daylight – he found his wife suffering from what he feared was an attack of cholera. He became so excited that he lost his mental balance, and in his frenzy he ran off to an undertaker's and ordered a coffin for his wife, and then went to a hotel, which was on the corner of James and Main streets, drank a glass of brandy, went up to a room and in less than 24 hours his body was conveyed to the cemetery. As it afterward proved, his wife did not have the cholera and she was well within a few days.

There have been many devices for connecting graves with electric alarms and other contrivances, so that if the person interred should come to life help could be summoned, but there has been no authenticated cases where it was ever of any service. There is no doubt that people have apparently died and yet been only in a trance. The other day a mother in a city in the United States fell into a trance, and as she was apparently lifeless, preparations were made for her burial. She knew all that was passing about her, but she had not the power to give any sign that she was still living. Her daughter protested against the burial of her mother, as she looked so natural and showed no signs of discoloration. The funeral was postponed from day to day till finally the mother returned to life, and at last accounts gave promise of returning health. She told of her efforts to speak, and of her consciousness of every act of those who were about her. Probably the new plan suggested by the Society of Medical Jurisprudence may prove beneficial in such cases.

—*The Hamilton
Spectator, January 22, 1900*

Government Quarantine

It is unfair to this county and to other border counties that they should be called upon to bear all the expenses of a quarantine service. Recently the municipalities in this county have been put to a large expenditure in the measures that were found necessary in order to care for the persons who came into the country infected by the disease of smallpox.

All cases of smallpox treated in this county during the recent outbreak were of individuals who came from the state of Michigan or other states or were residents of the county who were infected by these persons. The outbreak of smallpox in Quebec about the same time was traced to persons who carried the disease to that province from the states.

The Dominion government maintains quarantine stations at Atlantic and Pacific ports where passengers coming to this country from foreign countries are inspected. There is no good reason why the government should not protect the people of Canada from infectious diseases by land as well as by sea.

The Dominion government should be asked to recoup this county for all its expenditure during the recent outbreak of smallpox and also make arrangements at Windsor and other border places for quarantine stations. It is to be hoped that our members will call the government's attention to this matter without delay.

—*The Windsor Evening
Record, April 21, 1900*

The Milk Supply

It is becoming increasingly evident that the patience of the Vancouver public has about reached its limit on the question of the milk supply. It is not an uncommon remark that pure milk is not to be obtained in this city, and while we think that is somewhat beyond the fact, it cannot be denied that much of the article which is distributed to consumers as milk is either highly adulterated or has been robbed of practically all its qualities as a food-stuff before it is given to the public.

It is also said that much of what is sold in Vancouver is made from a preparation which is brought in packages in the form of powder and to which water and other liquids are added for the purpose of giving it the appearance of milk. It is not at all unlikely that this charge may be made with absolute truth against many of those who profess to supply the public with the genuine article.

The fight for pure milk in Vancouver has been carried on for nearly 10 years now and really with little, if any success. At times vigorous protests on the part of the citizens have resulted in an improvement in the quality; but this has only been for a short period; as soon as the vigilance of the public was relaxed those among the milk vendors who have no desire to deal honestly or conscientiously with the citizens and who will not do so except under compulsion, went back to their old and fraudulent methods.

Those fraudulent methods are more in evidence today than they ever were before. They are so because the milk dealers who employ them are satisfied that no punishment will follow the sale of a fraudulent article. In fact, that is the state of affairs today in Vancouver.

The city has no power to punish milkmen for selling an inferior or adulterated article, or in fact for selling anything that looks like milk so long as it does not act as a quick poison to which the death of one drinking it can be directly traced. That deaths have occurred as a result of the use by the public of much of the stuff which is sold as milk in Vancouver there can be little doubt.

A great deal of what is distributed today will make an adult ill if he drinks it by the glass. What, then, must be its effect upon children, upon infants, whose only food is milk. Undoubtedly, much of the sickness and even of the mortality among infants, especially during the summer weather, must result from the impure milk given them as food.

It is essential, then, in the interest of the public, that this question should be dealt with promptly and effectually. Its discussion on Monday evening at the meeting of the central ratepayers' committee has once more introduced it to public consideration, and Mr. James Eadie, in pressing it upon the attention of the meeting, as he did, showed good public spirit.

Mr. Eadie has apparently gone into the question very thoroughly and understands what steps should be taken to bring about a reform in the milk supply. Certain changes in the law must be made and power must be given to the city by the federal parliament to make regulations for the sale of milk and to punish those vendors who do not comply with such regulations.

Of course, it has long been known that it was necessary for the city to secure such power, it has been known since Mr. Justice Clement, some years ago, reversed a finding against certain milkmen given by Magistrate Alexander. The action of Magistrate Alexander in inflicting a penalty upon dishonest milkmen was cordially approved by the public and would have remedied the abuse which was indulged in by the milk vendors, but the supreme court judge pointed out that without special authority from the Dominion parliament the city was unable to impose penalties.

Since that time, matters in regard to the sale of milk have been going from bad to worse. Dr. Underhill did, indeed, press for action by the city council, which would enable the city to regulate the milk supply, but the city council, as usual, ignored a matter so unimportant as the health of the community.

—*The Vancouver Sun,*
June 12, 1912

18

Here's to Better Health

Cleaner Paper Money

The public will welcome any action on the part of the Dominion Government designed to keep the paper currency of the country in a condition of reasonable cleanliness. That paper currency is a fertile disseminator of disease is beyond question.

It is impossible that this should not be the case when we consider through how many hands currency notes pass, and the time they usually continue in circulation before they are destroyed.

In this respect too, the Government bills do much greater damage than those issued by the banks. As they are of smaller denomination they circulate more freely, and are more exposed to contagious conditions.

No doubt the banks will be willing to go to the slight trouble, it will cost them, to return soiled Dominion notes to the treasury, and obtain new ones in exchange. The public should be educated, too, to insist on having clean and

crisp bills when doing business with the banks, and if they once get into the habit of refusing to put up with those which have long been in use the sanitary condition of the currency will soon be established.

When we consider the immense work performed by our one-dollar bills, and give attention to the absolute filthiness of most of those in circulation, it is difficult not to blame the government at Ottawa, for deciding, on what ground the public are at a loss to understand, not to coin Canadian silver dollars.

There are three good and sufficient reasons why the government should include silver dollars in the country's coinage: they are more sanitary than paper currency; they would drive out American money in favour of that of our own minting, and their use would assist materially in the development of one of the great natural resources of the Dominion.

—*The Vancouver Sun,*
May 13, 1912

State insurance

Under the provisions of national health insurance in Britain insured persons were paid $40,000,000 in sickness benefits in 1922, and $16,000,000 in disablement benefits. Over 6,000,000 persons received medical treatment, involving 44,000,000 attendances.

It is a dozen years since the national insurance bill was passed, and it has done much to achieve the primary object in view, namely, to secure to every man, whatever his position, a reasonable chance of obtaining the medical advice that is open to those who are better off.

There are other respects in which the measure has fallen short of expectations, notably in the reduction of sickness and disablement by reducing their preventable causes. The bill's provisions looking to that end have been virtually a dead letter.

The principle of state insurance is sound and its guarantee of adequate medical attendance to those in need of it means much to the nation. It means more efficiency in the workshop as well as less suffering in the home. In the matter of national insurance, Canada might well take example from the motherland.

—*The Toronto Evening*
Star, November 13, 1923

Smoking Ban

It is reassuring to know that Calgary school authorities have no intention of following their Edmonton counterparts in giving consideration to allowing students to smoke on school property.

Responsible citizens will concur with the viewpoint expressed by Mr. Glenn Holmes, chairman of the Calgary Public School Board, who describes the Edmonton moves as "a ridiculous situation."

Judging from a 1962 survey by Calgary's health department, smoking among senior and junior high school students is a serious enough problem without giving it further encouragement by allowing it on school property.

The 1962 survey showed that 46.4 percent of all boys and 33.1 percent of all girls in Calgary's senior high schools indulged in the habit. Furthermore, there was evidence that many students in the junior high grades also smoked.

In view of the evidence that smoking presents health hazards and that the majority of students who do smoke receive poor grades, it is only proper that the habit should be discouraged.

The move by some Edmonton authorities towards condoning this habit is one more sample of the type of adult permissiveness towards immature young people which our society could well do without.

While Calgary school officials are to be commended for retaining their rigid stand against student smoking on school property, their authority is limited. In the final analysis the main responsibility rests with the parents of these young people, and it appears that many parents are not exercising this responsibility in an effective manner and discouraging their children from taking up the smoking habit.

In addition, it is clear that the law prohibiting sale of tobacco to persons below a certain age is being flagrantly violated. The 1962 survey revealed that 56.7 percent of student smokers purchased their cigarettes at a store near their home. From this, it would seem that many retailers are only too willing to supply young people with tobacco, regardless of what the statutes might say. It is time this law was more vigorously applied.

—*The Calgary Herald,*
December 22, 1965

Saving Medicare

When medicare was introduced in Canada during the late 1960s, the great fear spread by its opponents was that it would lead to a massive and uncontrolled growth of public spending on health. The real danger was always the opposite – that governments, over the years, would tend to bleed money from health care to finance fresh new attempts to win the affection of the voters.

That, in fact, is what has happened. In the past decade, health costs have risen much faster in the United States, where free enterprise medicine is the rule, than in Canada, where governments are in control. And the result of this is that, in some provinces, the very foundations of medicare are in danger.

Doctors, dissatisfied with their incomes from provincial medicare schemes, have taken to billing their patients for extra payments on top of what the government insurance pays. And provincial governments, encouraged by new federal-provincial cost-sharing arrangements to chisel on medicare and spend the money elsewhere, are relatively indifferent to the fact that the extra billing can deny medical care to the very ones medicare was supposed to help most – families on low incomes.

Despite urgings from repentant Liberals, whose cost-sharing formula created the problem in the first place, it is no longer possible for the federal government simply to order the provinces to mend their ways. What Ottawa can do, and what the new government proposes to do, is subject the provinces to a degree of moral suasion by reminding them, clearly and publicly, of the original aims of medicare.

There is no better man to do that job than Emmett Hall, the retired supreme court justice whose report laid the foundations for national health insurance. Mr. Hall's original report was a little overloaded with the liberal pieties of the day but at least it got its priorities right. Some of our provincial governments – happily not that of Quebec – need a reminder.

—*The Montreal Star,*
September 19, 1979

236

E. Coli Tragedy was Preventable

Walkerton's horror turned to outrage yesterday.

The explosive allegations of Dr. Murray McQuigge, the area's medical officer of health, demand both action and answers.

McQuigge said local authorities knew a week ago that the town's water was contaminated but didn't tell the public.

Worse, for three days after they got the lab tests showing the water was unhealthy, they assured McQuigge the water system was safe and secure.

"We wasted two days looking for a food source of contamination when they could have told us right away it was in the water. And we could have told people right away not to drink the water," he said.

Finally – amid growing evidence, including a fine piece of detective work by Owen Sound pediatrician Kristen Hallett that pointed to deadly E. coli in the water – McQuigge ordered his own tests. When confronted with the results, local authorities confirmed that the water was contaminated.

They also revealed that the chlorination system operated only intermittently in the critical days after a storm on May 12.

The storm's heavy rains may have washed cattle manure containing the E. coli strain into the water system. No one knows yet.

It is beyond comprehension, however, that health officials would not be told immediately of the test. It may be criminally culpable. Certainly it opens town authorities to huge legal liabilities.

The excuses offered by Public Utilities Commission chair James Kieffer and Mayor Dave Thomson were unacceptable. They still haven't read the alarming lab report.

The Ontario Clean Water Agency has been called in. But everyone associated with the debacle is still in place.

How can people have confidence in them after what has happened? The province should remove the water system from the town's control – effectively a trusteeship – until it's known what happened and who did what.

The environment ministry, in fact, has an inquiry under way. But the ministry may have had its own role in this tragedy.

Until 1996, the environment and health ministries did 400,000 tests of local drinking water a year. This job was downloaded to towns like Walkerton and testing was privatized. Apparently, Walkerton had just started with a new lab – the previous one went out of business.

Did downloading and privatization put Walkerton and other towns at risk?

Environment ministry inspectors were also cut. Did having 60 fewer staff members to test drinking water, groundwater and hydrogeology also open a way to this tragedy?

Two years ago, farms were exempted from local by-laws and lawsuits for problems caused by the runoff of animal waste, chemicals or pesticides.

Did the removal of these legal sanctions lead to sloppy management of farm wastes that are the prime suspect in this tragedy.

Both former environmental commissioner Eva Ligeti and provincial auditor Erik Peters criticized the environment ministry's water management. Were problems fixed or did they play a role?

In brief, was Walkerton's tragedy purely the lethal offspring of local blunders and nature run amok? Or was it an inevitable, cumulative consequence or weakening the policies protecting Ontario's town water – and health and life itself?

We need an inquiry. We need to know how to protect every community from the nightmare Walkertown is going through.

—*The Toronto Star, May 26, 2000*

(*Editor's Note: More than 2,300 residents in Walkerton, a town of 5,000, were sickened by the tainted water. Seven died. A public inquiry, compensation awards and criminal convictions followed.*)

Toronto Can Curb SARS Damage

For Greater Toronto's 4.5 million people, the warning by the World Health Organization's Dr. David Heymann that there's "a great risk" of getting SARS here came as a body blow. It also flies in the face of facts. Toronto is safe to live in and safe to visit. This city should not be made a pariah.

Mayor Mel Lastman is understandably "shocked" and angry. Dr. Sheela Basrur, Toronto's chief medical officer of health, regards the warning as a "gross exaggeration." Dr. Donald Low, chief microbiologist at Mount Sinai Hospital, calls it "a bunch of bullshit," which seems about right.

Stringent, effective measures to contain SARS are in place. While 320 Canadians have probable or suspected cases, most have survived. Sixteen have died. The experts say the outbreak is not out of control.

So, rather than waste energy bemoaning the WHO's nervous-Nellie alarmism, Toronto officials should put their outrage to positive use by crafting a plan to cope with the long-term damage to the city's image and economy after this episode of severe acute respiratory syndrome is contained. And Lastman must have federal and provincial help.

Prime Minister Jean Chrétien must recognize that the Toronto region accounts for a fifth of the entire nation's economic output. Ontario Premier Ernie Eves worries about "tens of billions" in damages. Every Canadian has a stake in the city's well-being.

Hong Kong has just budgeted $2 billion to help businesses, health officials and residents cope. We can do the same.

In an emergency meeting today, Toronto Council should focus on the immediate human impact. That means working with Ottawa and Queen's Park to channel prompt and effective financial and social support to the hundreds of city residents who are in quarantine. People who comply deserve to know that they won't lose homes or go hungry by missing two weeks' pay. They must be able to call for help getting groceries, medical prescriptions and other necessities.

That done, the mayor should launch an immediate multi-million-dollar, long-term communications blitz to set the record straight on SARS, to counteract hysteria and to polish the city's battered image. He should take New York City after the 9/11 attacks as a model. We will need a solidly financed, forward-looking strategy to get our message out, to sell our merits and to attract visitors and investment when the worst is over.

This healing can begin at home. We need to mobilize Toronto's civic spirit to show the world that we're not afraid to be out at restaurants, cinemas, ball games, cultural events and the like. You may get depressed cheering the Jays, but you aren't likely to get SARS.

Let's show the world how scared we aren't.

—*The Toronto Star, April 24, 2003*

19

Sober Advice

Manitoba Prohibition

Premier Hugh John Macdonald has introduced his promised prohibitory liquor law with the Manitoba legislature. If adopted (of which there seems no doubt, as the government has a good majority), it will go into effect one year from its passage. When the proposed law goes into force no man except a druggist will be allowed to sell liquor. And the druggist himself will find himself curbed in handling intoxicants.

If a man is sick and produces a certificate from a doctor, the druggist will sell him spirituous drinks, but not unless he is under the physician's orders. If either a druggist or an ex-hotelkeeper or anyone else seeks to minister to an illegal thirst, the law will impose a fine of not less than $200 and not more than $1,000 for the first offence and imprisonment of not less than three months with hard labour without the option of a fine for the second breach. In framing this bill, the premier has been very careful not to impose restrictions on manufacturers and wholesalers who are protected by the Dominion laws of trade and commerce. The province will not interfere with them, but as the brewers and distillers will only be able to fill individual orders for drug stores the prohibitionists expect to see their doors closed in a very short time.

Even the consolation of giving free drinks and sending complimentary bottles or flasks to their friends will be denied these dealers. This prohibitory act also takes away the last hope of the tippler, for no man, when the Macdonald bill comes into operation, will be allowed to bring in bottles, flasks and casks from outside the province for private use. The measure is designed to be full and sweeping and to be all that the most ardent prohibitionist could desire.

Already the liquor men of the province have presented a petition asking for compensation for the money they have invested in the business. The amount of compensation is fixed at $2 million.

—*The Windsor Evening Record, June 4, 1900*

The "Art of Drinking"

With the virtual certainty of the comparatively near future yielding a lifting of certain restrictions at least upon consumption of liquor in the United States, they are beginning to get ready for the deluge. In this, "higher learning" is lending its good offices.

For instance, one Dr. William Muhlberg, a former member of the faculty of Harvard University, comes to bat with the suggestion that there should be immediate education of Americans in "the art of drinking."

"It is not too soon," he says, "to begin educating people who want to drink in the art of using alcoholic beverages. In fact, such education is a definite responsibility of all organizations interested in public health." Dr. Muhlberg, says the despatch, "believes that the amount of alcohol imbibed should be limited to one ounce a day, which, he says, corresponds to one quart of light beer, half a pint of light wine, or two ounces of

whisky or brandy."

Now that "higher education" is ready to help out the boys in the U.S. who may be expectantly awaiting the promised land of unstinted guzzling, the thought arises that it might go further than this gentleman suggests.

How about colleges and universities across the line setting up "chairs" in drinking as she ought to be drunk? How about a Professor of Hoisting on every faculty? How about a "C.L.D." degree (Correct Liquor Drinker) at the end of your name? How about raising a huge endowment to provide scholarships all across the land calculated to advance the proper method of drinking out of a bottle, without getting your tongue in the road or spilling the contents all over your chin or your vest?

And what will your old-time drinker, that denizen of frontier saloons, think of this seeming professor-medico's proposal? If he is still extant he will scoff at it, and the shades of those worthies who have passed on will rise to rebuke it with a breath that may still reek to heaven. The acid test of manhood in these relics of yesteryear was a dozen stiff drinks on end without batting an eyelash and then drinking your mate under the table. Those fellows didn't have to be "larned" about drinking.

—*The Regina Leader,*
December 10, 1932

Penalties for Drug Peddlers

Following recent exposures of widespread use of habit-forming drugs by teenagers in some of the larger cities in the United States many persons in that country are advocating the death penalty for persons convicted of peddling or giving dope to minors.

While few Canadians would agree with any such suggestion one cannot escape the feeling that punishment for this lowest type of criminal – no matter whether he sells to minors or adults – should be much more severe than that usually meted out in our courts. One or two years in jail for an offender of this kind is hardly likely to deter racketeers from engaging in the lucrative but deadly traffic.

There would seem to be convincing evidence that U.S. dope rings are attempting to expand their operations to include Canada. In recent weeks arrests of peddlers have been made in Vancouver, Toronto and Montreal and a tie-up between those charged and operators south of the border has been alleged. Sentences of those convicted in Canada, therefore, should be severe enough to convince distributors that this is a poor country in which to attempt to get rich at the expense of unfortunate addicts.

Fortunately the RCMP assisted by police forces of Canadian cities have to date been successful in quickly rounding up peddlers and there has been no increase in the number of addicts in this country; indeed there has been a steady decrease for the last 20 years.

But it is quite probable there will be more and more attempts at invasion by U.S. dope racketeers as the drive against them in their own country gains momentum. One sure way to cut down on their activities here is to put those caught out of circulation for a long period.

—*The Winnipeg Tribune,*
September 3, 1951

Who Poisoned the Highball?

The findings of a group of New England doctors about what causes hangovers aren't exactly new. Most drinkers of alcohol, steady or occasional, probably were aware that the purer the alcohol the milder the hangover.

They may not have been able to put names to the gremlins which do the damage – now identified as "congeners" such as acids, esters, fusel oil and the like. Knowing their names won't make the morning-after headaches any better unless somebody is prepared to do something about it.

Maybe some government should pass a law making it unlawful to sell alcohol in any drinkable form that contains more than a certain minimum percentage of these congeners. But somebody will object to this suggestion on the ground that it would be a law for the rich and against the poor. For the better grades of alcoholic drinks cost like the dickens, while the impurer ones are the poor man's poison.

But if the government would take a smaller rake-off on the demon alcohol it might put better quality alcohol within the reach of all of us.

But again it will be objected – this time by the good people with the urge to reform their wayward brothers – that making liquor cheaper and better would promote sin. These people would be all for putting more esters and things into the liquor, arguing that the awfuller the hangover the more likelihood of true repentance. And anyway, tosspots deserve the awfullest kind of punishment.

But if there's any moral point in this business, we think the provincial governments ought to act. After all, they sell the stuff and their customers have a right to protection from impure potations.

If the provinces won't act, isn't there a federal pure food law? We'd like a legal opinion as to whether whisky merits rating as a food.

—*The Vancouver Sun,*
May 3, 1955

The Spirit is Fine, but the Law Won't Work

Although it is probably true that some individuals have used lysergic acid diethylamide (LSD) without suffering apparent ill effect, there is growing medical evidence that the hallucinatory drug can cause serious and injurious reactions. Panic, fear, homicidal and suicidal urges have been observed. We are told that LSD-induced psychosis are on the increase.

When known dangers such as these are associated with evidence of increased use of LSD in Canada, particularly among young people, it is probably to be expected that some form of legislative response will follow, aimed at discouraging use of the drug, cutting off the supply, and registering social disapproval.

The bill which was given first reading in the Senate on Tuesday night seems likely to score a direct hit only on the last of these objectives. It proposes that persons trafficking in the drug will face prison terms of up to 10 years. Possession of the drug would draw lighter penalties – a fine of up to $1,000 and up to six months' imprisonment on a first offence – but the onus would be on the person accused to show that possession was not for the purposes of trafficking. (This guilty-until-you-prove-you-are-innocent aspect of the bill will surely not survive the debate.)

The provinces have all welcomed the bill, but one suspects they were merely saluting the spirit of the contents, acknowledging that "something has to be done about LSD," rather than hailing measures they thought might work. It is difficult to believe that they seriously regard this as even the beginning of the end of the problem.

Canadian lawmakers are inclined to think that any and every situation can be dealt with by a law which provides heavy penalties for those who offend. This is a kind of hallucination that is not induced by drugs but appears nevertheless to be addictive, and it is much in evidence in the LSD bill.

Many doubts arise about the manner in which its measures would be enforced and the situation is further complicated by the existence of a number of plants or other commodities, innocently grown, perhaps, but capable of yielding drugs of the LSD type. This, of course, is possession without trafficking — but could you prove it?

The principal weakness, however, is the fallacy that outlawing LSD (it is, incidentally, already illegal to traffic in the drug) and penalizing the users will eliminate the problem. If the principle of this argument were sound we would long ago have seen the last of that other non-addictive drug, marijuana. Instead, arrests, seizures of supplies, and convictions occur with great regularity. The use of marijuana continues.

Governments cannot legislate out of existence something that people are interested in using or which excites their curiosity. Many people (not all of them young) take delight in kicking the Establishment, and, for some, the proposed laws against LSD will make its use almost irresistible. The imposition of heavy penalties is also likely to make it more profitable to traffic in the drug than it now is.

When these stimulants are weighed against the deterrent effect of fines and imprisonment, the bill seems to offer little to comfort those who are alarmed at the popularity of LSD. The next logical step would seem to be intensive education of young people to the dangers inherent in the use of the drug.

Considering the progress we've made in persuading people to give up tobacco, which will kill a good many of those who persist in its use, we'd better be looking for a third phase in our anti-LSD program. We're bound to need it.

—*The Globe and Mail,*
April 22, 1967

Prescription for Alcoholism

Alcohol is one of the most potent killers we have in Canada. That's the belief of Canadian doctors, as expressed at the Canadian Medical Association's annual meeting. They want something done about it.

Alcohol is a killer. It kills directly, through a variety of breakdowns of physical health. It kills indirectly; the majority of highway fatalities are blamed on alcohol-related circumstances. Alcohol destroys our social structure through loss of jobs, by breaking up families.

Doctors want the federal government to establish a royal commission to study drinking habits and associated health and social problems. The CMA says that Ottawa gets $2 billion a year in tax revenue from the sale of alcohol, but spends only a small fraction of that amount in helping alcoholics.

It is a national problem. And New Brunswick is very much a part of that national problem. For example, the provincial budget shows that the New Brunswick Liquor Corporation will have profits of $55,550,000 for the 1981-82 year. Less than ten percent of this is put into the treatment of alcoholics and in education programs.

A start on dealing with the alcoholism problem in the province has been made by the Alcoholism and Drug Dependency Commission under its chairman, Dr. G. Everett Chalmers.

The commission has treatment and rehabilitation centres at Ridgewood in Saint John, Lonewater Farm in Westfield, Fredericton, Newcastle, Campbellton, Bathurst, Moncton, Tracadie and Edmundston. It has about 70 detoxification beds and about the same number of rehabilitation beds.

The fact remains, however, that the amount of money allotted to the commission – $4.2 million this year – is a relatively small portion of the more than $55 million the government expects to make from liquor sales. The alcoholism commission could do more to salvage lives being destroyed through alcohol if it received a greater share of liquor profits.

A great many studies have already been made into the problems of alcoholism. Whether, as the doctors suggest, another study is needed may be debatable. What is irrefutable is that government action is needed.

Governments should heed the concern of doctors. For they are the ones who must cope first-hand with alcoholics, the break-down of health, the repairing – when possible – of bodies shattered and crushed in highway accidents.

—The Saint John Telegraph Journal, September 9, 1981

Transplants without Prejudice

Should an alcoholic be eligible to receive a liver transplant? Who will decide, and on what basis?

Medical students at the University of Western Ontario rcently tackled the issue of transplant ethics under the tutorage of Dr. Calvin R. Stiller, a renowned transplant physician at University Hospital in London, Ont.

In one hypothetical case, Stiller describes a candidate for a liver transplant, a 49-year-old father of two who has been active in community work but has lost his job because of drinking. He's now stopped drinking, but is near death and needs a liver transplant.

Should he get one?

The medical students say no, he shouldn't, because his cirrhotic liver is a self-inflicted disease.

In a second hypothetical case, Stiller describes a 59-year-old business executive, father of three, community leader, an overweight chain smoker, who has a family history of heart disease and often forgets to take pills for high blood pressure. Now, he needs a heart transplant.

Should he get one?

The medical students say he should.

In these two hypothetical cases, Stiller is quick to point out the inconsistency of their judgment.

He further surprises his students by telling them that an alcoholic liver transplant patient is more likely to reject a new liver than destroy it from drinking.

Survival rates for alcoholic liver transplant recipients, ruling out rejection, are about the same as transplants for other liver disorders. Most can live another 13 to 20 years if they give up drinking.

As it is, Stiller asks alcoholic liver transplant patients to stop drinking before he proceeds. Even so, he estimates 10 percent of recipients resume drinking afterwards, but points out this rate of recidivism is lower than for other alcoholism treatments.

Now that transplants are therapeutic, rather than experimental treatments, cost is not the prime issue. A liver transplant at University Hospital costs $83,000, or about the same as it costs to care for a patient dying of a cirrhotic liver.

As it is, alcoholics make up less than 10 percent of liver transplant recipients, usually because the booze has ravaged their bodies in other ways, making them unlikely candidates.

But should they be refused because of the social biases of a transplant surgeon as was the case with Western medical students? The answer is no.

—The Toronto Star, May 27, 1990

Decriminalize Marijuana

Canada's next prime minister will be an admitted marijuana user – a violator of the Narcotic Control Act.

Both leading candidates to succeed Brian Mulroney have confessed to smoking dope.

And unlike U.S. President Bill Clinton, Kim Campbell and Jean Charest have confessed to inhaling it, too – and getting away with it.

But half a million Canadians haven't been so lucky. They've been photographed, fingerprinted and dragged to court like common criminals for possession of pot.

And many of them have been stuck with a criminal record that can severely restrict their ability to travel, to get into professions and to find, or keep, their jobs.

That's too high a price to pay in the case of a casual smoker or of a teenager who lights up a joint to satisfy the urge of curiosity – just as previous generations sneaked behind the barn for an illicit taste of whisky.

The widely ignored prohibition

also creates disrespect for the law, diverts police from more serious tasks and undermines their morale.

Antonio Lamer, now chief justice of Canada, was well aware of this inappropriate application of the criminal law.

As chair of the Law Reform Commission of Canada, he said, way back in 1977: "Thousands of Canadians are being labelled as criminals in our courts when it is hard to find anyone involved in these charades – and this includes the arresting officer and sometimes the judge – who feel they are dealing with criminals in any rational sense."

Former RCMP commissioner Robert Simmonds also questioned the "very, very harsh" penalties for possession.

While still in office, he suggested that being caught with a marijuana cigarette should be no more serious than being nabbed with an open bottle of beer in public.

It's far better to educate the public, particularly youth, about the danger of drug abuse – the same way we teach people about tobacco and alcohol – than to invoke the heavy hammer of the criminal law.

Having had the courage to bring their own use of marijuana out of the closet, Campbell or Charest will be in a good position to save others from the harsh consequences of the application of the law.

They should point the way to a new law, making possession of a small quantity of marijuana for personal use no concern of the criminal courts. If society wants to impose a penalty, a fine – like a traffic ticket – would do.

—*The Toronto Star, April 18, 1993*

Roadside Checks Still Have Their Place

Peterborough District Ontario Provincial Police statistics shatter any and all illusions about the value of Reduce Impaired Driving Everywhere (RIDE) programs. They show a shocking, 130-percent rise in the number of drunk-driving charges laid this year, compared to 1993. That's ample proof the program needs to stay and, indeed, be beefed up.

The RIDE program always looks ripe to the cost-cutters. It uses a lot of police officers, annoys innocent motorists, and can make police look like spoil-sports. Any police officer who's had to clean up after a traffic death involving alcohol or had to tell a family it's lost a spouse or child to a drunk driver knows better. And so should the taxpayers.

The RIDE program reminds sober drivers not to take that extra drink. It reminds groups to designate a driver who'll stick to tea, coffee, juice or soft drinks and get them all home safely. And it signals society's continuing disdain for those who do drink and drive.

District OPP officials are not sure what's happened this holiday season.

They do know they laid 76 charges for impaired driving in the four weeks leading up to Christmas, compared to 33 charges in the same period last year. They also know they issued 169 12-hour suspensions to drivers who scored a warning on roadside breathalyser machines. The figures for last year's holiday season was 91.

More cars were stopped across Ontario – but only eight percent more than last year. The local increase also far exceeds the provincial average of 29 percent more charges this year than last.

This year's results may be an aberration. They may signal more problem drinkers on the road. They may reveal more people using alcohol as an antidote to pain, be it financial or personal. Time will tell.

In the meantime, OPP officials should start planning now to beef up the district RIDE program in the summer months, when fine weather puts vacationers in the party mood. City police should also be reviewing their plans for RIDE.

Three charges of impaired driving were laid inside city limits this holiday season, compared to none in 1993. That seems like slim pickings, especially when city police stopped 7,000 cars in 1993 and more than 9,500 this holiday season. But every life saved is precious and every injury spared worthwhile. Balance the cost of one RIDE shift against the cost of caring for major injuries and RIDE looks like an even greater bargain.

Of course, RIDE is only one facet of the campaign to end drinking and driving. But so long as some drivers lack common sense, it's one of the most effective means available.

—*The Peterborough Examiner, January 3, 1995*

20

Getting Close to Home

The Latest in Red Tape

This is the tale of a waterpipe, a citizen and an exhibition of red tape at the City Hall. The citizen, a man who pays his taxes with regularity and liberality, has, as all good people have, a waterpipe in his domicile, and as occasionally happens in all households, a burst occurred in his pipe.

The citizen hastened away to the waterworks office and asked that the water be turned off, and the obliging and ever-willing clerks referred him to the Works Department. In this latter office, the similarly obliging and ever-willing clerks sent him back to the Waterworks office; the other department was responsible, they told him, and would be glad to see to it. In fact, the willingness of the officials was most apparent – a willingness to let some other department do the work. They were always overjoyed to help a citizen with a grievance – by referring him elsewhere.

The citizen spent just ONE WEEK going from one department to the other and extending urgent if not cordial, invitations to officials to visit his residence and apply a key to the pipes beneath the sidewalk, but no one at City Hall appeared in any way anxious to become his guest for even the few moments necessitated by the work.

Then a woman appeared on the scene, an angry woman, resident next door to the hapless citizen. The water which had flowed all week was getting into her cellar and she did not like it. Possibly she is a New Woman, for she achieved greater success in half an hour than the man had obtained

253

in a week. She told the officials she would not leave the office until a man was sent to turn off the water. He was sent , and he did the work in two minutes.

During that week of delay the citizen's household had no water, could not use their closet, and had to call on neighbours. A quantity of furniture stores in the lower part of the house had to be removed and stored elsewhere at considerable expense, and damage was done to the house. The cause of it all was the official nonsense at the City Hall, which seems to ever relieve each department of responsibility and load it on another, no matter which.

This incident affords an opportunity for a movement to abolish red tape at civic headquarters, and the sooner our people who are so heavily taxed are relieved of the annoyance which was piled so heavily on this one citizen is removed, the better for all concerned.

—*The Toronto Evening Star, July 3, 1895*

A Busy City

Calgary just now is a very busy town. Every train brings in crowds of people. The hotels are overflowing. The sidewalks of Stephen avenue will soon need renewing. The traffic is increasing daily.

The new comers are mainly composed of two classes: Klondikers and new settlers. The immigration people say this will be a record year for new settlement in Alberta. They are coming from all parts, principally Great Britain and the United States. There is a distinct improvement in the character of this year's immigration so far. They are a moneyed class and most of them practical men accustomed to work.

Eighteen-ninety-eight will be Alberta's banner year.

—*The Calgary Daily Herald, April 4, 1898*

Write It, Alberta

The use of both "Alberta" and "N.W.T." as part of the address of people living in Alberta is extremely confusing to outsiders. There ought to be uniformity in the matter.

The Herald favours using the full word "Alberta" after the name of the post office. There is nothing characteristic about "N.W.T." and when spelled out it has a decidedly forbidding effect. The contraction "Alba." is likely to be taken for Alabama, especially by postmasters in the United States.

We do not know that there is much to be said against the use of "Alta.," but for the sake of uniformity and safety we might as well put in the extra three letters. Alberta is a euphonious name and the district is one to be proud of. The more the word is used the better will the future province become known.

—*The Calgary Daily Herald, April 23, 1898*

Hardships of the Hawker's By-Law

In the passing of the new Hawker's and Peddler's by-law, the Windsor council in their zeal has unwittingly imposed a serious hardship on a class who can ill endure it.

No doubt the aldermen, when framing that bylaw, had in view the foxy banana man, who, by passing his licence around, beats the city at every opportunity, but the grimy son of Italy is not the only peddler who pushes a cart.

There are a few persons in the city who eke out a meagre and precarious livelihood by growing garden truck, and carrying it from door to door. How will these unfortunates raise the necessary 10 dollars for a licence? Probably they do not net 10 dollars' profit in the whole season. These persons are not aliens but citizens with a clear claim on the protection of their representatives.

Some modification of the terms of the by-law seems in order to relieve this class from a burden which they are not able to bear.

—*The Windsor Evening Record, June 15, 1900*

255

A Mayor's Manners

This is a free country. Mr. James Simpson is entitled to talk. As Mr. James Simpson he is entitled to talk as much as foolishly as may be Mr. James Simpson's habit. But Mr. Simpson might be reminded that a Chief Magistrate of Toronto should not indulge in personal habits that impair the dignity of his office.

In plainer words, Mayor Simpson is within his rights as well as his capacities when he makes himself look cheap; he is not within his rights when he makes Toronto look cheap. The Mayoralty of Toronto is not a place for the display of tawdry witticisms and adolescent rudeness.

That Mayor Wilton of Hamilton should return Mayor Simpson's regrettable discourtesy in the same small change of antique wit was natural. That he returned rather more change than he got will be found small cause for lamentation in Toronto or elsewhere. When a Mayor of a great city so far forgets his Mayoral manners as to refer to the Mayor of a neighbour city as the "Toonerville trolley office-holder of a town-pump municipality" he deserves what he gets in the way of repartee.

Mr. Simpson got it plenty. It is the one consolation of humiliated citizens of Toronto. "Half-balanced" must appeal to many of them as an apt and just definition of their Chief Magistrate's state of mind.

N.B. – Mayor Simpson having stopped talking for a moment, tired city dwellers might improve the fleeting silence by studying one sentence in an official communication from Queen's Park to Toronto City Hall. The sentence is from the Provincial Government's relief-cut order. It reads:

"The relief lists must be purged of all employable persons for whom work is available."

Those are the words: "for whom work is available." Relief payments to all "employable" single men are the payments that the provincial government is stopping on the first of August. That is the sum of the notification received by Mayor Simpson last Saturday. That is the island of fact wherefrom Mr. Simpson launched away upon his floods of tosh.

—*The Toronto Globe,*
July 30, 1935

Why was the Home Closed?

Trauma, tension – and an air of mystery – surround the precipitate closing of a privately-run nursing home in central New Brunswick. In a dramatic move a week ago, the provincial Health Department ordered immediate closure of the Bethel Nursing Home at Mill Cove, on the shores of Grand Lake.

Specific reasons for the closing of the nursing home have not been made public.

When the province closed the home, it cited safety and well-being of the one-hundred patients, who were transported to hospitals in Fredericton and Oromocto. And the operators of the home were subsequently given a list of conditions under which it could be re-opened.

But just why was the Bethel Nursing Home closed?

The government says it was closed because of conditions relating to nursing care and financial and administrative aspects of the operation. It says a copy of a consultant's report dealing with this situation was shown to the operators of the home – but not given to them.

What did the report say?

How were the conditions at the Bethel Home different from conditions in other nursing homes? What were the concerns which prompted the govern-ment to move in and order the home closed?

Given the upset of the patients and the concern of their families and the publicity generated by the whole situation, it is more than a private matter. So why did the government order this home closed?

Were the conditions which brought about the closure related in any way to the strike launched by some of the home staff who were members of CUPE? If that is the case, would the government act in the same manner if there were a strike at another nursing home? Is it now possible for a striking union to create, or help create, a situation under which the government will close down a nursing home?

There has been no evidence that this is actually the case. But what is the public to believe? If the government action was justified in terms of health care standards, why not make the report public?

A spokesman for the home has charged that the forced closure was a political move, designed to curry favour with the union and gain votes in the next provincial election. Is that charge to go unanswered? It should not.

Is there any reason for this secrecy?

The government has set standards for nursing home care and it is important that they be met. But in a high-profile case like this, where a nursing home was abruptly closed in the middle of a bitter strike, there appears to be ample reason for making the report public. Otherwise, the public is left to draw its own conclusion on the basis of skimpy details and inadequate information.

—The Saint John Telegraph Journal, September 16, 1981

Heart of a City

There is a sadness at coming to the end of any useful era in this life. And that sadness is being manifested in Saint John as some long-established family businesses close their doors.

Kennedy's Shoe Store is no longer that family-owned business. Jack's Clothing Store, opened in the Depression year of 1935 and expanded and improved through the years, is going out of business. And Scovil Brothers Limited – where generations of boys and men bought their first peak caps and first long pants, where generations of girls and women went to be outfitted for their first parties – is calling it quits. Scovil's dates back to 1889, and its Oak Hall designation was synonymous with clothing fashions for generations.

In all these recent closures, the proprietors cite high interest rates, the cost of financing inventory, the competition of chains and the lure of the malls, as factors. The high interest rates in particular are a real concern and the Saint John closings are an indication of the effect current monetary policies are having on small businessmen. Merchants will be looking for some signs of relief as the current session of

Parliament gets ready to consider a new budget.

But it must be understood that Saint John's uptown is by no means a dying place. In fact, there is a resurgence going on, with the Brunswick Square development, the new Delta Hotel, the parking garage, the refurbishing of the Trinity-Royal development area, the opening of new businesses on Prince William Street, and steel going up on the massive Market Square development.

And there are family business-es and independent stores which are not only surviving, but thriving in the uptown – Calps Limited, currently marking its 48th birthday, Jack Calp's, Bustin's Furniture, Paterson Ltd., Ideal Stores, Cowie's Jewelery, to name a few.

But the thrust of federal and local policies must be to recognize that there are problems. And policies and practices must be designed to meet these problems and make our uptown thrive.

—The Saint John
Telegraph Journal,
September 16, 1981

Disclosure Rules

Their discomfort at the new provincial disclosure rules was expected. But listing their financial holdings and debts for public viewing won't hurt any municipal politician.

The new rules come into force April 15, when citizens can ask city hall officials to see their mayor's and aldermen's financial statements.

There will be media reports on what the statements disclose but those expecting juicy tidbits will be disappointed. The province has asked only for a general statement of assets and liabilities, not a detailed list of every item, includ-ing the month's credit care purchases. And that is entirely appropriate, given the scope of municipal government today. In many municipalities, elected office has become a fulltime occupation.

Of course, the rules were set to deal with fallout from a few specific cases, none of them in Peterborough. But all municipalities should be treated the same.

Some local aldermen have reservations. Alderman Paul Ayotte worries about nosy people snooping into his personal business. There will be some. But who cares if a few people know that Alderman Y has a mortgage and Alderman Z owns a cottage? Most forms will reveal perfectly ordinary people with perfectly ordinary assets and liabilities. Better facts on file than gossip in the streets.

Ayotte's idea of a provincial commissioner ruling on each request or charging $5 or $10 a peek is more bother than it's worth. Alderman Dean Wasson thinks only big city-politicians have hidden agendas and that Peterborough is small enough for everyone to know their city council members' business. He is wrong on both counts.

There are valid concerns about disclosure deterring some people from seeking office. But the public spotlight is already bright enough to discourage many. Public service also demands huge chunks of time many otherwise excellent candidates refuse to give up. Disclosure won't deter candidates seeking office because of a single issue or because they really believe they have something to contribute. And who can complain when they know the rules before the run for office?

No law is complete without some means of enforcement. Unfortunately, the province decided the new disclosure rules needed a local disclosure commissioner, with all the expensive trappings that go with it. Surely some other independent official could have been found should the need ever arise. Why must taxpayers always console themselves with the fact the good outweighs the bad?

—*The Peterborough Examiner, January 9, 1995*

21
Taking a Stand

An Asylum for Eastern Harlots?

It is to be lamented that the vice of prostitution is sullying so deeply the first page of Calgary's history. Already we find the advent of the harlot in town. It may be difficult to stop them from coming here, but it certainly is the duty of the police to stop them from plying their nefarious ways of living in our very midst.

We find the lesser offences of drinking, gambling, etc. crushed by the police with remarkable zeal, yet this greater vice to which we allude, can stalk about our town at noon-day, proclaim to the public its devilish purposes, and yet be winked at by the authorities.

If the den of iniquity which has recently flaunted its sign on Section 15 is not at once swept out of town by the broom of public duty, it will be due to the fact that the authorities are recreant to their trust. If the den to which we refer is allowed to continue its operations, it is merely a question of a few weeks before we have in our midst an exodus from the east of a small army of those characters.

The people of Calgary are asking themselves the question if the police are going to allow this promising town to become the asylum for the harlots and prostitutes of the east.

—*The Calgary Herald,*
March 5, 1884

Out of Joint

It is a singular fact in everyday life that the average man believes himself capable of running some other man's business better than the man who is running it. Nobody is just in the position that he fancies himself endowed by nature to fill. The right man is never in the right place. Verily it is a queer world.

The man has yet to be discovered who is not fully qualified to run a newspaper better than the editor, and natural born hotel keepers are to be found in every town by hundreds. Bank managers know nothing about banking. The men who know exactly how a bank should be run never have so much as a post office savings account. You can meet them in any bar.

If they had their way bank failures would be unknown and five dollar bills would be more plentiful than mosquitoes. In fact things would fairly hum, and such trifles as ratios, sinking funds and reserves would cut no ice at all. But short sighted bank directors continue to overlook these heaven born financiers and consequently we must groan in slavery and envy the other fellow's fat bank account.

Then take politics or law; how often the wrong man gets a seat in parliament. Any half dozen men who have had three Scotch whiskies apiece can tell just how to run that particular department, or amend a bill, or give judgment on a difficult case that the judges have not sense enough to see through.

There is the other fellow drawing the salary and here are six men that know more than he does and telling people all about it, without any salary at all! No wonder Hamlet pronounced the times out of joint a thousand years ago. They are still out.

But it is when we come to railways and war that the exasperating injustice of the whole thing is laid bare. There is not a brakeman, or a conductor, or a telegraph operator, to say nothing of the section hands, who could not run the old road 10 times better than the superintendent or the manager, or even the president. At the same time, however, they do not know as much about running the road as the country merchants, the Patrons of Industry, or the drummer who travels on a reduced ticket.

There was never a man in these walks of life who did not understand railway management from Dan to Beersheba. It is safe to say that in the smoke of a Pullman almost any day in the week enough railway wisdom can be found running to waste to manage the whole C.P.R. with the Grand Trunk thrown in.

But numerous as they are, the men who can run railways are not a patch on those who could conduct a war. The home of great military geniuses is the United States. They are not hampered by modesty. We were informed on the train the other day, by a blustering Yankee from Seattle, that "every person in the United States of America is a general."

It seems positively cruel that only one or two of them can be appointed to positions of supreme command. It makes a man fairly wild to think that there are thousands of men driving beer wagons, pushing whiskers, and writing on yellow journals, who could run armies and navies, yet they are given the cold shoulder.

In fact all over this disjointed world square men are in round holes. The real bank managers are sawing wood; men of the greatest legal ability are digging post holes or punching steers; expert railway superintendents are measuring calico, weighing sugar, or wasting their time on telegraphic tickers; great editorial writers are driving mules, or leaning against a bar, and the men who ought to be in jail are holding some of the fattest jobs in the country.

What a queer world it is.

—*The Calgary Daily Herald, May 28, 1898*

Ugly Toronto

If a Canadian had said it he would be accused of jealousy or spite. But take it from a Dutch-born painter and resident of Toronto, Frank De Bruun Valerius, Toronto is "one of the ugliest cities in the world… a unique monstrosity."

Too true. Canada's second city lacks the Old World charm of Quebec City, the cosmopolitan air of Montreal, the panorama of mountains and harbour that surrounds Vancouver. Toronto is, in truth, just a small town grown enormously large without taking on the aspect of a metropolis. Luckily for the traveller, a splendid four-lane highway bypasses the entire city.

—The London Free Press, September 9, 1958

End the Sunday Sham

Attorney-General Gordon Conant's statement at Oshawa on the so-called blue laws is a refreshing pronouncement, lifting the veil from the sham surrounding this long outmoded legislation.

To be enforceable, a law must impress the public as sensible at least. The laws governing Sunday conduct are so far behind public opinion that they have become "more honoured in the breach than in the observance."

Were literal execution of them attempted it would make a joke of the authorities. The fact that they are on the statute books tends to breed disrespect for all law. Since they have fallen into disuse in some respects and their violation is generally ignored, they ought to be amended to conform with modern conditions and thought.

The Sunday golfer could be haled into court and fined, but the most ardent advocate of Sunday observance would hesitate to raid the country clubs and arrest an army of "first citizens." The family picnic party, as the attorney-general points out, violates the law in many ways, yet the custom of Sunday afternoon outings in the car is so common that the legal aspects are not considered. Strangely, however, the citizen without a car or country club privileges may be "caught" for violations no more serious when a wave of law enforcement strikes.

If the police observed their obligations strictly, they would padlock the bathing beaches and halt numerous other pastimes which have become commonplace, but they would encounter firm public opinion.

Probably some citizens living in the past believe the old ways will return. They cling to the hope, at least. In the meantime the law pretends they never departed, although it has recognized the change in a thousand other ways.

The absurdity ought to be removed by appropriate parliamentary action. Sane and practical legislation, applicable alike to all classes of citizens, conforming with modern conditions, can be enforced. Let us rid ourselves of legalized deception and come out into the open.

—The Globe and Mail,
December 1, 1938

Sinners All

Nobody talks back to a preacher in the pulpit; that is, while he is preaching.

And there is danger in this, more for the preacher than for his congregation, because it sometimes makes him believe that his words are divinely revealed.

Social Credit leader Robert Thompson fell into this trap when he told a Toronto church audience that God prefers a Communist to a neutralist Christian.

Many would agree that a Christian should be positive in his attitude; but the way Mr. Thompson puts the matter, it would appear that he has a direct line of communication to the heavenly seat.

One of the primary Christian principles is humility, the realization that God is not always on our side.

A lady during the American Civil War said to Abraham Lincoln: "At least, Mr. President, we can be sure that God is on our side."

"The question," replied Mr. Lincoln, "is not whether God is on our side but whether we are on God's side."

Whether God would rather have a man be a Communist than a middle-road Christian belongs to the realm of pure theological speculation. The truth probably is that He regards us all as His children.

And the best policy for any man, instead of making judgments on the basis of labels, is to concentrate on the fact that he himself is a sinner.

—*The Toronto Telegram,*
December 7, 1962

Stop Sniggering

There is no better time than now for us to stop sneering and sniggering about failures in the United States' rocketry program and to start applauding.

Let's clap loudly, for American rocket people have successfully propelled to the environs of Venus an electronic capsule which is telling us – from a distance of 36 million miles – a lot of things we want to know about that distant planet.

Not that this is the first distinguished accomplishment on the part of the Americans. In their very diversified space program they have achieved many "firsts" before this.

The Russians, competing in the space race, have tended to play to the grandstands. And they have done exceedingly well. They placed a medallion on the moon – the space age's equivalent of planting a flag on a newly discovered shore – and they have sent men whirling round the earth in sealed capsules.

The United States successfully has orbited men, too. They have not succeeded in putting their national mark on the moon. But they have scored less spectacular successes that will probably be of more use to mankind in the long run.

The great difference between the American and the Russian experiments is that the Americans have performed them in full view of the public, exposing their failures as well as their successes. The Russians have announced experiments only after they had been initiated successfully.

266

However, there have been a great many Canadians – not all, but many – who have felt an impulsion to cheer when the Americans failed and look with awe on Russian successes.

From any point of view, this is stupid.

The people of the United States are our partners on this continent; they share the same territorial home. There is no spite fence between us. Our wealth and their wealth in a very real sense is shared. Their scientific achievement and those of our own people are shared. And our mutual protection to a large extent is going to depend on all these factors.

The people who snigger on the news of American failures do not belittle the United States; they belittle themselves.

Of course it would be nice if Canada could produce bigger and better rockets and space capsules than her more populous and richer neighbour. We can't. To try even to compete with the American space program – or the Russian program, for that matter – would impoverish our economy. Instead we can co-operate; and the scientific minds among us do this profitably. Our scientists helped create the electronic brain of the newest U.S. Telstar (this one called Relay).

This is the right approach. It is in our best interests and should stem from our best instincts.

Some of us have spent too much of our energies booing the American team. Instead, let's stand up and cheer.

—The Toronto Telegram,
December 17, 1962

Hardship? Humbug

God rest you, merry gentlemen, let nothing you dismay… Wassail well. Deck the halls of the office of the Minister of Immigration and Citizenship with holly boughs and ring bells gaily.

Because you see, merry gentlemen, the Indians of northern Manitoba are not actually dying from starvation. Isn't that a pleasant thought? Doesn't that make you feel warm and comfortable inside? Oh, they're living in misery, of course, living in squalid surroundings and garbing themselves in rags.

But, according to the Honourable Minister of Immigration, Richard Bell, they are not actually starving.

So, the Honourable Minister contends, we should not concern ourselves with supplying the Indians and the Métis with food and clothing and other comforts. The plight of these people, in the cold poverty of the north, is being revealed – the Honourable Minister says – "for publicity purposes only."

Publicity for what? Well, publicity to illuminate a dark corner of our national life. Publicity to call attention to want. Publicity to call the attention of Canadians to a situation where they can help at this Christmas season.

The fact that Mr. Bell exploited the situation to call attention to ministerial ineptitude and sheer political idiocy is an unexpected by-product.

The Salvation Army has called attention to the plight of these poor people. *The Telegram* sent a competent reporter into their hovels to find out how they were living and report it to the people who are living elsewhere in comfort.

The impact of the reports moved the hearts of many people to send contributions of clothing and money. The Royal Canadian Air Force was prepared to transport these comforts to the Indians and Métis. But the Government called off the airlift because it was "unnecessary."

Who is presenting a false picture? Who is lying – the Salvation Army or Mr. Bell?

The Minister of Immigration who, through some hideous accident is charged with the care of our neglected Indian population, apparently does not like "publicity" about the condition of his charges. Imagine the idea of the Salvation Army publicizing misery. From the plush warmth of the office of the Minister came the reassuring word that no one is actually dying in the Indian community.

From *The Telegram*'s reporter-photographer came facts and pictures telling and showing in detail the actual conditions in which these poor people are living. And from the office of the Editor of *The Telegram* today is being dispatched a collection of these photographs taken on the spot.

They're not pretty pictures, for Mr. Bell. Some are quite ugly. But the Editor is having them put in a nice, neat folder so that they can be put up on the mantel piece among the Christmas cards a minister receives in his office.

They won't look nice among

all those brightly-coloured greeting cards. However, if Mr. Bell behaves in conformity with the character he has displayed lately, he will turn the pictures to the wall. He doesn't like being reminded of misery.

In the meantime, Mr. Bell can rest assured that The Telegram, for its part, will continue to give all the publicity it can to conditions of misery and the agencies dedicated to the alleviation of misery. It will give, as it has in the past, publicity to the Salvation Army and other agencies of mercy.

And it will give a lot of publicity to Mr. Bell's mean record when he stands again in the "safe" Conservative constituency of Carleton. Let it be hoped that the party remembers the record when it chooses another candidate to represent it. And let it be hoped that it will react as intelligently as did the people from all over Ontario who were touched by a story of privation in our land of plenty and responded with positive action.

—*The Toronto Telegram,*
December 20, 1962

You MUST!

MUST is the word today.

Our society is rapidly degenerating into a MUST society.

The citizen MUST do this, he MUST do that.

All-knowing, all-powerful governments issue the compulsory edicts.

The citizens obey – or else.

Even in earlier, more relaxed times, when democracy was at its height in our land, there were municipal, provincial and federal laws, rules and regulations which had to be observed. Organized society cannot get along without certain basic rules.

But today, the rules and edicts have multiplied to such an extent that people cannot help but feel they are being hemmed in and smothered by them.

You MUST register for medicare.

You MUST have your car tested at a government testing station.

You MUST write in your birthdate on the application for the $50 property-tax rebate.

You MUST fill out your

income tax form, which will enable the government to grab a bit part of your hard-earned cash.

You MUST have a social security card and number.

You MUST prove that you were born and are of good character if you want a passport which will enable you to travel outside the country.

You MUST belong to the Canada Pension Plan and you MUST contribute to the unemployment insurance fund, even though you are unlikely ever to draw anything from it.

There are lots more, and they're increasing all the time.

Is this really what government is for? Do we elect people to dream up new ways of making life complicated and difficult for us? We do not. We elect governments to be our servants, not our masters. At least that is the basis of democracy, or used to be.

Sadly, a change is afoot. Now it is the ambition of our politicians – some more than others – to rule over us, to manage, not simply our public affairs, but manage us, the people. More and more new ways are dreamed up to replace the individual citizen with the great, managed blob of humanity in which identity is lost except for numbers in computer filing cabinets.

The Alberta government's medicare brochure is full of MUSTs. "Dependents who MUST be registered." "A person ceasing to be a dependent MUST register separately with the commission." "Members of the Canadian Forces or RCMP MUST register their dependents only." And so on.

Can the citizen who doesn't want this medicare program created by his elected representatives muster out of it? Not on your life. Let him try and he will be summarily punished.

Compulsion is the essence of Socialism. From Socialism you go to autocracy and dictatorship.

We are turning back the clock very rapidly these days. When will we know that dictatorship has actually arrived? When we finally are mostest with the MUSTest.

—*The Calgary Herald,*
May 13, 1969

The Lottery Drug

There is something profoundly sleazy about the spectacle of our provincial ministers of justice gathering in solemn conclave to negotiate casinos and lotteries.

There was a time when justice ministers concerned themselves with rather more noble matters: the rights of the individual, reform of the criminal code, protection of the citizen, reform of the Constitution. Perhaps they still do; they did manage to get self-righteous about the RCMP in their Quebec meeting. But what really seems to turn them on these days is the chance to get together like so many Mafia capos to plot how to rook the suckers out of a few million more bucks.

There was no great harm done when Montreal introduced its modest lottery to the Canadian scene. What is indecent is the frantic pursuit by the governments which followed, of ever newer and more seductive ways to relieve the citizens of their money. Grossly one-sided games of chance which were called rackets when operated by private enterprise are now being peddled by provincial governments.

Those governments are not the least deterred by evidence that the lotteries and games of chance draw a vastly disproportionate amount of money from those who can least afford it – from the poor and discouraged to whom a lottery ticket may seem the only chance to escape from dreariness.

Whether the dream is worth the price is something for the conscience of the justice ministers. Like other peddlers of fake nirvanas, they might argue that it is not their business to protect citizens from their own gullibility. But do they really imagine that it is their duty to exploit that gullibility.

—*The Montreal Star,*
September 17, 1979

271

Even Those Who Err Must Have Their Say

As modestly successful authors go, Salman Rushdie, 41, had been only run-of-the-mill. His first novel, *Grimus*, came out 14 years ago.

The Bombay-born Briton attended Rugby School and King's College, Cambridge, working as an advertising copy writer, enjoying chess, table tennis and politics. His novels of this decade included *Midnight's Children*, for which he won the Booker Prize, and *Shame*.

It is technique that has changed life for Rushdie. His writing uses "magic realism" – in common with Argentina's Jorge Luis Borges and Britain's John Fowles. It is a style that blends the fantastic with reality. Rushdie used it in his newest work, *The Satanic Verses*, a book he describes as being in part "a fictional departure" on the birth of a religion.

However, the fantasy is too close to the realism of Mohammedanism for the liking of some Muslims. Book-burnings in Bradford, England, swelled a tide of notoriety, bringing Rushdie strong sales for what had begun as a so-so market, and a $1.7-million contract for this and his next novel from the author's American publisher.

On Tuesday, Ayatollah Ruhollah Khomeini put out a different sort of contract on Rushdie, urging his Iranian Revolutionary Guards to kill Rushdie and his publishers. A mob of 3,000 stoned the British embassy in Tehran.

It is much too easy to leap up on our high horses and condemn either Rushdie for his supposed profanations or Khomeini for his arrogant and bloody defence of his religion.

Yet we, too, can be very quick to seek to censor others. Canadians and others showed considerable sensitivity during the first screenings last year of Martin Scorsese's movie, *The Last Temptation of Christ*. Just as many opponents (and champions) of Scorsese had not seen the film, many critics (and defenders) of Rushdie's work have not read *The Satanic Verses*.

At the University of Western Ontario, Philippe Rushton recently stirred the furies with a view ranking Orientals and whites above black races in genetic superiority. He has tried to relate "genetic purity" to the might of the German army in the Second World War, and lack of it to U.S. failures in Vietnam. The university defended Rushton's academic freedom to research and expound views, even if they appear unreasonable and repugnant, despite outcries of racism.

Without a protected academic freedom, we cannot think, experiment, create. We cannot develop the new Galileos and Newtons and Einsteins. The less-gifted researchers who advance flawed or spurious hypotheses are soon exposed, but at least the process must be there to let both emerge and be challenged, or to let them stew in their own juice.

Ours is not a world of unanimity or consensus. Not even neighbours or family members always agree; yet we would not deny their right to their views. We must similarly allow the Rushdies and Rushtons of the world their right of expression as well, even if we personally find these utterances reprehensible.

—The Regina Leader-Post, February 17, 1989

Alberta's Gamble

The first step in treating an addiction, they say, is admitting that you have a problem.

In recent days, Alberta Premier Ralph Klein seems to be in the midst of acknowledging that he has a problem with video lottery terminals in his province. But the measures being taken by Mr. Klein seem directed more toward preserving VLTs in Alberta than toward weaning his government away from its rather unseemly reliance on gambling revenues.

VLTs are not your run-of-the-mill type of gambling diversion:

They're fast – it takes just a few seconds to play one game and there are no breathing spaces needed between one game and the next.

They don't directly use cash, operating instead on a system of credits that appear on the screen. Unlike slot machines or lotteries, you don't see the amounts of money leaving your hands until the end, when you go to redeem or pay up on your credits. Usually, you're paying. It's been calculated that every dollar put into a VLT returns only 92 cents to the players. The return declines to about 70 cents the more you play.

They're accessible. Just drop your family in a restaurant and slip away to drop your wages into the machine.

In the face of renewed anxiety about VLTs in Alberta and a growing move in Calgary to banish the 1,200 machines there, Mr. Klein is going some distance to placate the critics. His government passed a motion last week in the legislature calling for the play speed of VLTs to be slowed and for the screens to display the cash, not credits gained and lost.

He has also convened a "gambling summit" to take place in Medicine Hat, right in the middle of the push in Calgary to gain 80,000 signatures on an anti-VLT petition.

Mr. Klein should get some credit for taking measures to address the concerns about the addictive properties of VLTs, even if his motives are traced more to desperation about revenues than to concern about citizens.

But the province hasn't moved at all to address the problem of VLTs' accessibility, which is being identified as one of the root causes of their addictiveness. Alberta's original goal was to put 8,000 machines in 1,200 places – it capped the number of VLTs a few years ago but didn't cap the number of locations. If you want to indulge your addiction, you hardly need to make a special trip.

The most worrisome part of Alberta's new reliance on gambling and VLTs (a total of $1.6 billion, or 62 percent of gambling revenues in the province came from VLTs in 1996) is the lack of research into its consequences. Governments have embraced and promoted gambling with apparently few considerations to its long-term effects. And not only have they unleashed it, but they insist on controlling it too. It may be one of the most blunt fiscal instruments we've ever seen.

One simple gambling summit is not going to fix that. Mr. Klein is tinkering at the edges of the problem, clearly reluctant to turn his back on the money that VLTs and gambling bring him. He should, as the Canada West Foundation and other critics have recommended, be just as serious about the costs of gambling as he is about the revenues. He's playing with his luck and Albertans' money.

—*The Globe and Mail,*
March 10, 1998

22
Inside the Fourth Estate

Yellow Journalism

The American nation is beginning to realize that it has been dragged into a war [Spanish-American] which has already cost millions of dollars and which may cost thousands of lives, solely through the mercenary sensationalism of the yellow jingos who run its newspapers.

Yellow journalism has been exploited to the highest degree by the *New York World* and the *New York Journal*. These papers have issued edition after edition in colours so gaudy and indiscriminate that each page looks like a dish of fried eggs with the yolks smashed.

The so called illustrations are of soldiers, sailors, exploding bombs and iron clads in action, while the reading material is alcoholic, vitriolic, electric and sensational.

One editor broke down under the strain and actually issued an edition declaring war several weeks ago. He was taken from the office of *The World* to the mad-house – a merciful change of scene, because he will notice the difference and the public will.

A clever English writer in New York has been describing some of the phases of this crazy journalism. "It is the evening editions," he says, "that are capping the climax of sensationalism and audacity. They are coining money out of the war scare, which they themselves have manufactured, and may yet see brought to a hideous reality. The yellowiest of all these papers, *The Journal*, actually printed 30 extra editions in a space of 12 or 14 hours, and sold a million and a half copies to the shop girls, store porters, errand boys, counter jumpers, and bar room loungers, who get their daily education out of this sort of mental pabulum.

"I brought the 21st edition for a curiosity, as I went into a theatre at 8 o'clock. After the second act I went out and got the 26th edition, and at 11 o'clock, when I was on my way home, I bought the 29th extra. Every day this is repeated in a greater or less degree. The news carts, which race madly about the town, clearing the streets like fire engines, have large placards on their side, announcing 'Latest War News!' The newsboys always yell: 'Extra! All about the war!' precisely as if we were in the midst of hostilities.

"The recipe for making a war extra is to get a line of fact or rumour and charge it with the carbonic acid gas of imagination, until it fills three columns, half made up of headlines in poster type. Here are some actual titles of recent articles: 'The Pope is with America,' 'Bismarck Says Germany Favors our Side,' 'Six New Warships Bought,' 'Spaniards call our Senators Dirty Pigs,' 'A Journal Woman Rides on a Dynamite Torpedo,' 'United States Rejects International Arbitration,' 'Britain's Minister Calls on the President to make an Anglo-Saxon Alliance.'

"The minor articles and pictures deal with the starving Cubans, contemptuous cartoons about Spain, accounts of cruel Spanish bull fights, or pictures of Sullivan, Corbett, Fitzsimons and Peter Jackson, the prize fighters, dressed in soldier clothes, each with a patriotic sentiment underneath, like: 'You bet your bottom dollar I'll fight,' credited to the ex-champion of the bruisers, John L. Sullivan.

"The evening papers have each a staff of 20 men on duty day and night, ready at a moment's notice to turn out a complete edition filled with hair raising war news and pictures, any one of which, if taken into a dairy, would sour all the milk.

"Another paper keeps three steamboats at sea loaded to the gunwales with war correspondents, pencils ready sharpened to puncture the Spanish cause.

"A theatre manager, trying to imitate patriotism for the sake of notoriety, spread an immense Spanish flag in the foyer of his theatre in a German and Jewish neighbourhood, expecting his audience to walk over it. Before the doors had been opened many minutes the banner was torn in shreds by an angry crowd, and the pieces carried off as trophies of war. This bit of savagery humiliated millions of Americans, who yet cannot deny that it shows what yellow journalism can do.

"A young woman, who essayed to sing the delightful ballad, 'In Old Madrid,' was hooted off the stage of one of our music halls, and when, in another theatre, the orchestra played a lively Spanish fantasia the people stormed the musicians with yells and missiles until they retreated under the stage. In all the theatres now it is considered essential to an evening's recreation for the orchestra, after each act, to play 'The Star Spangled Banner,' whereupon the entire audience rise, and sing and cheer until their patriotism finds relief.

"Those patriotic outbursts are not confined to theatres. A businessman entered a Broadway restaurant the other day and ordered a Spanish omelette. The waiter took his order, but soon came back and told him he would have to take his eggs some other way, as the cooks absolutely refused to make any more Spanish omelettes until Spain apologizes to the United States.

"The guest heartily endorsed the cooks' position, and changed his order. The proprietor of the restaurant, not to be outdone in patriotism, immediately struck 'Spanish omelette' from all his bills of fare.

"'Spanish' has in fact become the most unpopular word in the English language from an American point of view. During the past two months a New York firm that advertises a special brand of Spanish liquorice has lost half its trade. 'We have to swallow Spanish insults,' said one indignant citizen, 'but I'll be darned if we'll swallow Spanish liquorice.'"

It is no wonder that this correspondent concludes that "this endless flood of the most irresponsible sensationalism is breeding an unnatural volatility to the popular mind, and should a sharp crisis come there might be a flare up that would be infinitely dangerous" and the result has shown his prophesy to be a true one.

—*The Calgary Daily Herald, April 15, 1898*

The Fogogram

At last the *Telegram* frankly admits what many people have long said about it. Not only does it admit it, but loudly proclaims it. In the current issue of *Marketing*, the *Telegram* has a full-page advertisement, part of which we reproduce here in facsimile:

Covering Toronto like a Fog

Permeating every nook and corner of Toronto – seeking out family circles, in the homes of rich and poor alike – *The Evening Telegram* descends upon Toronto each evening like a veritable fog...

The *Telegraph* has said it. That is just what it does –"descends upon Toronto each evening like a veritable fog." Nobody could have said it better. It goes to show that our contemporary could tell the truth as well as anybody if its regular contents were not more carefully scrutinized than its occasional advertisements in outside journals.

It descends like a veritable fog on the city every evening, beclouding every issue, blurring every outline, rendering confused and indistinct all familiar objects.

In the fog it makes small men at times loom large against the background of the glimmering half dark, and big men are made to fade and seem indistinct.

The fog the *Telegram* makes is sometimes so thick you could almost cut it with a knife, and its readers have to grope in every direction to find their way about. Sometimes the fog smells like smoke, and at other times it is moist and dampish. But it is astonishing what a fog the *Telegram* creates daily for its readers, encompassing them in a thick, yellow, soupy pall, in which nothing can be clearly distinguished, everything taking on grotesque outlines. Fortunately those escape the fog who avoid *The Fogogram*.

—*The Toronto Evening Star, November 6, 1923*

Newspapermen

Chains of causation take odd turns. Because bandits killed a Manchester newspaper correspondent in China, discussion of the old question, *What makes a newspaperman a newspaperman?* has broken out in Ontario.

The *Chatham News* started its. According to the News, a reporter killed at his job, whether in China or Chatham, "makes the sacrifice gladly, convinced it is worth while so long as something is added to the sum of human knowledge."

Maybe, but the *News*'s editor had better get it in writing from his staff if he intends to carry the noble principle to extremes in practice. In *The Globe*'s 90 odd years of experience, ambition to become a human sacrifice on the altar of knowledge has figured remarkably little in the making of good reporters.

Moreover, in *The Globe*'s opinion, it would be a bad day for the newspaper business if it ever figured more. To go where he is sent, to get his facts, to write his story, to accept the risks of his occupation as and when they come – these things are a newspaperman's job, in China as in Chatham.

Death, if it overtakes him on the job, no more qualifies him for a martyr's crown than it would a deckhand or a steelworker. A reporter determined to die "gladly" for the honour of the first edition is wasting his gifts on the newspaper business. He ought to be black shirting it in Italy.

—*The Toronto Globe,*
August 31, 1935

Douglas Social Credit

The Alberta legislative session just concluded revealed the extremist complexion of Premier William Aberhart's administration. The whole bag of Fascist tricks was exposed and no one need be under further illusion as to the desire of the government to place the citizens of this province under a Hitlerlike domination. Thanks to the refusal of the Lieutenant-Governor to sign three measures, some of the most obnoxious legislation of the session has been held up.

One of the first moves in a campaign to establish a dictatorship has always been to muzzle the press so that only information in line with government aims and policy or highly favourable to the rulers will be given to the public.

Mr. Aberhart and his group of would-be little Hitlers have adopted a well-defined technique in passing a press control act, one of the measures which failed to secure vice-regal approval. If the "social credit" government could have got away with this first invasion of the domain of free utterance and opinion, there is little reason to doubt it would have gone further in later sessions. At least that has been the experience in all autocratic countries. Repression grows on what it feeds on.

Another development of the session was the passage of an act to license trades, businesses and occupations. This legislation aims to place the livelihood of every citizen of Alberta, outside of a few exempted occupations or professions, at the complete mercy of the government.

The government re-enacted a measure which, if it means anything, is a defiance of the Federal Constitution and Federal authority to disallow improper provincial legislation.

This, too, was held up.

It has awarded members $10 a day in addition to the sessional indemnity provided by law for doing all this.

It has passed an act which wipes out one of its main campaign promises, a recall system. At the first moment when the electorate sought to avail themselves of its provisions, arbitrary as they were, the recall machinery was abolished in order to protect the premier himself.

A further development of the session was the passage of a resolution providing for the dismissal of the Royal Canadian Mounted Police from this province, one of the most famous, most efficient and most trusted police forces in the world. Such a change cannot be justified on the grounds of economy or efficiency. The purpose is to supplant the Mounted Police by a force appointed by and subservient to the attorney-general. All dictatorships have their own special police.

These sessional fruits have not been the invention of Premier Aberhart but were the results of direct intervention and guidance by Major C.H. Douglas, founder of the Social Credit movement. The government's program represents expressly Maj. Douglas' own conceptions of how government in Alberta should be conducted.

All this attempted regimentation of the lives and activities of Alberta citizens is ostensibly "social credit." Actually, it is so closely in line with the strategy of certain European dictators that one is free to wonder whether "social credit" has become merely an easily succulent phrase, and Fascist tyranny the real objective.

—*The Calgary Herald,
October 5, 1937*

(Editor's Note: On March 4, 1938, the Supreme Court of Canada disallowed the Alberta Social Credit government's law forcing Alberta newspapers to disclose news sources to a government board, and also to publish government rebuttals to papers criticizing the government. The same year, The Edmonton Journal, representing Alberta newspapers, was awarded a special Pulitzer bronze plaque for editorial leadership in defence of the freedom of the press in Alberta.)

Star Continues to See Red

Commenting on Ontario Attorney-General Gordon Conant's observation that democracy must discipline itself to escape the alternative of dictatorship, *The Globe and Mail* assumed "a disciplined dictatorship is one in which the people use the ballot conscientiously for the general good, and not to promote 'isms' or selfish causes."

Evidently it ruffled the fur at the *Toronto Daily Star*, which saw red right away. "Our contemporary," whines *the Star*, "wants Canada, its provinces and its municipalities to take the first step toward a dictatorship by depriving the masses of their votes, or at least, by depriving selected groups of their votes. Somebody, it thinks, should discipline democracy; and democracy means the people as a whole."

Democracy means a form of government, and not the method favoured by the *Star's* satellites, the Communists. If the people fail to recognize and correct the weaknesses of their system, if the conflict of dogmas and preachments and the battle of classes can be developed to chaos, there will be a better chance for Red doctrines to infiltrate the body politic.

In fact, this is what the Reds are hoping for and waiting for, and apparently what the *Star* is fighting for. Why warn the people that democracy must discipline itself, that selfish causes must give way to the common welfare, and thus block the game? It would be too bad if Canada became a country in which the majority of voters went to the polls determined to put national interests before sectional views, and community welfare before group causes. It would be a terrible affront to the "isms" if the State did something to protect itself from the enemies of democracy. Let the merry confusion go on until democracy is wrecked!

Would the plunder fall to the *Star's* friends? We doubt it. They may fool some of the people some of the time, but that is all.

—*The Globe and Mail,
December 9, 1938*

Abuse and Neglect of Duty

Healthy doses of their own medicine have been poured down journalists' throats in an article published elsewhere in this paper today.

People whose business in a democracy is to furnish news and critical comment are on the receiving end of the same treatment administered by Publisher Mark Ethridge of the *Louisville Courier Journal*. More of such introspective examination would be wholesome for publishers and editors in Canada as well as the United States.

It's fashionable to attack the Hitlers and Stalins and Perons for imperilling the freedom of the press. But Mr. Ethridge throws the light of his soul-searching on more subtle but equally dangerous threats of smugness and indolence and that fat-catism which smothers altruism.

He also takes alarm at economic forces that have driven hundreds of newspapers into bankruptcy, into mergers with competitors or into the arms of chain journalism.

But smugness and laziness are the most unforgivable of all the evils. Mr. Ethridge accuses the American press of sinning against its own light.

It lost the battle against McCarthyism by outrageous default: in some cases, it even excused the infringement of personal liberties supposedly guaranteed by the U.S. constitution. The press was too blind to see that its own freedom depends on the liberty of every citizen. It was too deaf to realize that the bells tolling the death of tolerance were tolling for it too.

The spectacle of journalistic fat-cats purring contentedly under the petting of politicians should shame every newspaperman.

Such obvious devices as free junkets to flatter the ego and off-the-record statements to dull and distract the spirits of inquiry are a disgrace to the profession's traditions.

Fortunately most of the cats in Canada are somewhat leaner and more aggressive, but the tendency to relax must be constantly and conscientiously resisted. To the credit of Canadian newspapers, they almost unitedly repudiated McCarthyism from the start and stopped it cold on this side of the border. The press here is almost less worshipful of big business and big government and more concerned about individual rights.

That general description may sound like fat-catism of a different sort but each publisher and editor will know how well it fits his own operation.

Let them examine their own ethics and their own adherence to the fundamentals of honest news-

paper work. Let them give free rein to the self-critical analysis which Mr. Ethridge finds so cleansing.

If they judge themselves according to the standard of how well they have served in the defence of democracy they will know how true they have been to the obligations of a free press.

—*The Vancouver Sun,*
May 14, 1955

Is a Story Itself the News?

It was only nine paragraphs out of 108 pages, but one section of the *McAlpine Report* on racism caught our eye, as might be expected. It dealt with "the media."

In line with much of the report, it quoted others or raised questions rather than offering opinions and recommendations of its own.

It reminded us of a question often discussed among journalists: how to define the "news" in newspaper. It could be put this way: is a story about the news or is a story itself the news?

Reporting on organizations such as the Ku Klux Klan, the journalist must further refine the question. How far does he go in reporting hateful activities with-

out promoting the hatred?

That is where John McAlpine comes in. He notes in his report that concern was expressed to him about the Klan finding a forum for its message in the news media. But he is careful not to express that concern himself. He goes on to quote federal broadcasting regulations that prohibit "any abusive comment or any abusive pictorial representation on any race, religion, or creed."

Fair enough. But then Mr. McAlpine goes on to observe that there is no parallel restriction in respect of newspapers. True. He then asks, "If communication of the 'message' is proscribed should consideration not be given to placing restrictions upon its appearance in print?"

The question is also fair enough – but Mr. McAlpine does not attempt to answer it. We would answer it: No.

The analogy with broadcasting is not quite appropriate for a couple of reasons. First, the restrictions there are surely aimed at an entertainment medium rather than a news medium. No one is telling *The National* it can't report on Arab-Israeli conflict, or trouble in Northern Ireland, or even a cross-burning in the B.C. Interior.

The purpose of the radio and television regulations is to prevent the gratuitous dissemination of discrimination as fact masked in fiction.

The second place the analogy breaks down is in the basis for the regulations. Government can regulate broadcasting because the public owns the airwaves, and radio and television broadcasters lease them for a fee. The regulations are terms of the lease, but a publication requires no similar arrangement to transmit its message.

That does not condone irresponsibility in newspapers, which must always be careful to sort the news from the propaganda and to avoid being used. That is what we must do every day. Quite frankly, we don't want anyone else to do it for us, especially not governments or their agents.

If activities, however unpleasant, are suppressed from the news, you are more likely to find the sort of situation Mr. McAlpine also worries about, namely the insidious, clandestine spread of discrimination and hate. What's out in the open is easier to treat than a secret cancer.

—*The Vancouver Sun,*
June 29, 1981

Earnest Press

Trying to be a man of the cloth in the 20th century is not the easiest thing to do.

After all, back when popes were popes – and cardinals were cardinals – most of the time was spent in holy meditation or hanging around the court advising kings and despots on how to get rid of unwanted wives.

These days a pope has to go off to Central America and try and convert Marxists and guerrillas to the ways of God.

Cardinals have to show up as speakers at policemen's breakfasts. This requires fancy footwork.

We think Pope John Paul II has the right idea when he kisses the ground of every country he visits (he must do it for some obscure liturgical reason) even though there is scarcely a Costa Rican or Nicaraguan who does the same.

But when you put on the scarlet robes and ruby ring of the Church you must, we suppose, do and not do ordinary things and that may mean kissing a lot of ground.

But having made these concessions to diplomacy and high position is it necessary to ask the princes of the Church to refrain from having a sense of humour as well?

Last Sunday, Emmett Cardinal Carter made a couple of ethnic jokes about Jews and Catholics at the Metro Toronto policemen's 19th annual communion breakfast. Those present – including Jews and Catholics – laughed. But others, not present, wrote outraged letters of protest.

This is lunacy. Isn't it going more than a little overboard for the *Globe & Mail* editorial to tell the Cardinal that he should know better than to "truck in this intolerant trade?"

In fact, those who make such serious comments on such harmless incidents are doing the very opposite of what they profess to want. They are the ones who cause trouble by over-sensitizing people to racial slurs and cultural tensions.

It is like the Victorians whose endless concern about the delicate state of women turned some females into weakened individuals who could never be moved out of the bedroom.

For, ahem, Heaven's sake, let's allow a sense of humour and a little irreverence into this world. This over-protection, this spotting of a possible injury, slight or cultural boo-boo will do for racial harmony what the Victorians did for sex.

Sweep it under the carpet to fester into intolerance.

Couldn't we make fun of ourselves again? Allowing even a cardinal to poke fun at co-religionists of every persuasion?

—*The Toronto Sun,*
March 9, 1983

Let the Public Judge

Viewers tuning in the *fifth estate* on CBC-TV on Tuesday night must have been puzzled. Instead of the program's much-hyped investigation into the missing billions of Nicolae Ceauflescu, entitled "Evil's Fortune," they were treated to a profile of the Canadian scientist Gerald Bull, arms designer to the Iraqi government.

The reason: an hour before airtime, an Ontario court had placed a 22-day gag order on the broadcast, at the request of the Romanian government and its accountants, after a lengthy in-camera hearing. Even the terms of the injunction itself are secret. The court, in effect, said to Canadians: we can't tell you why we didn't show you why we won't let you see this program.

The notion that the public is best served chilled in ignorance has gained much currency of late. Racial activists would block publication or even compilation of statistics on the incidence of crime by race. Teachers' unions oppose standardized tests that would allow comparison of educational performance among difference schools or provinces. There are legitimate fears in such cases about how the information would be used.

But truth is rarely found in darkness.

No such concerns attend *the fifth estate* broadcast. The issue, so far as the public has been told, is rather an alleged breach of trust over the use of privileged material. This, too, is a frequent justification offered in defence of publication bans. The Thatcher government in Britain spent the better part of two years trying to suppress *Spycatcher*, former intelligence officer Peter Wright's tale of wrongdoing in the secret service, on grounds that he had violated his oath of confidentiality.

The Israeli government produced similar arguments last year in persuading a Canadian court to slap a temporary injunction on *By Way of Deception*, an insider's account of its own security apparatus. Even Buckingham Palace invoked a betrayed confidence in its ludicrous attempts to impose a worldwide ban on *Courting Disaster*, an irredeemably trivial piece of gossip by a former palace employee.

There are two objections to all such efforts to prevent the dissemination of information, one practical, one principled. The practical objection is that word gets out, willy-nilly. The government of Quebec, to take another example, was forced to abandon attempts to stop publication of the terms of secret contracts between Hydro-Quebec and 13 of its biggest customers, after they appeared in newspapers from Norway to Australia. Worse, Quebecers themselves could learn all from Vermont television. Will Canadians have to wait for a U.S. Station to broadcast "Evil's Fortune"?

The principled objection is simply this: in a democracy, the press is free. If breach of trust there be, there are ample legal remedies without resort to the affront of prior censorship. If editors and producers overstep the bounds of professional responsibility, they can be held to account after the fact. Sue if you must, but let the public judge the merits of the matter for itself.

—*The Globe and Mail,*
October 10, 1991

Improved Journalism is in National Interest

Much of the discussion surrounding a new Senate report on the Canadian news media has focused on two controversial areas: proposed limits on media ownership and sweeping changes to the CBC.

But there is much more to the report. Its 40 recommendations and 10 "suggestions" touch on almost every aspect of newsgathering in this country.

And it provides a clear road map for moving ahead.

While this newspaper takes issue with some recommendations, such as giving elected politicians oversight over media mergers, it heartily supports many proposals in the Senate committee's *Final Report on the Canadian News Media*.

The authors of this three-year study outline several solid ways to strengthen journalism, including simplified access to official documents through Canada's freedom-of-information laws. The existing system is so slow, costly and limited in application that it acts more as a hurdle to be overcome than an efficient way to receive documents.

The committee's call for reform is especially timely given Prime Minister Stephen Harper's recent retreat from promises to reduce official secrecy. For example, by creating 10 new grounds for allowing civil servants to quash access to information requests, Harper's government is moving to make it harder for journalists to obtain federal documents.

Citizens have a right to know what their government is doing and the Senate committee is right to press for more, and better, access to information.

The report also urges Ottawa to help fund "centres of excellence" devoted to research into journalism and the state of Canada's news media.

Similar centres for other professions already exist in universities across the country. Many are dedicated to the study of medicine, engineering and the social sciences. Journalism, too, is worthy of such an approach given that a free press is fundamental to democracy.

The senators also strongly urged newspapers and broadcasters to continue supporting Canadian Press, the only national news service. Some members have hinted they may soon pull out of the co-operative.

A strong national news service is critical for a strong press in Canada because it provides both large and small media outlets with the quality and diversity of news and commentary that ultimately benefits all readers and listeners across the country.

As well as recommendations aimed at government, the Senate committee lists 10 sound "suggestions" for Canada's news organizations.

Canada lacks a permanent, full-time research centre devoted to the study of Canadian news gathering, and the media here should support one. Such centres exist in the U.S.

Other suggestions include:

Having all news organizations develop a statement of clear and public principles to guide their coverage. The *Star* has long been steered according to the Atkinson Principles, a set of socially progressive guidelines developed by the newspaper's legendary publisher Joseph E. Atkinson.

Expansion of press and media councils in Canada, where people can go to have complaints about coverage heard and ruled upon by a tribunal.

Establishment of more "public editor" positions at newspapers to review complaints from readers. The committee noted the *Star* is the only daily newspaper in Canada with a public editor.

Federal officials, news organizations and anyone interested in improved public discourse would do well to study these beneficial changes proposed by the Senate committee.

Canada has been well served by its news media, but it could be served even better. And the Senate report shows how.

—*The Toronto Star,*
June 25, 2006